RADICAL ORIGINS

RADICAL ORIGINS

WHY WE ARE LOSING THE BATTLE AGAINST ISLAMIC
EXTREMISM—AND HOW TO TURN THE TIDE

DR. AZEEM IBRAHIM

PEGASUS BOOKS
NEW YORK LONDON

RADICAL ORIGINS

Pegasus Books Ltd.
148 W 37th Street, 13th Floor
New York, NY 10018

First Pegasus Books edition November 2017

Interior design by Maria Fernandez

Library of Congress Cataloging-in-Publication Data is available.

ISBN: 978-1-68177-548-7

10 9 8 7 6 5 4 3 2 1

Printed in the United States of America
Distributed by W. W. Norton & Company, Inc.
www.pegasusbooks.us

CONTENTS

Terminology   ix

Introduction   xi

PART ONE: LOOKING BACK TO THE ISLAMIC GOLDEN AGE   1

Muhammad and the Birth of Islam   9

Muhammad's Moral Mission   11

The Constitution of Medina—the Prototype of an Islamic State   12

The Caliphates   18

The Rashidun—The Right Guided Caliphs   19

The Umayyad Caliphate—God's Sword   23

The Abbasid Caliphate—The Light of the World   26

Summary   30

PART TWO: SAUDI ARABIA AND WAHHABISM   33

Al-Wahhab and Revolutionary Islam   38

The First Wahhabi Emirate: Jihad Against Polytheism (1744–1818)   42

The Second Wahhabi Emirate: Regrouping and Consolidation

   (1823–1891)   44

The Third Wahhabi Emirate: Maturity and Orthodoxy

   (1902–1953)   47

The Ikhwan: The Original Wahhabi Ultra-Radicals   49

Wahhabism Becomes Salafism   52

Interaction with the Muslim Brotherhood   54

Oil—Saudi Arabia Becomes Rich   56

The Domestic Challenges of Contemporary Saudi Arabia   60

The Muslim Brotherhood and the Development
of Islamist Salafism   63

The Emergence of Jihadi-Salafism in Saudi Arabia   66

Summary   67

PART THREE: MODERN JIHADISM   69

The Logic of Terrorism   71

The Logic of Salafist Terrorism   78

Friend and Foe   78

Enemies Near and Far   83

The "Just" War   86

The "True" Faith   89

Ideological War   97

The Goals of the Salafist Movement: Sharia   101

The Role of Theology   103

"We Love Death as You Love Life"   108

The Particular Challenge of Salafism   110

Conclusion   113

PART FOUR: AN ISLAMIC CHALLENGE   119

The Amman Message and the London Declaration   122

An Islamic Rejection of Salafist Arguments   125

    The Right to Rebel   125

    The Laws of War   129

Conclusions   133

PART FIVE: EXPORTING HATE   137

Spreading Propaganda   142

Hate Preaching in Britain   145

Abu Qatada   149

Abdullah al-Faisal   150

Abu Hamza al-Masri   151

Omar Bakri Mohammed   152

Implications   153

The Stages of Radicalization   156

    Stage 1: The Bottom of the Pyramid: "We Are Oppressed"   159

    Stage 2: "They Are Attacking Our People"   167

    Stage 3: "The Band of Brothers"   172

    Stage 4: Violent Jihad   174

Summary   177

PART SIX: A CASE-STUDY: SALAFISM IN THE BALKANS   181

Islam in Yugoslavia   187

The Muslim Population and the Balkan Wars   189

Postwar Salafist Involvement and Narratives   190

    Bosnia   192

    Kosovo   192

Similarities and Differences   196

The Salafist Interpretation   197

PART SEVEN: IRAQ AND SYRIA   199

Salafism in Iraq   205

Salafism in Syria   210

Salafist Groups Not Aligned to Al-Qaeda   211

Al-Qaeda's Official Faction: Al-Nusra   214

Al-Qaeda's Offspring: ISIS   216

Global Repercussions   223

Summary   227

PART EIGHT: THE ANTIDOTE   233

The Role of Saudi Arabia   240

The Role of Religious Leaders   246

Recommendations

     For Western Policy Makers   253

     For Teachers   253

     For Journalists   256

     For Policy Makers   258

     For All of Us   265

Epilogue   271

References   275

Index   289

TERMINOLOGY

The Abbasid dynasty: The third major Islamic dynasty. Noted for the intellectual activity that dominated up to the 11th century when the dynasty started to decline.

Jihad: In conventional Islam, any struggle to improve oneself and come closer to God. In Salafist terminology, invariably this means going to fight against unbelievers in a violent struggle.

Mardin Fatwa: A key document in Salafist ideology. Divides the world into an "abode of war" and an "abode of peace" (where what they see as true Islam rules). In turn is used to justify attacks not just on non-Muslims but also on those seen as being insufficiently pious, as their realms too fall into the "abode of war."

The Muslim Brotherhood: Emerged in the post–World War II era as an opposition to secular socialist states such as Egypt and Syria. Many of its leaders fled to Saudi Arabia, where they worked as engineers and in the universities. Modern-day violent Salafism is in part a fusion of the ideology of the Muslim Brotherhood and Saudi-sponsored Salafism.

Rashidun Caliphate: The rule of the first four caliphs after the death of Muhammed.

Salafism: The ideology that the Saudis now use to replace Wahhabism when they wish to spread their version of Islam.

Takfir, **Takfirism:** Another key part of the Salafist ideology. This argues that Muslim leaders who ally with the US/West, and any Muslims who do not condemn them (or fail to meet the demands of Salafist Islam in other ways), are apostates. This makes them legitimate targets for violent attacks.

The Umayyad dynasty: The first "imperial" Islamic dynasty established after Islam had spread across the Middle East, North Africa, and to the borders of modern-day India.

Wahhabism: Emerged in the 1760s in what is now modern-day Saudi Arabia. Claims to be a return to the purity of the early days of Islam.

ABBREVIATIONS

AQ: Al-Qaeda
AQI: Al-Qaeda in Iraq
ISIS: Islamic State in Iraq and Syria—also known as *Daesh* or ISIL or IS.

INTRODUCTION

T his book focuses on the major issue of our times: how to deal with the global rise of Islamist fundamentalism. This has been a growing issue ever since the defeat of the Soviet occupation of Afghanistan in 1988 and the deployment of US ground troops to Saudi Arabia in 1991 to deal with Saddam Hussein's invasion of Kuwait. Initially, the Islamist insurgency was mostly organized by a relatively structured organization that took root in Taliban-controlled Afghanistan—Al-Qaeda. Following the astounding success of the Islamists in the Afghan war in the '80s, the organization went from "defending Muslim lands" to a global offensive against all "enemies of Islam" that culminated in the 9/11 terrorist attacks on US home soil. This triggered President George Bush's "War on Terror," an ill-defined conflict between the West and Islamism that rages to this day and which has come to define much of our understanding of geopolitics so far this century.

In the fifteen years since 2001, Al-Qaeda (AQ) itself has suffered many major defeats: it has lost most of its safe bases and most of its leadership, to a point where today it is but a shadow of the organization that struck fear on the American Main Street. Yet their radical interpretation of Islam has flourished and spread well beyond their former heartlands. When the so-called Islamic State of Iraq and Syria (ISIS) first asserted itself and proclaimed the reestablishment of the "caliphate" in the Levant,[1] they usurped Al-Qaeda as the dominant force in global jihad and relegated our public enemy number 1 to a mere sideshow. Al-Qaeda had, for most practical intents and purposes, been defeated.

But even as Al-Qaeda currently flounders on the margins, we are now even farther from winning "The War on Terror" than we were on day one. ISIS has not merely taken over the mantle from Al-Qaeda: it has upped the ante on ideological extremism, on reach, on organization, on resources, and on the sheer brutality and violence towards those it does not see as true believers,[2] both in the regions where it has some degree of physical control, and throughout the world through ever-growing jihadist networks.

This book argues that there has been a fundamental flaw in the Western approach to Islamic extremism. So far, our response to the global jihadi insurgency has been too focused on the areas where the militants have claimed physical control, like Afghanistan in 2001 and Iraq and Syria today. Indeed, military misadventures like the 2003 invasion of Iraq have no doubt made matters worse, by setting the scene for the rise of ISIS in that area. Rather, I argue, we should have focused on those global jihadist networks that are, even as we speak, expanding ever more into the undergrowth of our societies, on the economically, socially and culturally marginalized edges. This is where resentment against our civilization, our "way of life" seethes more than in the bazaars of Raqqa or Mosul, and where for many young Muslims caught in vicious cycles of petty criminality and a deep existential lack of direction, the opportunity to assert an identity separate from their

---

1   Azeem Ibrahim, "The Resurgence of Al-Qaeda in Syria and Iraq," (Washington: SSI, 2014).

2   Amnesty International, "Absolute Impunity: Militia Rule in Iraq," (London: Amnesty International, 2014); Human Rights Watch, "Iraq: Women Suffer Under ISIS," Human Rights Watch, 2016 https://www.hrw.org/news/2016/04/05/iraq-women-suffer-under-isis.

"decadent," "Western" surroundings and fight for something "bigger than themselves" so often proves to be irresistible.[3]

There are, of course, very many reasons why young people—and it is overwhelmingly young men—become radicalized. As many reasons as there are radicals themselves, we like to say. Social and economic factors, of course, but also political disenfranchisement, identity politics and the perceived erosion of traditional notions of masculinity, sexual frustration, alienation from family, problems with law enforcement, religious illiteracy and no doubt many other factors combine in different ways to push so many young, active people towards destructive and self-destructive ends.

But it has to be noted that these factors are not unique to young Sunni Muslim men. Across the world, they are extremely common for young people of all nationalities, races, and creeds. Yet it is nevertheless uniquely Sunni young men that go from seething in this poisonous soup of deprivation and resentment to terrorism, suicide bombing, and indiscriminate killing of innocent civilians on a mass scale. If only the underlying factors were enough to drive someone to such indiscriminate killing, then why do other groups who are even more marginalized not commit similar violence on a similar scale? Why are young blacks in inner-city United States not blowing themselves up in crowded public spaces, or why are Palestinian Christians in European ghettos not doing anything of the sort? In effect, at the end of feeling marginalized there must be an ideology that can convert that feeling of anger into the means to carry out acts of violence.

In many ways the use of suicide bombings has become the one thing that differentiates extremist Sunni terrorism from other violent responses by the excluded. It is, of course, not unique to them. The Hindu Tamil Tigers in Sri Lanka also used it extensively but in the context of their self-styled liberation struggle. The secular PLO certainly sent its fighters on missions that were guaranteed to end in their deaths. Equally Shi'a Muslims have also engaged in suicide bombing,

---

3   Karen Armstrong, "Wahhabism to ISIS: how Saudi Arabia exported the main source of global terrorism," New Statesman, 2014 http://www.newstatesman.com/world-affairs/2014/11/wahhabism-isis-how-saudi-arabia-exported-main-source-global-terrorism.

but it is always done for well-defined, narrow strategic purposes and within the formal structures of bigger political organizations. This is not to excuse or justify it in any way, but at least the Shi'a fighters have a well-defined idea of what they are dying for.[4] Mass indiscriminate killing of civilians for no obvious immediate tactical purpose but in the name of some poorly understood "higher purpose" is indeed uniquely specific to Sunni jihadism—and flows from the core ideology of Salafism that those who do not share their beliefs are, at best, flawed Muslims but most likely are either apostates or a threat to true believers.

This understanding starts to move us beyond the "push factors"— those factors that push so many young people to desperation and petty criminality all over the world. There is a very specific reason why Salafist beliefs in turn create a small minority within their community who wish to kill all who do not share their own beliefs. This means we must look at specifically those unique "pull factors," those factors that shape the response to these conditions so specifically in young Sunni men that they alone go out to commit indiscriminate mass murder, and claim to do so in the name of their religion, with such depressing regularity.

I argue that the difference between young Sunni Islamists and so many other young people who share similar frustrations and despondency is that they are uniquely exposed to an ideology that rationalizes and indeed encourages specific kinds of violent responses to their conditions. Sunni Islam is currently the only large religion in the world which has a strong—and growing—strand of thought that justifies and implicitly condones indiscriminate violence against anyone who is not a member of the inner religious group.

This strand of thought is militant Wahhabism—a sect of Islam that emerged in what is now modern-day Saudi Arabia in the early 18th century, and which has come to be the kingdom's state religion. Wahhabism, or as it is more politely called these days, Salafism, is not, as its

---

4   Andrew L. Peek, "The Roots of Lone Wolf Terrorism: Why the West's Homegrown Jihadists Are All Sunni," Foreign Affairs, 2016 https://www.foreignaffairs.com/articles/middle-east/2016-01-12/roots-lone-wolf-terrorism?cid=soc-tw-rdr.

proponents like to claim, simply a strict interpretation of mainstream Islam, a revival of older beliefs that has happened many times over the centuries, akin to the fundamentalist claims of many Christian Bible–literalists. Rather, like so many of the extreme sects of the Christian Reformation, it was a new ideological creation masquerading as a return to the simplicities of the early Muslim Golden Age. But unlike the historical "Golden Age" of the first caliphates, Wahhabis see all "non-Muslims," including the other "People of the Book"—the Christians and the Jews—as opponents. What is more, they also see all non-Salafist Muslims as deviants and apostates who had diverted from the original tenets of Islam. As such, these Muslims deserve even harsher treatment than nonbelievers. They are to be given one chance to convert to the Salafist creed. If they refuse, they are to be ostracized, or, sometimes, killed. And the early Wahhabis killed with considerable enthusiasm.

Contemporary Salafism has moderated its murderous urges to quite a large extent. At its most benign, it merely insists that believers should treat "nonbelieving" Muslims, and, of course, those of other faiths and none, as deviants to be kept at arm's length lest a "true believer" be corrupted by the habits and ideas of the outsiders.[5] Believers are discouraged from helping non-Muslims or seeking their help in return,[6] and even to speak well of non-Muslims. It is not just a belief that stresses rigor of faith;[7] it is a belief that regards the rest of the world as an active spiritual and moral threat, and which imposes on the "true Muslim" the need to stay well away from all who do not share their radical Salafist beliefs.

In short, even at its most benign, Salafism is a creed and ideology that dehumanizes everyone who is not regarded as a pure "true Muslim" and actively urges intolerance and discrimination as a moral and religious duty. It should be hardly surprising that this kind of

---

5   Roel Meijer, ed. *Global Salafism: Islam's New Religious Movement* (Oxford: Oxford University Press, 2009).

6   As we will see, much of what constitutes Salafist beliefs is in direct contradiction to mainstream interpretations of Islam.

7   Ali Al-Arian, "Why Western attempts to moderate Islam are dangerous," AlJazeera, 2016 http://www.aljazeera.com/indepth/features/2016/01/western-attempts-moderate-islam-dangerous-160118081456021.html.

worldview lends itself so easily to terrorism. The logic of seeing everyone else as corrupted can easily become the logic to argue that they are not even really human. That their sins are such that both the individuals and their societies should be destroyed whether these are Muslim or not, in part to protect those who are pure and in part to bring the benefits of religious purity to those mired in darkness.

Again, we need to be careful here. We may find such beliefs repugnant and offensive, but they are not that unusual. Many religious belief systems have a militant fringe who wish to convert others so that they can be rescued from their own sins[8] or who are sanguine about the fate of nonbelievers.[9] Equally many belief systems, both religious and secular, have spawned movements that seek to remove themselves from what they see as a corrupt world—and one that threatens their own beliefs by its very corruption. Equally, conversion of nonbelievers is not exactly just a theme in Salafist beliefs: almost all faiths have engaged in this, often with extreme violence. In addition, constructing a flawed myth of the past to justify current actions is scarcely limited to just Salafists.

This theme is perhaps the fundamental issue in this book. Many self-identifying groups, whether on religious, political, or ethnic grounds, tend to have a fear of corruption due to engagement with other people. Sometimes this can produce essentially benign if closed groups, such as some ultra–Orthodox Jewish sects, Christian groups such as the Amish, or those with socialist or green beliefs who opt to live in a separated commune. However, such separation always carries a risk—whether of malign control within a separated group or the desire to force others to accept your preferred lifestyle.

On the other hand, a constructed fear of a group of "others" under the control of an outside power and aiming at undermining "our" society is depressingly common in Western European and North American politics. As an example, for two and a half centuries Protestant England made sure

---

8   Shmuley Boteach, "Godlessness has doomed Britain," Jerusalem Post, 2011 http://www.jpost.com/Opinion/Columnists/Godlessness-has-doomed-Britain.

9   Katherine Stewart, "How Christian fundamentalists plan to teach genocide to schoolchildren" The Guardian, 2012 https://www.theguardian.com/commentisfree/2012/may/30/christian-fundamentalists-plan-teach-genocide.

that Catholics were excluded from public life, as it was feared they would serve the pope, not the Crown. Republican secular France regarded those Catholics who did not accept the primacy of the French clerical leaders with deep suspicion on the same grounds. Fears that socialists were all being controlled by Moscow as part of a well-orchestrated plot were common in post–World War II America. The dehumanization tactic has also been employed by others in history. When the Nazis came to power, they started their persecution of the Jewish community not by mass murder but by identifying them in public and then taking away certain rights, jobs, and then homes and possessions. By the end, Jews seemed "otherworldly" (and dirty, marked, and alien to "civilized" society), so that when the Final Solution was implemented, they had already been cast out by their former neighbors. Thus we need to be clear why we identify modern-day Salafism as such a unique threat.

Disagreeing with something, especially if it describes us in terms we find to be repugnant, is not a reason to break with a long liberal tradition of acceptance of differences. Even the fact that Salafism contains a violent core is not sufficient. The same charge can be levelled at both those from the radical political left and, increasingly, the newly energized far right.[10] Most people in both groups are not violent, many explicitly reject violence, but some use very similar arguments and beliefs to justify extreme violence.

Equally if we are to simply reject all Salafists—or, worse, all Muslims—we play into their hands. They believe that Islam is under attack and that Muslims are at risk whenever they live in a state not based on Sharia law. As we will see later in this book, they repeatedly use events such as the Bosnian civil war to justify their belief that Muslims are always at risk—even in the most integrated of societies. Their leaders would like little more than to be proved right that Muslims have no place in Western societies. However, if we are to see Salafism as a fundamental threat, there is an important question: How are we to respond to its many nonviolent adherents?

---

10   Arie Perliger, *Challengers from the Sidelines: Understanding America's Violent Far-Right* (West Point: Comating Terrorism Center, 2012); Dale Watson," The Terrorist Threat Confronting the United States," FBI, 2002 https://archives.fbi.gov/archives/news/testimony/the-terrorist-threat-confronting-the-united-states.

Before we can answer this question, we need to understand what we are dealing with. At the moment Sunni extremism is being presented as something unique—as will be further argued and developed in this book—yet it is perhaps less new than even its own adherents would like to believe. But it is one of the major threats facing the modern world, so we cannot downplay it. But, to repeat, before crafting a response we must understand what we are dealing with.

Salafism, reflecting its Wahhabist roots, is also, unsurprisingly, very strongly anti-intellectual. Whereas traditional Islam is a highly literate and intellectual religion, with a plurality of carefully developed traditional schools of Islamic jurisprudence, and where learning about the theology and history of the religion requires a rigorous curriculum of many years of study, Salafism leans more towards a simple-minded Qur'an-based literalism, makes little appeal to the centuries of rich theological thinking and jurisprudence, and puts little emphasis on the social and moral importance of the mosques. As we will see, few of its leaders actually qualify as Islamic scholars. This DIY protestantism is also exactly the model of ideological dissemination that sustains modern-day self-radicalization, one of the most common ways in which young people become radicalized.

There are thus two ways in which Salafism lends itself perfectly to jihadi radicalization: the first one is in the attitude it encourages towards the outsiders, and the second in the attitude it encourages towards any careful study of Islam.[11] In both cases, behind the veneer of the self-righteous drive for moral purity lies an attitude of contempt: contempt towards people not exactly like the "believer" and for ideas that are not exactly like the "creed." That this attitude spills over into excesses of violence should not be surprising. If anything, it should be surprising that it does not do so more often.

The first wave of Wahhabism had, as we shall see in later chapters, every bit of the zeal and murderous brutality of today's ISIS. But in the second part of the 20th century, the Wahhabi religious establishment

---

11   Andrew Lebovich, "How 'religious' are ISIS fighters? The relationship between religious literacy and religious motivation," Brookings Institute, 2016 http://www.brookings.edu/research/papers/2016/04/how-religious-are-isis-fighters-lebovich.

and their House of Saud allies have toned down on the violence, for reasons of political expediency. What they have not toned down on, however, is the attitudes towards other people and other ideas. Nevertheless, the orthodox Salafism of the leaders of Saudi religious establishment today is indeed pacific.[12] When they decry terrorism and violence in the name of Islam, they are being honest and their conversion to what they call "quietest Salafism" should be seen as real.

But they make no apology for sharing those same attitudes towards outsiders that the jihadis also adopt. And will insist that their creed and those attitudes—the very same creed and attitudes that Saudi-funded imams teach in Saudi-funded mosques across the world—are not linked to jihadi violence. Yet the research into radicalization yields, time and time again, the exact opposite conclusions: the Salafi tenets and the attitudes towards other people and other ideas that they engender are the recurring factor that sets apart jihadis from other equally marginalized and brutalized young people. And it is particularly noteworthy that none of the jihadis from non-Arab backgrounds, such as those committing attacks in Europe who come from North Africa or the Indian subcontinent, draw inspiration for their acts from the Islam of their parents and grandparents, who come from long traditions of open, liberal Islamic jurisprudence. They inevitably talk the language of the Salafist, and share the Salafist disdain towards the thoughtful theology and jurisprudence of their cultural background, opting instead for the simplistic, pamphlet Islamism that gives voice to their personal grievances.

Yes, in Europe and North America we now face a direct threat from groups like ISIS and what remains of Al-Qaeda, who still organize and direct some attacks. The recent massacres in France and Belgium[13] are chilling reminders of the threat they still pose. However, the much greater, deeper, longer-term but currently hidden threat comes from the dissemination of Salafist teaching. A lot of it is ad hoc, via the

---

12   Charles Allen, *God's Terrorists: The Wahhabi Cult and the Hidden Roots of Modern Jihad* (Philadephia, PA: Da Capo Press, 2007).

13   Lincoln Clapper, "The Saudi Connection in the Belgium Attacks," Geopolitical Monitor, 2016 https://www.geopoliticalmonitor.com/the-saudi-connection-in-the-belgium-attacks/.

Internet, as some groups of young men, or even lone individuals, self-radicalize through social media, forums, or other media. Most recent attacks in North America seem to fit this pattern, often involving second-generation American Muslims who have become radicalized. But equally, Saudi Arabia invests billions of dollars every year, money they get from us when we buy their oil, into building mosques and funding clerics to disseminate their Salafist state religion all over the Muslim world and, in tandem, all over the West. As we will see in the example of Kosovo, there is a depressingly close correlation between Saudi religious funding and the subsequent growth of violent jihad.[14]

This is why any response to the rising tide of global jihadism must start with an examination of radical Salafist interpretations of Islam, and why any coordinated effort to stop its global dissemination must start by confronting the state that sponsors this ideology—Saudi Arabia—head-on. Equally, our response to Salafism must always be aware that we are not fighting a group of people but rather an ideology. So victory will come not on the battlefield, or in a secret undercover war, but from overcoming that ideology. The more our politicians use binary language of "us" and "them" and argue that all Muslims are the problem, the more we actually feed the underlying beliefs of our Salafist opponents. The only way to resist the logic of our enemies is to emphasize not the often fictitious differences between us that the Salafis insist upon but rather the humanity we all share and the interest that most of us, Christian, Muslim, Jewish, or atheist, share in living a peaceful life in a fair and safe society. Just like mainstream Christianity, or mainstream Western secular humanism, mainstream Islam responds to those exact same needs and interests of safety, civility, and neighborliness. That is why, after two Islamists stabbed a priest to death in Rouen, France, in July 2016, the Muslim community in the town joined their Catholic neighbors for Mass in their cathedrals and churches, and for the wake for the deceased priest. It is only to the Salafist radicals that this obvious gesture of humanity and decency might be shocking.

---

14 Carlotta Gall, "How Kosovo was Turned into Fertile Ground for ISIS," *New York Times*, 2016 http://www.nytimes.com/2016/05/22/world/europe/how-the-saudis-turned-kosovo-into-fertile-ground-for-isis.html.

RADICAL ORIGINS

PART ONE
LOOKING BACK TO THE ISLAMIC GOLDEN AGE

Today's radical Islamism is filled with strange contradictions and paradoxes. If it were to have one explicitly stated goal, it would be to "bring back the Golden Age of the Islamic caliphate." This is very odd for quite a number of reasons. The one reason that strikes the observer straightaway is that it is a kind of reactionary antimodernism that is nonetheless intermingled with aspects of modernity, not the least of which are modern weapons and modern propaganda strategies, notably, the Internet, with 7th-century styles of corporal punishment, forced amputations, lashing, stoning, and all the rest, under the guard of Kalashnikovs, filmed on smartphones and broadcast on Twitter.

This matters for two reasons. One major theme in this book is we need to stop seeing modern-day Salafist terrorism as in some way something new or unique. As we will see both at the level of ideology and in terms of tactics, they are the (unacknowledged) heirs to many previous movements based around a violent rejection of the status quo. However, having said this, if we are to deal with this latest incarnation of this particular problem, we need to understand exactly what it is that drives today's Salafists. As indicated in the introduction to this book, an acceptance of violent jihad is rare even among the Salafist community, but there are aspects of the underlying ideology that make the journey to violence relatively easy. If we are to deal with this threat (and it is a serious threat), we need to do so in a manner that will first break the link between ideology and violence and, at the same time, to discredit the ideology.

Despite the contradictions in modern Salafist thinking and practice, so far their seemingly reactionary goals and the apparently modern means they use to achieve it have gained considerable traction, not least in the minds of alienated young Muslims in the West. However, this tension between using modern methods and a desire to return to an idealized past is not new in the history of terrorist movements. The late-19th-century Russian *Narodniks* made effective use of the new train network (and the technology provided by modern explosives) to plan their attacks even if their stated goal was to return Russia to some fanciful rural idyll.[1] This helps stress an important secondary theme in this book: Islamic terrorism is but the latest incarnation of something that certainly has been used as a form of protest throughout modern history—and often as an explicit revolt against that very modernity. As with their unacknowledged predecessors, we have the apparent contradiction of young people completely at ease with the technologies of the modern world, but using those assets to pursue a goal of re-creating a form of state that has not existed for over a millennia (and it is very dubious if it ever existed in the form they now claim to seek).

Firmly identifying Salafism as an antimodernist current underpinning much of what is happening today in the Middle East, as well as in Muslim communities all across the world, is a fundamental theme of this book. To understand this reactionary Islam we must understand its history, and how it in turn fits in with Islam and its history.

In this chapter we start by looking at the remarkable story of the rise of Islam and its place in world history. This will help us understand both the ideology of reactionary and violent Islam, and the psychology of those who are seduced by this ideology. Westerners are generally unaware of the history of many regions across the globe, especially those regions where Islam is the dominant religion. Often they are ignorant of their own history. In the United States, for example, for most people "history" begins in 1776. And if that is not bad enough, most people's understanding of the history of Islam is basically nonexistent.

This gap also affects how young Muslims living in the West learn both the history of the West and the history of Islam. This gap allows for erroneous teachings to take root. We need to acknowledge how and why the Salafists distort the history of Islam to suit their agenda. In effect, we need to answer the question, How can a group of young, Western-born, Western-educated Muslims find the ideals of 6th- to 7th-century Arabia in any way attractive? Well, perhaps if you consider that within just a couple of generations of emerging on the scene

---

1   Derek Offord, *The Russian Revolutionary Movement in the 1880s* (Cambridge: Cambridge University Press, 1986).

Islam built the largest empire the world had ever seen seemingly out of nothing more than the desert sands, you would not find it so surprising. To the believers, even at the time, this could not have been anything other than a miracle bequeathed by God. It is a miracle that still captures the imagination. Just like we here in the United States thought we had a "Manifest Destiny" to expand across a continent.[2] Imagine how the "heirs of the caliphate" must think then when they believe that they too can claim a past where Islam spread across the known globe. And imagine how they must think about what went wrong, and why the "Muslim World" as it stands today seems in such a state of decay.

But as is usually the case with reactionary ideologies, many things in the Islamist frame of thought are very upside-down. The story of the rise of Islam in this chapter will illuminate the way in which Islamism, with its backwards reading of history, is in fact inconsistent and intellectually self-defeating. By the lights of mainstream Islam, and by the lights of history, these ideologies are a bitter betrayal of everything Islam meant to the Prophet and his followers, and a blunt rejection of everything that made Islam great throughout its history.

Herein lies the irony of ISIS, and of similar groups: they harken back to an age of "moral purity" in the Islamic Golden Age of Muhammad and the first caliphs. This is what they use to justify subjecting people to medieval punishments in semi-arbitrary fashion, and bitter discrimination and oppression of any individual or group that deviates from their narrow view of the world.

Such barbarity was not common in the early caliphates, yet it *was* found in some communities outside the caliphates where Islam had spread *without* the core structures of the new religion and state. The early success of Islam was indeed linked to a moral mission. In that much ISIS is correct. But that moral mission was not to impose one fixed, unquestioning dogma or a stale reading of the Qur'an that may not change under the pain of death. It was a mission to bring peace, tolerance, and liberty to all people—regardless of ethnic group or

---

2   Hugh Brogan, *The Pelican History of the United States of America* (London: Pelican, 1985).

5

religion and, to a lesser extent, gender. Islam, I will argue, was successful precisely because in the context of the time it was a moral step forward for the people that came under the administration of the Muslim caliphs. And it can never hope to be successful if it ever represents a moral step backwards—or as in the case of today's Islamic radicals, 1,400 years' worth of steps backwards.

Even so, we must nonetheless acknowledge that Islam's early history, and indeed its history since, has not exactly been one of perfect moral rectitude. There have been many wars. There was much bloodshed in the early history of Islam. What by modern standards we would call atrocities were committed—and the fact that this was the common etiquette of war at the time should not stop us from describing the facts as they are. There are many critics in the West who point to this history of bloodletting as evidence of Islam's inherent backwardness. But such criticism is ill thought out. Of course people from the 6th, 7th, and 8th centuries had views we would now regard as morally backwards—and this applies whether they were Muslims or Christians or Jews or from other faiths at the time. The Persian Zoroastrians killed some seventeen thousand Christians in and around Jerusalem when they captured the city in 615 A.D. In turn, the Christians killed many Jews in revenge when the city was retaken in 630 and the survivors were forbidden to live in the city. Later on, the behavior of the early Crusaders was a shock not just to their notionally Muslim opponents but also to the adherents of the various Eastern forms of Christianity.[3] And none of what I am saying here is to defend any excess carried out by any state or any religion over one thousand years ago.

But no early caliph went to war with the express purpose of subjugating or converting Christians or Jews.[4] And when Christians,

---

3   Amin Maalouf, *The Crusades Through Arab Eyes* (London: Al Saqi, 1983).

4   Quite the opposite. Some Umayyad caliphs and their governors were actively trying to prevent people from converting to Islam. According to Qur'anic injunctions, *dhimmis*, or non-Muslim citizens of the caliphate, would be liable to pay an extra tax, the *jizya*, so that they would be protected "on equal terms" by the Muslim community and allowed to be subject to their own religious laws and authorities. This tax constituted a large proportion of the income of the state, and when Umar II greatly reduced the number of people who had to pay this tax, it led to serious cutbacks in military spending that would eventually bring down the Umayyad dynasty.

Jews, and even pagans found themselves under Muslim rule, they were always given due protections by law and treaty. No early caliph took ghoulish pleasure in cruel punishments and the suffering of the vanquished. And even when protecting the *Ummah* (in other words the realms where Islam was now the state religion) required carrying out acts of violence or brutality, the decision to take the course of war was never taken lightly. That was a standard of probity that did stand above the normal practice of Christian Byzantine emperors or Zoroastrian Iranian shahanshas. And it represents a level of morality squarely above the practice and the intent of the so-called Islamic State in Iraq and Syria today.

If this is the case, then we need to understand where the ideology behind today's Islamic State comes from. Of course, as with any large religious group, at times Islam has spawned more or less tolerant sects. Equally there has always been a debate about the reasons why Islam has shifted between being outward looking, driving forward scientific discoveries, and its sometimes more reactionary periods. This book primarily argues that it is the perverse and reactionary reading of Islam and its history that allows for such poisonous ideologies to develop. In particular, the Wahhabi strand of Islam that emerged in the early 18th century has become the taproot for all modern Islamic extremist movements.

This points to an important issue. Wahhabism, for all its fundamentalist zeal, for all its harkening back to "the original, true religion," is ironically an 18th-century invention. It has about as much to do with the history and theological development of Islam in the first centuries after Muhammad as Mormonism has to do with the early Christian church.

For the moment I will set aside discussion of this strand of modern Islam and use this chapter to provide a short, but hopefully accurate, depiction of the history of Islam as it is known in the mainstream Muslim tradition. I will also take into account recent scholarship from non-Muslim sources about the historicity of these events. Readers with a background in Islam should not find anything here that is particularly surprising. But Western readers who are not familiar with Islam and its beliefs will.

How so? You will be surprised how much the Message of the Prophet has in common with Western ideals of democracy and human rights. This is no joke. For example, what do you think the most Islamic country in the world is? Iranian-born professor of International Business and International Affairs at George Washington University, Hossein Askari, conducted a study into how closely 208 countries and territories organized their societies in terms of law, politics, and business to resemble the principles outlined in the Qur'an.[5] So you might think of Saudi Arabia? It is the place of the two most holy sites in Islam, Mecca and Medina. But you would be wrong. Or perhaps Indonesia: the largest majority-Muslim country in the world. But not so. According the professor's study of the values of different countries in the way they run their societies and public administration, the most Islamic country in the world is: Ireland. Followed by Denmark, Luxembourg, Sweden, the UK . . . you are perhaps noticing a pattern. The highest-ranked Muslim-majority country is Malaysia, at number 33. Next up is Kuwait at 48.

In 1899, Muhammad Abduh, a respected Islamic scholar who had travelled to the West and met with many scholars of his day at Oxford and Cambridge Universities, at Paris, Vienna, and Berlin, was appointed grand mufti of Egypt, that country's highest religious authority, and leader over the hugely important Egyptian centers of Islamic scholarship. Upon returning from his travels he is reported to have said, "I went to the West and saw Islam, but no Muslims; I got back to the East and saw Muslims, but not Islam."[6]

Professor Askari's study simply reflects that the world has not moved much in this respect in a hundred years. This chapter will hopefully shed some light into what these two eminent scholars mean. It will also inform much of my critique of Wahhabism in subsequent chapters.

---

5   Damien McElroy, "Ireland 'leads the world in Islamic values as Muslim states lag',"
     The Daily Telegraph, 2014 http://www.telegraph.co.uk/news/worldnews/europe/
     ireland/10888707/Ireland-leads-the-world-in-Islamic-values-as-Muslim-states-lag.html.

6   Shahab Ahmed, What Is Islam? The Importance of Being Islamic (New York: Princeton
     University Press, 2016). p. 174.There is no actual hard evidence that Abduh said this
     exact thing, but he produced many publications articulating just this sentiment, and
     it seems that many of his contemporaries, and his followers in the early 20th-century
     Islamic Modernist movement did in fact agree.

MUHAMMAD AND THE BIRTH OF ISLAM

T he story of Islam begins with the story of the life of its prophet, Muhammad. Muhammad is believed to have lived between 570 and 632, in the fiercely tribal and often brutal world of the Arabian Desert. By all accounts, his life was not an easy one—but his achievements are all the more spectacular for it.

According to Islamic tradition,[7] Muhammad was born in the Quraysh tribe of Mecca, who were at the time in charge of the city. However, Muhammad's family belonged to a marginal clan of the tribe, the Banu Hashim, and was neither especially wealthy nor politically powerful. But what really made life difficult for Muhammad as he was growing up was the fact that his father, Abdullah, died before he was born. Growing up without paternal protection in a tribal society puts one very much on the edges of society. In keeping with Arab traditions at the time, Muhammad is believed to have been sent by his mother to be raised by a Bedouin family in the desert outside the city—this was considered to be good for young babies, making them healthier and better prepared for later life in the desert sands.

While the young boy's life prospects had already been seriously hampered, perhaps an even more significant event in the early life of the Prophet was the loss of his mother when the boy was six. It is difficult to imagine what emotional and psychological impact that would have on anyone now. But the circumstances in which this happened to Muhammad were all the more dramatic. His mother, Amina, had fallen ill in Mecca. She decided to take the young Muhammad with her and to try and make their way to the oasis town of Yathrib, where they had family who could tend to her health and look after the boy. But halfway along the journey her health declined dramatically. The caravan they were with left them in a small oasis for her to rest and recover her health. But she never did. She died shortly thereafter. And the young Muhammad was left for several days in the oasis tending to the body of his mother, until the next caravan came along.

---

7   Tariq Ramadan, *The Messenger* (Oxford: Oxford University Press, 2007).

Being marginalized by society is one thing. Being left utterly alone for days, seemingly abandoned by the universe, in such a way at such a young age is quite another. It is impossible to imagine quite what an impact that could have had on the young Muhammad, but one thing is certain: the Prophet forever after had a burning concern for the weak, for those marginalized or left outside of society, for those who have nobody to protect them and little ability to protect themselves. In that, it seems, he honored the memory of his mother for the rest of his life.

When he was finally found by the next caravan to pass through the oasis, he was fortunate enough to come under the guardianship of his paternal grandfather, Abd al-Muttalib, according to tribal custom, and later, at the age of eight, under the guardianship of his uncle Abu Talib, the new leader of the Banu Hashim clan. With Abu Talib, the young Muhammad began a life as a merchant. He is known to have travelled with the Banu Hashim trade caravans towards Syria and other trading centers early in his teens. This would allow him to accumulate not only some degree of wealth but also social status. He built a remarkable reputation for honesty and integrity, and by his twenties, he had already earned the appellations *al-Amin* ('faithful' or 'trustworthy') and *al-Sadiq* ('truthful'). As a consequence, he was often sought as an impartial arbitrator in trade disputes between competing merchants, and thus constructed a healthy network of acquaintances and business relations built on trust and respect.

Through his reputation as an honest and highly capable merchant, he came into the service of Khadija bint Khuwaylid in 595. Khadija was a forty-year-old widow who had built one of the most successful and wealthy trading businesses in Mecca, and was thus one of the most powerful people in the city. She dispatched Muhammad on a trading expedition to Syria. When Muhammad came back with a substantially larger than expected profit, Khadija proposed to the twenty-five-year-old man. Though it was highly unusual for an older woman of such high status to propose to a younger man of lower status, the match did seem to make sense, both to Muhammad and Khadija, and also to their respective families—the match was quickly agreed. And it was a fortuitous match too. By all accounts, the two fell in love, and were happily married for the next twenty-five years. And despite Arab society at the time having polygamy as a norm, Muhammad and Khadija remained in a monogamous marriage for as long as Khadija was alive.

Muhammad had thus risen, in little over twenty-five years, from desolate orphan to a respected and well-connected pillar of his society. But his society was still harsh and brutal, one in which most orphans did not rise the way he had been lucky enough to. Instead, orphans, women, widows, the poor, anyone on the edges of society were living in very precarious conditions, at the mercy of powerful merchants and warriors. They could be robbed of the little they had, physically abused, traded as slaves or even killed, with relatively few repercussions. And though he rose to a position of security, Muhammad had not forgotten what it was like to be in such a precarious condition. He had achieved success and a great measure of personal happiness, but he remained profoundly disenchanted with the lack of justice in his world.

MUHAMMAD'S MORAL MISSION

Muhammad's disenchantment led him over the next fifteen years to take periods of seclusion and spiritual retreat. He would go up into the mountains surrounding Mecca at different times of the year, often with Khadija and his family, to get away from it all. There, he would meditate, pray to the gods of his time, and reflect upon the condition of the world around him. He was trying to make sense of the injustices in society. But more than that, he seems to have had a deep anxiety about finding long-lasting solutions to those injustices.

It was after fifteen years of being tormented by these problems and concerns, to the point where he needed frequent refuge from society, that Muhammad is said to have had his first revelation of the Message of God in the cave of Hira above Mecca from the voice of Archangel Gabriel (or *Jibra'il* in Arabic): "Recite in the name of your Lord Who created / Created man from a clot of congealed blood. / Recite: and your Lord is Most Generous / Who taught by the pen—/ taught man what he did not know." (Surah Al-Alaq 96:1-5)

The *Qur'an*, or 'the Recitation,' is the collection of revelations Muhammad received throughout the rest of his life. Like the other Abrahamic religions, the first and most fundamental tenet of Muhammad's message is the Oneness and Uniqueness of God, *al-Tawhid* in Arabic. This God, *Allah* in Arabic, is also the God of Abraham, Moses, and Jesus. And "there are no other gods beside [him]" (20:14). This message was not what the Qurayshis wanted to hear. They were keepers of the Ka'aba in Mecca, the holy shrine of the Arabic peoples in the region, where the idols of all the tribal gods were held. And they derived much of their wealth from the pilgrimages and trade generated by the shrines. They would go to great lengths to dissuade Muhammad from proselytizing his revelations, and later, to great lengths to try and remove him from Mecca, and Arabia.

But Muhammad was undaunted. His God was the only true God, but also a God of justice, a God who made all people equal and in the eyes of Whom all people were of equal moral worth, to be judged only on their individual merits. This God created the weak and vulnerable in the same way he created the rich and powerful—and demanded that they should be equally protected. Women, children, the infirm, the poor and wretched, all demanded the same consideration and dignity as the most exalted in society.

THE CONSTITUTION OF MEDINA—
THE PROTOTYPE OF AN ISLAMIC STATE

But this was not just about theology, or religion. This was to be the moral foundation of a new kind of state—an *Islamic* state, in accordance to the Will of God. Yet Muhammad would not initially have the opportunity to implement such a state in Mecca. The Quraysh had no time for Muhammad's message or for his God. And when it became clear that Muhammad would not bend to their status quo, not even Muhammad's position and power could keep him, and his small band of new followers, safe. Muhammad did not seem intent to leave

Mecca, and he and his community tried to stay on despite increasingly severe repression, including being banned from buying food in the local markets for nearly two years. But when a shift in the internal politics of the city meant that the small community of believers came close to being massacred, they had to leave.

And thus the *Hijra*, the 'migration,' from Mecca happened in 622. The Prophet and his followers moved north, to Yathrib, where the local tribes invited Muhammad to serve as an adjudicator and impartial administrator in the diverse but internally fractured town, with its fiercely competitive Arab pagan and Jewish tribes and clans. Yathrib became known subsequently as *Madīnat an-Nabī*, 'the City of the Prophet'—today, Medina.

The *Hijra* is hugely significant in Islam. It marks the beginning of the Islamic calendar. It is not the birth of the Prophet, or even the first revelation, that marks the beginning of the Islamic age. Rather, it is the *Hijra*. And it is very important to explain why. In leaving Mecca, Muhammad and his followers did not just flee their hometown for fear of persecution. As I have mentioned, Arabia at this time was an intensely tribal society. People could not simply leave their town, their community and their tribe and clan, their blood relations. The tribe was sacred, as much as one's tribal god was sacred. In leaving Mecca, Muhammad and his followers were not simply seeking an easier life elsewhere. They in fact committed as heinous a heresy as one could have in the Arabian society of that time.

Remember, Muhammad had had his first revelation at the age of forty, roughly around the year 610. And though he spent the twelve years prior to the *Hijra* in Mecca, telling the Meccans and any visitors to the town who would listen that their gods were not gods at all, that there is no god but the one God, he suffered in order to live and preach his message. Yet when he and his community decided to leave Mecca, to leave their tribes behind, this was considered a much more serious transgression. And from that point on, the Meccans would pursue Muhammad wherever he went. He was marked for death.

The decision to leave Mecca was thus nothing short of a revolution—both political and moral. It was the first time in Arabia that a group of people formed a community of ideology, underpinned in this case by Muhammad's message of submission to just one God, and such a community superseded the traditional communities of blood, the family, and tribe, which formed the foundation of Arab society at that time. It is this fundamental shift in the conception of what underpins social relations that marks the proper beginning of the Islamic age. That is why the *Hijra* is year 1 in Islam.

And what happened next is equally fundamental. Upon arrival in Yathrib/Medina, Muhammad did not find a city in the way that Mecca was a city. Rather, Yathrib was an oasis that hosted a number of villages, each small settlement being dominated by a variety of tribes: for example the Banu Qaynuqa, Banu Qurayza, and Banu Nadir, who were Jewish; or the Banu 'Aws and Banu Khazraj, who were Yemenite pagans. Each tribe was fiercely independent, and competitive, and they had long histories of feuds with each other. It is in this tense environment that Muhammad and his new community were invited and asked to serve as mediators.

Muhammad's initiative was to establish a new state, a new *kind* of state—an *Islamic* state. The fundamentals of this state were codified in the Constitution of Medina[8] and were very much the practical application of the principles of all humans being equal under one God that Muhammad's prophecies urged. The Constitution:

1. Established all the people of Yathrib as "one nation [*Ummah*] separate from all peoples." This, note, was regardless of their tribe, clan, or religion;[9]

---

8   It is unclear whether this constitution actually existed in the sense in which we think of constitutions today, as a written/codified legal document establishing a state. The earliest historical evidence of the existence of such a document dates to one hundred years later. If it existed in such a form, it would be perhaps the first example of a written constitution in the world. In any case, all scholars do agree that some kind of formal agreement or treaty was established between all the tribes of Yathrib, the new Muslim immigrants, and Muhammad. And there seems to be a broad consensus on what this agreement would have contained.

9   Today, the word *Ummah* is used to refer to the transnational "Muslim community," what most Muslims would refer to as the Islamic Nation. Note what a different meaning the word had for the Prophet!

2. Established peace between the tribes and banned all private justice: all disputes were to be mediated peacefully, according to law;

3. Forbade the tribes to wage war without his authorization;

4. Guaranteed the freedom of religious belief and practice for all citizens;

5. Ensured that representatives of all the constituent groups of Yathrib would be present at any consultation in matters of state or foreign affairs;

6. Codified protections for women;[10]

7. Established a system of taxation to support the functioning of the communal aspects of the society, especially in times of conflict and hardship;

8. Declared the land of Medina as holy ground, upon which none of the signatories of the pact could spill each other's blood.

This is clearly not entirely the foundation of a modern liberal state, but it went further along the way towards such a state than any other state in the middle of the 6th century A.D. And further along the way than many Muslim-majority countries have gone today.[11] Nor was this by any means a perfectly egalitarian state. The rights of women were still relatively lower. The citizens of the state continued to belong to sub-communities: for example, if two Jews had a dispute between them, they would not be arbitrated under the general state law, but rather under Jewish law.[12] And while Muslims were necessarily the

---

10 Though by no means equal rights in the modern sense. But it is still important to note that these protections were a substantial improvement on the way women were previously treated, as little more than chattel.

11 This was the fundamental point of both Muhammad Abduh and Professor Askari earlier in the chapter.

12 Though whether this is a plus or a minus is open to debate.

guardians of the state, non-Muslims could hold any kind of public office, except that of leader. That was reserved for the leader of the Muslim community. But as a political settlement, it was more positive than anything Arabs had experienced before. And it established the template for governing a diverse, plural, and vibrant population, which, in due time, would go on to conquer much of the known world.

Not that this new kind of state was without its growth pains. Infamously, the Jewish Banu Qaynuqa were accused of breaking the treaty of the Constitution and suspected of having closer relations to the Meccan Quraysh, with whom they had extensive trading links, than to Muhammad and his new state. This led to a series of open conflicts between the group and Muhammad's new state, and their eventual expulsion from Medina. And indeed, Muhammad's ongoing conflict with Mecca, up until his final victory over the Meccans in 627, created many tensions within his new state. But the moral and political principles underlying this new kind of state proved rock-solid despite these birth pains. And perhaps they even achieved sharper definition in the conflicts that threatened to undermine them.[13]

Muhammad's young state at Medina did survive the five-year onslaught of the Meccans' army, even though they had superiority in numbers. And, through the wise building of alliances with other

---

13 A particularly problematic episode for the Treaty of Medina happened during one of the last fights between the Meccans and Medina at the Battle of the Trench. Mecca attacked Muhammad with a force of 10,000 against 3,000, so Muhammad decided to fight defensively. He fortified the Medina oasis and built a large trench across the most obvious entry route to the oasis. The rest of the oasis is shielded by volcanic mountains. This held off the Meccans for two weeks, and their supplies started to run out. But the Meccans seemingly managed to strike a deal with the Jewish Banu Qurayza, so that they would attack Muhammad's forces from within Medina. This alleged break of treaty, at such a critical point for the survival of the young Muslim community, prompted a swift and brutal response: after a brief trial the traitors were executed. This would have been a standard response to treason according to the norms of the time. But it nonetheless remains a hugely contentious issue for Muslims and Jews alike, to this day. People from both sides argue bitterly about the rights and wrongs of what occurred. But what cannot be denied is that the Constitution, for all its merits and high ideals, was no longer a pure and innocent institution. Nonetheless, as we shall see, this did not lead to a special animosity between Islam and the Jews in the centuries immediately after these events. Indeed, the Jewish Golden Age happened in Muslim-controlled Spain later in the Middle Ages. Anti-Semitism within Islam is a rather more recent phenomenon, often associated with Wahhabism.

neighboring Arab tribes,[14] Medina ultimately asserted itself as indomitable in Arabia. The final confrontation was not a military one. Rather, Muhammad managed an unusual political coup against the Meccan Quraysh. In 628, Muhammad and his followers set out from Medina to Mecca, to perform the *Hajj*, the traditional Arab pilgrimage to the Ka'aba. This journey had been part of the pre-Islamic pagan religions of the region. But to perform the *Hajj*, one has to be unarmed. The Muslim community thus went towards Mecca, into the hands of their enemies, completely unarmed or ready for battle. The Quraysh did not accept them into Mecca. But it would have been against everything that their own traditional religion stood for to spill the blood of pilgrims to the Ka'aba, hence Mohammad's motivation to approach Mecca in just this fashion. So the Quraysh and the Muslims came to an agreement: Muhammad and his followers would be allowed to perform the *Hajj* in the following year, provided they agreed to a truce and a set of otherwise rather humiliating demands from the Quraysh. At the time, this might have seemed like a defeat, but the decision to pursue peace rather than war would reap huge benefits for the Muslim cause.

Muhammad and the Muslim community finally returned to Mecca in 629, and during their visit to the Ka'aba, they also impressed the civilian Meccans with their righteous behavior. They were already winning hearts and minds. But the following year, 630, the Quraysh broke the truce with Muhammad and attacked one of his allies. His extended web of alliances now came into play, and he managed to bring together a huge force of ten thousand against the Quraysh transgressors. He marched onto Mecca. The Qurayshes' forces could not hope to match him, and they were expecting to be wiped out. But Muhammad did something completely unexpected next. He declared a general amnesty. And he declared that no one should be forced to join his Muslim community or submit to it. But he did go straight to the Ka'aba and cleansed it of all the idols of the Arab pagans. None of the Meccans, or indeed any of the pilgrims to Mecca, were ever

---

14   Many of these alliances were achieved through marriage, and Muhammad practiced polygamy. He is supposed to have had between nine and thirteen different wives as a consequence of this alliance-building exercise. This is something that often raises eyebrows for modern readers, but it was entirely common practice in Arabia at the time.

forced to convert or subjected to any brutality. But the idols were not to be tolerated in the shrine of God, built by Abraham (as the Ka'aba at Mecca was traditionally believed to be). In this respect, Muhammad was returning the shrine to its original focus on a single deity shared with earlier Jewish and Christian traditions.

Subdued, Mecca was then absorbed into the *Ummah* of Medina. The inhabitants were afforded the same rights and protections, as well as the same duties, as the citizens of Medina. And then, Muhammad simply went back home, to Medina. With the Quraysh pacified, much of the rest of Arabia quickly submitted, voluntarily for the most part, to the new order. Entire tribes were also converting to the new religion, even though there was no requirement to. The new model of society, underpinned by the new religion, prevailed over the rest of Arabia. The *Jahiliya*, the Arabian pre-Islamic "age of ignorance," had ended.

In 632, Muhammad returned one last time to Mecca to perform the *Hajj*. Here, he delivered what would be his last sermon. *Be righteous, and do not stray from the path. All men are equal before God: Arab and non-Arab; white or black; Muslim and non-Muslim. Always do the justice of God.* This was his message. A message that would reap his young community huge rewards as it expanded. But a message that, unfortunately, seems to have been quite forgotten by many of those who proclaim the loudest today that they themselves are Muslims. After this last sermon, Muhammad returned to Medina and died soon after, surrounded by his family and his followers.

THE CALIPHATES

By the time of Muhammad's death, this template of society, of government, spiritual and temporal, was ready for prime time: it was ready to take over the world. Most neighboring regimes were grounded on discrimination against those who did not share either a defined faith (Christianity to the Byzantines, Zoroastrianism for the Iranians) or a particular ethnic identify. Such rigorously stratified societies not only practiced slavery but also discriminated in every respect against those who were seen to be excluded.

But the Arabian *Ummah* itself was not ready just yet. Neither the Muslims nor the other groups of Arabia had yet contemplated what would happen to the new order once Muhammad died. Muhammad himself always repeated that he was only human. And that he had no special powers—that the only miracle of Islam was the message. But the Muslim community had nonetheless found it deeply traumatic to hear that their Prophet had simply died. Many of the tribes of the new *Ummah*, upon hearing the news, promptly withdrew from the political pact. The pagan tribes argued that they were not bound to the Muslim community but had only submitted to Muhammad himself. And many of the Muslim tribes started fighting over the succession to their communities.

This situation was exacerbated by interference from the two super-powers neighboring Arabia: the Byzantine Eastern Roman Empire, and the Iranian Sassanid Empire. Both had watched with concern how Muhammad had brought together the people of what traditionally would have been a tribal no-man's-land and fashioned them into a new and vigorous state. Neither wanted a competitor power on their borders. So they both sponsored various splinter groups within Arabia, and encouraged tribal and sectarian divisions. It is in this hugely volatile political situation that Muhammad's family and closest followers had to come together to ensure that their community and the new social order in Arabia would survive.

THE RASHIDUN—THE RIGHT-GUIDED CALIPHS

Most of the leaders of the Muslim community rallied around a man called Abu Bakr. He had been one of Muhammad's closest friends, one of the earliest converts, was a father-in-law to Muhammad and had been with Muhammad when they escaped from Mecca for the *Hijra*. He was also one of the oldest and most proven of

Muhammad's followers, so most Muslims felt he had the most authority to take over the leadership role in the new community. He was thus duly elected caliph, or "deputy" of the Muslim community. This was not an election in the way we think of a democratic election today, but it was a decision reached by consensus by a council of representatives of various groups within the community. So in a sense, a process not too far removed from how a US state would nominate a senator.

But it was not quite as straightforward as that. The closest male relative of Muhammad was a young man called Ali ibn Abi Talib. He was the son of Muhammad's uncle Abu Talib, who had taken Muhammad under his wing all those years ago. He was married to one of Muhammad's daughters, Fatimah. And he had also been one of Muhammad's closest followers, friends, and allies throughout. Many thought that Ali would be Muhammad's natural successor, especially given the blood ties. There are also verses in the Qur'an which, according to some particular readings, seem to indicate that Muhammad designated Ali as his heir and successor (e.g., 5:55 and 5:67).[15]

Ali was not present at, and it seems he was not aware of, meetings that were being conducted to establish the succession. He is believed to have been tending the dead body of Muhammad at that time, as he was supposed to do according to his relation to the Prophet and tradition. When he found out that the succession had been established, he objected to the procedure. He did not accept the outcome for some time, and he also had many followers who supported him instead as the rightful leader of the Muslim community. In time, this group would come to be known as the Party of Ali, today known as the Shia, the second-largest denomination in Islam after the Sunnis.

---

15   5.55. "Your guardian and confidant is none but God, and His Messenger, and those who, having believed, establish the Prayer in conformity with all its conditions, and pay the Prescribed Purifying Alms (the *Zakāh*), and they bow (in humility and submission to Him)."

5.67. "O Messenger (you who convey and embody the Message in the best way)! Convey and make known in the clearest way all that has been sent down to you from your Lord. For, if you do not, you have not conveyed His Message and fulfilled the task of His Messengership. And God will certainly protect you from the people. God will surely not guide the disbelieving people (to attain their goal of harming or defeating you)."

The division between the two main branches of Islam was thus originally a political one. But in time, the two also developed deep doctrinal and theological differences.

The conflict between the Sunnis and the Shi'a would go on to dominate much of Muslim history, and it is one of the fundamental conflicts in the Middle East to this day. But at the time, the divergence between Abu Bakr and Ali was not in fact that deep. Though he felt betrayed, Ali eventually conceded that it would not be in the interest of the Muslim community for there to be a succession civil war, and he eventually accepted Abu Bakr's election peacefully.[16] With that matter resolved, and with the acceptance by the Muslim community that succession should be decided in this quasi-democratic fashion rather than dynastically, Abu Bakr and the Muslims could focus on reestablishing order in Arabia.

But the next three decades would nonetheless be ones of constant conflict. On the side of the Muslims, Abu Bakr (632–634) would be succeeded as caliph by other Companions of the Prophet: Umar (634–644), Uthman (644–656), and finally, Ali himself (656–661). There continued to be internal tensions and differences, but the main threat now was from the outside. Both the Sassanids and the Byzantines were still intent on breaking apart the new Muslim state, and so the four caliphs were forced to follow a consistent foreign policy: they had no choice but to wage war against both powers.

And they did so with stunning success. They started with overrunning the entire Arabian Peninsula, and then added Syria (637), Armenia and Egypt (639), North Africa (652) and Cyprus (654), amounting to two thirds of the territory of the Byzantine Empire, while the entire Sassanid Empire was conquered in steps from 633 when they conquered Mesopotamia (today's Iraq), until 651, when they got as far as today's territories of Afghanistan and Pakistan. This is how in just three decades, the companions of Muhammad built on the legacy of the Prophet to create an empire that rivaled that of Alexander the Great.

---

16 Different traditions give different timescales for how quickly Ali conceded the leadership contest, but all say that he did so within six months.

But the gains were not just territorial. The caliphs didn't just occupy land. They renovated or rebuilt the local infrastructure in their new territories, they built new settlements, and brought Muhammad's Qur'anic law, as well as the model of the state of Medina, to the territories they conquered. Furthermore, many of the people in conquered territories found Islam itself as a religion to be a natural development of Judaism or Christianity, and they converted in large numbers, whereas the Zoroastrian religion dominant in the former Sassanid territories had always been an exclusivist cult for the elites, and the general population relished the fact that in the new state, they could belong to the same religion as their leaders, on equal terms.[17]

Alexander the Great had built a similarly large empire, covering much the same areas, but after his death the empire imploded and the successor states would spend much of the following two centuries fighting each other until Rome's expansion ended their squabbling. The Islamic expansion, by contrast, would continue for at least the next two centuries, and then would usher in an age of innovation and science that was comparable to the European Renaissance, five centuries later. The difference is important: while Alexander spread Greek culture and language, his successors mostly remained a small Greek elite separated from the local population and absorbed with their own dynastic struggles. The reason for the difference in success was Muhammad's model of an Islamic state: an inclusive state, where all people were part of the same *Ummah*, irrespective of tribe, nation, or religion, with largely equal rights and obligations, tolerant and indeed protective of a plurality of customs and beliefs and with a very strong ethos of social justice. The bottom line is that while the remnants of the Roman Empire and Europe were eating themselves alive and setting the stage for the Dark Ages, fighting each other, fighting Christian

---

17 At least in principle. For a long time, there was still a sense that the Arab Muslims should be at the top of the imperial and social hierarchy, but in time Muhammad's message of racial and ethnic equality would prevail.

heresies, suppressing pagans and the writings of pagan Greek and Roman scholars and philosophers; the caliphs and the successor Muslim empires were building a state in which people *wanted* to live, which attracted the brightest and most talented from all over the world, including wise religious leaders, philosophers, scholars, and what would in time come to be called "scientists."

THE UMAYYAD CALIPHATE–GOD'S SWORD

However, expansion also brought tensions, not least between religion and the need to govern the new lands. Much of the early history of Islam can be understood as a struggle between the moral teachings of the Prophet and the earlier social and political instincts of the Arab *Jahiliya*—the pre-Islamic dark age of paganism in the Arabian Peninsula. To some extent, that can probably be said about the struggles in the Middle East today. But it was certainly the case in the political circumstances that led to the fall of the early Rashidun caliphate and the emergence of the Umayyad dynasty as the dominant political force of Islam. To many fundamentalists, 661—the year when Muawiya ibn Abi Sufyan became the supreme political power in the Islamic state after a five-year-long civil war that lasted during the entire caliphate of Ali—is the end of Islam's Golden Age. It is when the moral purity of the caliphate became irrevocably tainted. This view is broadly shared by Salafis, Wahhabis, and jihadis, but also many others. In addition, the majority of Sunnis and Shi'as also take a pretty dim view of the Umayyads. For all their good points, this was to be a deeply flawed dynasty.

Upon the death of Ali, his successor and grandson of the Prophet, Hasan ibn Ali, concluded a treaty with Muawiya to end the civil war and acknowledge the latter as the caliph of the Muslim community. But this new leadership was not going to be run in the republican fashion, as had the Rashidun, with leaders serving as deputies of Islam elected by popular constituencies, under the provisions of the Constitution of Medina. Rather, it was going to be more of a traditional, dynastic and imperial administration. In this sense, at least, the new regime of Muawiya represents a fundamental regression from the message of Muhammad and the spirit of his leadership.

The Umayyad record of government is mixed and highly contentious. Their dynastic approach was widely resented, and the period to 750, when they were finally deposed, saw wave after wave of rebellions and no less than three *Fitnas*, or civil wars. They are also widely regarded as having built not so much a Muslim caliphate as an Arab empire. The message of racial equality that Muhammad preached was widely ignored. Arab Muslims were regarded as the top of the social hierarchy. Non-Arab Muslims were held as inferior, and were for the majority of this period subjected to much the same taxation regime as non-Muslims. Non-Muslims were largely afforded the protections prescribed by Muhammad, but there were periods of brutal repression, against Jews, against Christians, but especially against Persian Zoroastrians: in direct contradiction to the Qur'an, there were periods when the Zoroastrian clergy was slaughtered *en masse*, and Zoroastrian temples were destroyed.[18]

But it was under their rule that the caliphate achieved its largest ever expanse: from Morocco and Spain to northern India. And this brought Islam to the territories that are its heartland to this day. Save for Spain, Portugal, and Sicily, everywhere the Umayyads went, Islam is now the dominant religion. And it was a well-organized and well-run empire, with adequate infrastructure, adequate trade and communication links, a well-functioning post office, eventually its own stable currency, and a place where civilians could for the most part travel safely from one end of the world to the other. This was no mean feat in the 7th and 8th centuries. In the subsequent centuries, these territories would come to be the center of civilization, trade, and scientific development for the entire world.

They ruled over not an Islamic empire but a multiconfessional, highly cosmopolitan empire. For most of the period, the share of

---

18 According to the Qur'an it is strictly prohibited to kill the priests of other religions or destroy places of religious worship.

Muslims in the empire was far below 10 percent of the population. It is more appropriate to say that they ruled over a secular state that allowed for certain specific political privileges for Arab Muslims. Indeed, one of the main causes of the repeated rebellions was the belief that the caliphs themselves were Muslims just in name: for most of the Umayyad caliphs, everything from their style of government to their private behavior was secular. And despite an emphasis on Arab Muslims running the state, Christians and Jews very often found themselves in chancellorships, governor's seats, and indeed a role in imperial marriages—Muawiya's wife and the mother of the second caliph, Yazid I, was a Syrian Christian.

Even with the regressive tendencies of the Umayyads, anyone who was not a strict Orthodox Christian as required by the Byzantine emperor or a strict Zoroastrian as required by the Sassanid Kings was still safer and better off in the caliphate—and they paid lower comparative tax rates too. As far as we can tell, the repressions against religious communities during the Umayyad period were rarely, if ever, primarily driven by religious animosity. Save for one or two Umayyad caliphs, they did not seem to have cared all that much about Islamic orthodoxy themselves. By and large, the repressions happened when, at a local level, some group was perceived to be a threat to the state or to civil order. This also explains why the Zoroastrian faith was especially targeted, because it had always been and remained a fundamentally Persian-nationalist imperial cult—the imperial cult of another emperor and of another civilization. This was not going to be tolerated, especially by a succession of caliphs who were constantly challenged throughout the empire, on many, many grounds.

History in the Islamic world was established as a separate scholarly discipline during the dynasty of the Abbasids, who would follow the Umayyads. This matters, because when the history and achievements of the Umayyads were finally recorded in writing—under a new dynasty, a century after the events occurred—the Umayyads were never going to get good press. But for all the Umayyads' follies, and for all their achievements, it is nevertheless accurate to say that the Abbasids, their successors, gave Islam its Golden Age.

THE ABBASID CALIPHATE-THE LIGHT OF THE WORLD

The Abbasid revolution of 750 put an end to the Umayyads as caliphs of the Muslims.[19] It has been described as one of the "most well-organized revolutions"[20] in history, and had been in the making for many years before the events. According to tradition, the fundamental drive for the revolution was precisely the Umayyads' pre-Islamic tendencies, with regards to inheritance and dynasty, tribal and ethnic considerations, and even points of doctrine and theology: for example, the Umayyads styled themselves as "deputies of God," rather than "deputies of the Messenger of God," which many Muslims found deeply offensive. In all, by the 740s, the Umayyads had alienated the religious "minorities"[21] that had suffered from sporadic repressions and the non-Arab Muslim converts who were not treated as first-class citizens. Shi'a Muslims had hated the Umayyads all along because they rose to power at the expense of Ali and on the back of killing Ali's successor, Hasan ibn Ali. Additionally, an increasing number of Sunni Muslims were losing patience with the impieties and indiscretions of the caliphs. And when Marwan II moved the capital of the caliphate from Damascus further north to Harran, they even lost support in their heartlands in Syria. They had dug themselves into a hole.

This brought together virtually every constituency in the empire against the Umayyad dynasty, and the Abbasids very skillfully managed to unify this campaign to promote their own candidate for caliph: as-Saffah.

The Abbasids moved the capital from Syria to Iraq, first at Kufa and then to the newly built Baghdad, in 762. For the next four centuries, until 1258 when the Mongols invaded and sacked Baghdad, the city would be the cultural and scientific center of the world. What would

---

19 Though a branch of the Umayyads would survive in the splinter Emirate of Cordoba in Spain.

20 Hala Fattah, *A Brief History of Iraq* (New York: Checkmark Books, 2009)., p. 77.

21 They were minorities in the political sense but still largely outnumbered the Muslim community.

become Islamic civilization, art, culture, architecture, science, and even theology, religion, and law, achieved its definition in the Abbasid period. This is what historians and what mainstream Muslims both call the Islamic Golden Age.

The Abbasids were true to their promise of racial equality between Muslims. They were not always as true in their promise for protection of religious minorities, but in this they followed the Umayyad model of targeting groups according to the degree to which they were thought to pose a threat to the state and civic order. And still miles ahead of the chaos of schisms and heresy hunting in Europe during this time. But more than anything, the period is marked by the most astonishing cultural openness towards every new idea from every corner of the world, which would not be seen again until the Scientific Revolution in Europe five hundred years later. Throughout the period, the Abbasids remained true to the *hadith* (the collection of observations about the life and acts of the Prophet) that "the ink of the scholar is more holy than the blood of a martyr."[22]

The Abbasid caliphs sponsored the House of Wisdom in Baghdad, where scholars from all over the world, Muslims and non-Muslims, spent decades and even centuries translating into Arabic every single notable text from any civilization they could get their hands on: Greek, Roman, Persian, Indian, Chinese, and many others. Indeed most of what we now know about classical Greek and Roman culture, science, and philosophy from the European Renaissance, we originally learned from the Arabs, after the Christian Church in Europe had spent a millennium suppressing these "pagan" writings.

And when they translated it all, they started to expand on this body of knowledge. Out of the Greek tradition of skepticism and medical empiricism, the scholars of the House of Wisdom developed methods of inquiry that by any account must be described as empirical science, complete with an experimental method, well over five centuries before the idea would emerge in Europe with Copernicus and his contemporaries.

---

22   Note the dramatic difference in attitude from those today who claim to want to reestablish the Golden Age of the Islamic caliphate.

They developed mathematics and geometry. Al-Khwarizmi developed the Indian numerical system into the Arab decimal numeral system we still use today; he also invented algebra. Al-Battani used this to calculate the length of the solar year, the actual time Earth takes to revolve around the sun completely, to within two minutes of the currently known figure. And he also calculated the tilt of the earth's axis relative to the sun. Omar Khayyam, meanwhile, developed the quadratic equations that we still use today,[23] while al-Tusi developed trigonometry as a full, separate field of mathematics. Al-Kashi developed decimal fractions and calculated π to 17 decimal figures.

Al-Haytan discovered through experiment how the optics of the human eye work, with light reflecting off surfaces and being taken in and processed by the retina. Ibn Sina pioneered empirical medicine, and his *Canon of Medicine* was the standard text for physicians in Europe till the 17th and 18th centuries, while in the Islamic world his work continued to be developed and expanded on by many others. Jabir ibn Hayyan developed laboratory techniques and the experimental method for chemistry.

We could spend pages listing scholars and achievements that predated and, in truth, enabled the European Renaissance and subsequent scientific revolutions. But the point is this: this was perhaps the first example in history of a long-term, state-sponsored cultural and scientific research program, and it is what made Islam the most advanced civilization on earth. These scholars, Arab and non-Arab, Muslim and non-Muslim,[24] and their patrons were the foundation and the highest expression of this glorious age.

Empires come and go. And the Umayyad achievement in building the largest empire to that date could have easily failed and then be

---

23   As well as a corpus of elegant poetry, some praising the virtues of alcohol and others based on his somewhat casual love life.

24   Indeed, it may surprise the reader to find that it was not just people of other religions who were tolerated but also people of none. Ar-Razi, a physician of great renown, is the best known of them for his staunch rationalist rebuke of theology and holy books in general, but many other rationalist philosophers would have fallen in the deist, agnostic, or atheist camps. Yet in the "Islamic" countries of Saudi Arabia and Bangladesh today, expressing even mild skepticism is likely to get you killed in the street.

forgotten by history. After all, this empire had only lasted for one hundred years. And other such large empires that came and went overnight left little in the way of a cultural legacy, such as the Mongol Empire, which eventually brought the Abbasids to their knees. But the Abbasids themselves had not built an empire. They took an empire and built a true, global civilization within it. It is that civilization that is the legacy of Islam. That is the reason why Islam is still so important in the world. Without the Abbasids, the Message of the Prophet would have remained the exclusivist religion of a tribal and racist military elite that quickly came upon the world, and would have just as quickly been beaten back to Arabia. The Message of the Prophet had always been a universalist message of tolerance, peace, and intellectual plurality and openness. It is the Abbasids who took that message to heart and gave Islam to the world.

But this is not the Islam you'll get in ISIS recruitment videos. In fact, at this point you may be struggling to understand how we got from the House of Wisdom to desecration of Palmyra and Nineveh. This examination of that about-face is to come.

As history tells us, this Islamic Golden Age was not to last. It ended with the Mongols sacking Baghdad in 1258. Muslims remember the Mongol eruption from Central Asia as something that threatened the very existence of the Islamic civilization. In contrast, in Europe the Mongols only got as far as Germany, and didn't stay long. In the Abbasid caliphate, by contrast, they practically razed most of the empire to the ground, and then took it over, in turn creating a series of splinter khanates. And the vibrant and vigorous cultural and scientific ecosystem that the Abbasids had created in Baghdad would never really recover. The centers of Islamic civilization and culture would move westwards towards Cordoba in Spain and later towards Constantinople, from where they would bequeath the Europeans the intellectual underpinnings of the Renaissance. But perhaps it was already time for the light of civilization to move on to other places. By this point in time the Abbasid Empire was already stagnant, and complacent, riven by internal political divisions. And culturally too, acclaim moved from the scientists and innovators to more traditionalist "revivers of the faith," such as al-Ghazali, who in the eyes of traditionalists is celebrated for having shifted the entire intellectual discourse in the East to one based on theology and faith. His influence is so substantial that some historians have subsequently named Ghazali the second-most influential Muslim after the Prophet Muhammad.

In the turmoil of the 13th and 14th centuries, and in a cultural environment that was becoming increasingly closed off, introverted, and reactionary, the genius of the Abbasid Islamic Golden Age was progressively lost[25] following the fall of Baghdad. And even though the Ottoman caliphate would revive a significant amount of the political power and cultural vigor of Islam from this period, Islam would never again be the Light of the World, the most advanced civilization in the world and as dominant to global culture as it had been at the height of the Golden Age. And to this day, more and more parts of the so-called Islamic World seem to be slipping ever backwards towards a new *Jahiliya* (the pre-Islamic dark age in Arabia), where the name of the Prophet matters more than his message, and where *"Allahu Akhbar"* ('God is Great') is chanted in the name of death and war, not in the name of peace and enlightenment.

SUMMARY

T hus there is a clear line of descent from the community established by the Prophet to the scientific and cultural glories of the Abbasid Empire. This is not because all the rulers were wise and learned—they were not—nor is it because those who spread the new faith always followed the option of peace and tolerance; they did not. What stands out is the fact that the message of Islam survived all these vicissitudes of fate and the differing characters of men. In addition, like any vibrant intellectual community, Islam faced competing interpretations and the emergence of different traditions.

---

25   Ruzwan Mohammed, *Caliphate Reloaded: Past, present and future Muslim discourse on Power* (2016).

The most fundamental difference, and one that matters today, is between the Sunni and Shi'a communities. As we have seen, at first this was basically a matter of politics and the line of succession of the caliph. The early Rashidun caliphs broke the tradition of inheritance following kinship. This perhaps made it easier for the early caliphs to unify the disparate tribes of modern-day Saudi Arabia and to generate a genuinely multiethnic state. That Ali himself finally became the last of the Rashidun caliphs indicated that the early split could have been healed. This goodwill was lost by the great, but flawed, Ummayad dynasty. The death of Ali's sons at Kerbala opened a permanent fissure that came to take on both religious and political overtones.[26] Once a political division had opened, matters of doctrine started to emerge. While both strands of Islam have their own differences, a common thread in Shi'a jurisprudence is that the leader of the community must have certain religious values.[27]

Equally, the Ummayads diverged from the approach of the early caliphs in other ways. In many ways they came to see themselves more as the inheritors of the Roman and Greek Empires. It was not just the devout who were offended when they styled themselves as the "deputies of God" or rulers indulged in all the vices of a traditional Mediterranean dynasty. To be clear, this in itself did not make them bad rulers, but, combined with the dynastic approach and racial policies, it left them very vulnerable. Equally, the narrative of the dissolute caliphs of the Ummayad dynasty was to become a key part of the argument of subsequent fundamentalists of subsequent eras who argue it was at this time that mainstream Islam lost its connection to the true faith.

As I have argued above, this is nonsense. The subsequent Abbasid dynasty both reached back to the early messages of tolerance and the inclusive polity preached by Mohammad, and created the basis for a

---

26   However, we should still be careful about reading back today's sectarian strife to earlier periods. Egypt was ruled by the Shi'a Fatimid dynasty from the 9th to the 11th centuries. Neither the arrival nor the fall of the Fatimids led to sustained religious strife, as most inhabitants simply adjusted to the whims of their new rulers.

27   It is for this reason that the modern-day Islamic Republic of Iran reserves certain key posts for religious clerics while allowing a degree of democracy in other aspects of the governance of the country.

religious, cultural, and scientific flowering. Again, we are dealing with men with all their foibles, strengths, and weaknesses, but the result of their rule was to place Islam at the center of the world. And this was not because of their adherence to scriptural literalism but because they welcomed scholars and ideas from across the known world. Like all empires, they weakened and fell. If the Mongol invasion was what finally destroyed them, in truth the dynasty was already in decline from the 11th century. The arrival of the Seljuk Turks from Central Asia had already weakened their control of modern-day Iran and Iraq. Equally, the Crusades fragmented Muslim rule in Syria, Lebanon, and Palestine.

As with many empires in decline, somewhat malign intellectual currents started to appear. When one's world is crumbling, blaming the loss of divine protection becomes common. And of course, God only withdraws his support from those who no longer follow the true faith. In this argument, it was God, not the merits of the regime adopted by the early caliphs and the external forces, that had created a Muslim empire, and the fall of that empire must be due to the loss of God's support. This argument has reverberated across the centuries and found its modern expression in the Wahhabism that arose in modern-day Saudi Arabia in the middle of the 18th century.

By turning its back on the cultural and intellectual achievements of the Ummayad and Abbasid dynasties, this claimed to reclaim the truths and simplicity of the early caliphs. It is the core root of modern-day violent Salafism and Islamic extremism. How it emerged, and its basic belief systems, are the focus of the next chapter.

PART TWO
SAUDI ARABIA AND WAHHABISM

The radical Islamism that we are facing today, whether it is Al-Qaeda, ISIS, or lone wolf radicals, is in many ways a very recent, modern phenomenon, born in the 1950s as a result of a fusion between Saudi Wahhabist beliefs and the radical Islamic traditions of groups such as the Muslim Brotherhood. However, the ideological and politico-historical developments that led to its rise did not happen in a void. It is, for example, possible, indeed easy, to draw a genealogy of the thought and developments in the Islamic world that would lead to the development of derivative ideologies of Islam that would allow for these kinds of extreme violence. And in order to truly understand radical Islamism in the form of jihadism, Al-Qaeda, ISIS, Boko Haram, and other such movements, we must indeed trace the history of thought that gives rise to the possibility for reading of Islam in such a peculiar, unorthodox way.

As we will see in this chapter, the story of how this version of Islam arose is closely entwined with the history of Saudi Arabia. Understanding this often symbiotic, sometimes hostile, linkage is critical to understanding the intellectual underpinnings of Salafist violence, the challenge of how to deal with the majority "quiet"[1] Salafists, and the complex problem of how to engage with Saudi Arabia.

At an intellectual level, the crux of the matter is that "Islam," as understood by jihadists, is a reactionary, suspicious, intolerant, violent, anti-intellectual, anti-cultural ideology. It is an ideology of violent hatred towards anything and anyone who deviates, however slightly, from its own views on right belief and conduct. But as we have seen in the last chapter, that is in direct opposition to the letter, the spirit, and the practice of the Islamic founders and centuries of Islamic history. Islam, like any religion, has adherents who are more or less tolerant of those who do not share its beliefs, and this has been reflected in its

---

1   In other words the peaceful form of Salafism that is now officially promoted by Saudi Arabia.

history. However, on balance the record is one of a religion predicated on peaceful universalism, order and tolerance, a religion of inclusive learning and progressive social order. However, this history is now used by jihadists as the "model" for their ideology—one that is its exact opposite?

Naturally, as with any ideology, the roots of this reactionary reading of "Islam" are idiosyncratic and can be traced to social and intellectual manifestations of man's baser nature all through the history of the religion. You will be able to find Islamic scholars scattered throughout this long and complex history who contribute individual pieces towards the emergence of contemporary jihadist beliefs. And you will occasionally find individual instances of violent reactionary behaviors by Islamic states.[2] But the same applies if you look at Christianity. The cruelties of the Inquisition were driven by intellectual underpinnings, and the idea of spreading that faith by violence has been depressingly common.

But the real game changer for Islam was the rise of the ideology of Wahhabism.[3] This is where the problem of a reactionary tendency in Islam becomes entwined with the modern-day state of Saudi Arabia. Wahhabism is the wellspring of the majority of modern reactionary Islam, and it is the mother ideology to Sunni reactionary jihadism—effectively responsible for just about every instance of Islamist terrorism and extremism not directly associated with Shi'a Iran. The movement was established by Muhammad ibn 'Abd al-Wahhab (c. 1703–1791) in the Najd desert, now central Saudi Arabia. It represents a fundamentalist movement in Islam that in many ways paralleled the Reformation in European Christianity, two centuries earlier. Like the leaders of the Christian Reformation, Wahhabism started from the observation that contemporary Islamic practice deviated from the founding texts of

---

2   One example of this was the invasion by the very austere Berber Almovad dynasty of Islamic Spain in the late 12th century. The new dynasty displaced the religiously tolerant Almoravid rulers and actively persecuted Christians, Jews, and those Muslims who were seen to be too relaxed in their interpretation. Local rebellions ended their rule, but they probably hastened the end of Islamic Spain by destroying the relative unity of the Islamic kingdom centered on Andalucia.

3   Allen, *God's Terrorists: The Wahhabi Cult and the Hidden Roots of Modern Jihad*.

the religion, the Qur'an and the *hadiths*. So its defining characteristic at the time of its emergence was a desire to purge Islam from what it saw as "unsanctioned innovations" in Islamic practice that arose after the time of the Rashidun, during the Islamic Golden Age and subsequently.[4]

To understand what the movement is about, and how it works, one need only highlight its extreme *iconoclasm*. One of the first concerns of Al-Wahhab and his followers was the then wide-spread practice of reverence towards Islamic saints, which included visiting tombs and shrines dedicated to these saints. Al-Wahhab and his followers saw these practices as diverting worship from the unique, indivisible (*tawhid*) God, and thus a form of polytheism or idolatry (*shirk*). This is the worst kind of blasphemy against God, according to any reading of Islam, but the habit of visiting tombs and shrines of saints was far from idolatry, reflecting a wider (across all religions) practice of linking prayer to certain locations. But for Wahhabis, this became an all-consuming concern. Even reverence towards the Prophet Muhammad can sometimes be seen as suspicious, and Wahhabis discourage visitations even to the tomb of the Prophet himself.

But Al-Wahhab did not stop there. He went further and claimed that any Muslim who engaged in such practices, or indeed any practices that deviated in any way from the letter of the Qur'an or the practices of the Rashidun as he himself interpreted them, was no Muslim at all. He reinstituted the practice of declaring non-Wahhabi Muslims *takfir*, or 'apostates.'[5]

The majority of Muslims, who follow mainstream traditions, had not engaged in this practice of declaring other believers to be apostate since the very early days of Islam because the Prophet Muhammad forbade it. In effect, this declaration was so serious that it put someone outside the wider community, so it could only be applied when sanctioned by legal and religious authorities. But then the Wahhabis set themselves against the entire Muslim world, and effectively declared every Muslim that did not belong to their sect to be outside of the *Ummah*. And though

---

4   Malise Ruthven, *A Fury for God: The Islamist Attack on America* (London: Granta, 2002).

5   David Commins, *The Wahhabi Mission and Saudi Arabia* (New York: IB Taurus, 2009).

strictly speaking Wahhabism also urges nonviolence, violence against those outside of the *Ummah* is very easily justified. When Muslims are deemed apostates for refusing to acknowledge Al-Wahhab's reading of the sacred texts, then Wahhabism sanctions their death.[6]

In normal circumstances, such a borderline-suicidal little cult emerging in the middle of nowhere in the back end of a barren desert would have next to no relevance to world history, and would wither away and die before it even had the chance to be chronicled for the history books. Yet today, Wahhabism is the religion of state of the Kingdom of Saudi Arabia, and it is the most actively proselytized form of Islam around the world.[7] The reason for this linkage is critical to understanding the issues of radical reactionary Islam and of jihadism in the present and the future. In effect, we have a powerful, wealthy state that controls the most holy places in Islam, which was born as a marriage between a single dynastic family looking to take power and a local, reactionary interpretation of Islam.

AL-WAHHAB AND REVOLUTIONARY ISLAM

The movement of Wahhabism from historical aberration to now being the most vocal sect of Sunni Islam has occurred in three distinct phases:

1. A jihadi or "revolutionary" phase, as preached by Al-Wahhab himself and his immediate followers, roughly in the period 1744–1818. In this stage, the sect of Wahhabism sets itself against the entire Muslim world by declaring all Muslims not belonging to the sect as *takfir*, against whom it is legitimate to wage jihad.

6   Allen, *God's Terrorists: The Wahhabi Cult and the Hidden Roots of Modern Jihad.*

7   Yousaf Butt, "How Saudi Wahhabism Is the Fountainhead of Islamist Terrorism," Huffington Post, 2015 http://www.huffingtonpost.com/dr-yousaf-butt-/saudi-wahhabism-islam-terrorism_b_6501916.html.

2. A consolidation phase, roughly between 1823 and 1891, in which it became more theologically conciliatory. At this stage, it could no longer engage in active war with all other schools of Islam due to unfavorable political conditions, even though it still regarded itself as the sole true religion. Of note, this phase is when Wahhabism and the House of Saud made their alliance—one initially of convenience to drive the Ottomans from the Arabian Peninsula.

3. A mature phase, between 1902 and 1953, during which Wahhabi authorities acquiesced the absolute temporal supremacy of the House of Saud as "keepers of the Two Mosques" (Mecca and Medina), despite the fact that the House of Saud did at times adopt policies directly at odds with Wahhabi theology. This in turn is the point at which modern Salafism was created.

Despite this incremental movement from uncompromising dogmatism towards some pragmatic accommodation to the political realities around them, Wahhabis have lost remarkably little of their dogmatic zeal over the intervening two and a half centuries. And in some ways, their intransigence may have been a great source of strength for the ideology. To those looking for simple answers, a radical framework, kept austere and plain, can often be highly attractive. At times it will remain a minority viewpoint in part due to its sectarian intolerance, but its radicalism—and consistent and closed worldview—can attract wider support if it can pose as the one true defender of a community.[8]

---

8 This is not just an issue within Islam. The brief electoral popularity of hard-line pro-Soviet Communist Parties in Western Europe after 1945 can be traced to their pivotal role in the various resistance movements to German occupation. Ideologically and organizationally, they had been well suited to take the lead in the resistance and were also able to gain access to Soviet support and weaponry—thus earning themselves a reputation for being well equipped. In effect, they drew in wider support because they were effective, well organized, and ruthless—at a time when many were desperate to find some way to strike back at brutal occupiers. This has a modern aspect—reports from Syria suggest that some of the local support for ISIS has nothing to do with ideological affinity and much to do with their relative effectiveness in fighting opposition groups or as a vehicle for those seeking revenge on the Assad regime.

In times of stress, extremists can gain the support of a wide group of people.

The story of this persistent intransigence begins with the founder, Muhammad Al-Wahhab himself. He believed that Muslims in his time had strayed from the authentic teachings of Islam and had entered into a deep state of pre-Islamic ignorance (*Jahiliya*). As mentioned, he accused his fellow Muslims of saint worship, seeking intercession from and calling upon the pious dead and venerating the Prophet Muhammad, all of which were condemned by Al-Wahhab as folk practices and "innovations." But this was not merely a case of harmless ignorance. Al-Wahhab believed that such beliefs and actions compromised God's divinity, and therefore led Muslims to a state of polytheism (*shirk*). And then, he decreed that unless Muslims repented and adopted the Wahhabi way, they could be legally put to death.

To his followers, this message was as powerful as it was simple. If it was not in the Qur'an or the *hadiths*, then it was an "unsanctioned innovation" and, in all probability, blasphemy. Immediately, the simplistic logic behind this thinking also betrays two things. Though greatly respected by his followers and held up as a great reformer and reviver of Islam by populists, most Islamic scholars, then and now, point to the fact that Al-Wahhab lacked a sound Islamic education in both theology and jurisprudence. By ignoring the reality that the world changes, and that Islam provides a framework to deal with such changes, Al-Wahhab ignored every established school of Sunni jurisprudence. From the inception of his mission, both his message and the subsequent actions of his followers were condemned as a heresy by Sunni scholars from across the Islamic world. Needless to say, Shi'a scholars have never had any sympathy for his arguments either.

The second is that his followers, especially those keen to wage jihad against their *takfiri* neighbors, were generally equally ignorant of the finer points of Islam and the significance of the cultural developments within Islam beyond the period of the Rashidun caliphs. It was all very well *interpreting* reverence to saints as something uncomfortably close to misguided polytheistic worship and arguing against the practice.[9] But the fundamental role of pluralism of belief, of freedom of conscience and tolerance in Islam can only be overlooked by someone without a sound understanding of both the texts and the history of Islam, especially in its Golden Age. And the practice of branding people *takfir* on account of their beliefs was something explicitly prohibited by the Prophet Muhammad himself. In effect, early Wahhabism made little progress outside a small group, as to many Muslims its approach and argument were clearly deeply flawed.[10]

But the appeal of al-Wahhab's message went beyond its comforting reliance on simplistic, "ancient" truths. It also fed off the entrenched tribalism of the Arab communities of the Najd desert and the fear and dislike of outsiders that can often be found in closed, marginalized communities. Al-Wahhab accused the Muslims around him of falling into a state of superstition, heresy, and blasphemy by following corrupt religious practices and holding onto deviant religious beliefs under the auspices and direct protection of the Ottomans, who ruled over "the Two Mosques," and thus also held the title of Sunni caliph as a consequence.

In other words, the Ottoman Turks and their empire, which ruled over Arabs in much of the Middle East, had usurped both Arab lands and the true Arab faith. And were now contaminating the faith with all sorts of alien, inauthentic innovations.[11] Thus any Arab tribes that were less than keen on Ottoman rule over Arabia were now gifted this ideology of "true, authentic, Arabic Islam" as a rationalization and catalyst for rebellion. Or indeed, as an excuse for any local tribal lord to subdue neighboring tribes on account of their "heresies." It did not take long for just such a tribal lord to emerge. The alliance between the House of Saud and Wahhabism was one designed with strictly secular goals—taking power in the center of the Arabian Peninsula.

---

9   Michael Crawford, *Ibn 'Abd al-Wahhab* (London: Oneworld Publications, 2014).

10   Mohammad Hashim Kamali, *Principles of Islamic Jurisprudence* (London: Islamic Texts Society, 2005).

11   Of note, at this time the Ottoman Empire was undergoing a major reform of judicial interpretation of Islamic law—in turn making it vulnerable to allegations from strict traditionalists that it was turning from the true core of Islamic beliefs.

THE FIRST WAHHABI EMIRATE:
JIHAD AGAINST POLYTHEISM (1744-1818)

I n 1744, after having been expelled out of his hometown of 'Uyayna
because of the unrest caused by his reforms, Al-Wahhab was invited
by the ruler of the nearby town of Diriyah, Muhammad ibn Saud, to
join him. The two made a pact which their descendants have honored
to this day: Ibn Saud and his dynasty would protect and propagate the
Wahhabi dogmas, and in exchange the Wahhabis would grant religious
support to the rule of the House of Saud. Thus an essentially dynastic
and secular project was able to cloak itself as a religious revival.

Soon after forging the relationship with Muhammad ibn Saud, in
1746 Al-Wahhab issued a formal proclamation of jihad against all
those who opposed his doctrine. By 1773, the Wahhabi-Saudi alliance
had established and fortified itself in Riyadh, still its capital today,
from where they would extend their conquest throughout the Najd
plateau—and beyond. As they continued to expand their territories
through violent conquest, a veritable purge occurred. All Muslims they
encountered were either forcefully converted to the sect of Wahhabism,
fled, or were killed. What was to follow could only be described as a
reign of terror. The parallels to today's situation with ISIS will not be
lost on the reader.

In 1802, the Wahhabis attacked Karbala (situated in modern-day
Iraq, some sixty miles southwest of Baghdad) and decimated the most
sacred shrine of the Shi'as, the tomb of Hussain, the grandson of the
Prophet Muhammad. Lieutenant Francis Warden, who authored Britain's first official report on the Wahhabis, noted that they carried out
mass murder, "slaying in the course of the days, with circumstances
of peculiar cruelty, above five thousand of the inhabitants."

In 1803, as they sought to impose their interpretation of Islam, the
Wahhabis laid waste to Islam's holiest sanctuary, the grand mosque of
Mecca that contained the House of God (Ka'aba), killing many scholars
and destroying the tombs of saints. The following year, they entered
into Medina, Islam's second holiest sanctuary, destroyed the tombs of
the companions of the Prophet Muhammad, and pillaged the tomb

of the Prophet himself. When the Wahhabis returned again to Mecca in 1805, they destroyed more mosques, domes, and tombs, trashing relics and ornaments.

The iconoclasm of the Wahhabis still continues to this day. And it still always provokes condemnation from around the Muslim world. But imagine the shock waves that the initial attacks must have sent throughout the lands of Islam at the turn of the century. This was probably the first time that something like this had happened to the Muslim world, and at the hand of *Muslims*, no less. Echoes of the Mongol invasion resounded strongly, but at least in that case, the Mongols were making no claims to be representatives of their religion.

The Ottomans, for their part, only began taking notice of the Wahhabis when they overwhelmed Ottoman-administrated al-Hasa in the east and the Hijaz in the west of modern Saudi Arabia—the latter region containing both of "the Two Mosques," Mecca and Medina. Their initial reaction was to issue doctrinal refutations against this new creed, comparing the Wahhabis to the earliest splinter sect in Islam, the Kharijites, who also developed violent, extremist tendencies. But when both Mecca and Medina fell, the Ottomans woke up to the fact that the Wahhabis presented both a real temporal threat to the political authority of the Ottoman sultan and also a challenge to his spiritual authority as caliph and "keeper of the Two Mosques." They dispatched an Ottoman-Egyptian army directed by the talented Egyptian governor Muhammad 'Ali Pasha.[12] His orders were to reclaim the Hijaz and restore the empire's order.

By 1818, the first Wahhabi emirate lay in ruins. It was crushed and defeated. 'Abdallah ibn Saud, the head of the Saudi dynasty, and several members of his family were taken prisoners, paraded through the streets of Istanbul, and then beheaded. Other members of the Al Saud and Al Shaikh families either fled, were placed under house arrest, or exiled. As far as mainstream Islamic scholars were concerned, a

---

12 A highly talented soldier and administrator who had organized Egypt's recovery from Napoleon's invasion. The Ottomans came to regret their early sponsorship when, in 1839, he was to make Egypt *de facto* independent. Subsequently he came very close to conquering modern-day Syria and Palestine before being forced to withdraw when Western powers backed the Ottomans.

heresy that resulted in a rebellion against the legitimate Ottoman ruler of Islam had been rightfully exterminated.

THE SECOND WAHHABI EMIRATE: REGROUPING AND CONSOLIDATION (1823-1891)

E xcept that neither had the heresy been eradicated, nor had the two families that led it been completely subdued. The House of Saud regrouped and consolidated in its heartland around Riyadh in Najd. Al Shaikh also endured, even as its members were scattered. Wahhabism had already spread throughout the Arabian Peninsula during the first emirate, and the descendants of Al-Wahhab found a warm welcome with many of the local warlords who were left over after the collapse of the first state.

And once the chaos that followed the collapse had subsided, the House of Saud and some of their Wahhabi allies were able to rebuild much of their previous state in Najd. Yet the second emirate was in a radically different position from the first. It did not have the means to pursue aggressive expansion in new territories, as it had before. At times, it barely held together.

The Saudis were given breathing space due to their isolation. The Ottomans did continue to keep a watchful eye over the situation but generally were reluctant to intervene directly again, as long as the Wahhabis did not seem capable of mounting another attack on the Ottoman-administered al-Hasa and the Hijaz. And the first war had been costly. Military operations in the Arabian plains were always going to be a logistical strain, and there was very little reason why anyone would go to the effort of controlling that territory given the high cost of administering it and the very low yields for doing so.

The Saudis' alliance with the Wahhabis endured but with complications that hinted at future problems. The House of Saud was no longer the only protector of Wahhabi doctrines as rival families also converted to Wahhabism, asserting their own ambitions for power and territory. And some descendants of Al-Wahhab, in turn, supported these alternative claims to power. This meant that the period of the second emirate was largely dominated by tribal rivalry and intra-Wahhabi infighting.

The emerging Saudi emirate was most seriously undermined in 1838, when Muhammad 'Ali, now the governor of Ottoman Egypt, overthrew one descendant of Al Saud in Riyadh and replaced him with another, Khalid ibn Saud, as the new ruler of the Najd. Wahhabi scholars were divided over the move. Some chose to recognize what was *de facto* non-Wahhabi, Egyptian rule, while others chose to emigrate because they deemed the land to have now become "infidel land." So while the lands remained Saudi, it was no longer obvious whether they were also *"genuinely"* Wahhabi lands. This somewhat uneasy relationship between the House of Saud and Wahhabi purists has continued to the current day. In many ways this is the key issue—they coexist; at times their interests are as one, at others they diverge.

Having made a form of reconciliation with the Ottomans—or more strictly come to terms with the Ottoman settlement—the Saudis now found themselves attacked by some of their former allies. For this they used language that was to be repeated by bin Laden after the Saudis called in US aid following Saddam Hussein's invasion of Iraq declaring the aggressor to be an infidel. In opposition to the Saudis, some Wahhabi exiles used the xenophobic fatwas of Sulayman ibn 'Abd Allah ibn Muhammad (d. 1818), the grandson of Muhammad ibn 'Abd al-Wahhab, to argue their case. Sulayman had written two small tracts that revolved around the importance of having loyalty to Muslims and enmity towards non-Muslims (*al-wala' wa al-bara'*), probably produced during the first war between the Wahhabis and the Ottoman-Egyptian army. Sulayman argued that Wahhabis could not befriend the Turks or any of their allies—in this case, Khalid ibn Saud. If they did so, then their lands ceased to be truly Islamic.

He also argued that "true" Muslims (Wahhabis) could not travel to the land of the idolaters (Turks and their allies), since even this risked contaminating their faith. After the installation of Khalid ibn Saud, this interpretation meant that even Saudi lands were now uninhabitable for "true" Wahhabis. He cited his grandfather, al-Wahhab himself, who had written that true faith required showing "open enmity toward the idolaters." But showing open enmity towards the new Saudi ruler in Riyadh would likely get one killed, so many chose to leave and found refuge among the leaders of rival tribes. In effect, a religious dispute within the Wahhabists as to what constituted a land pure enough for them to live in also fused with a territorial dispute between different tribal groups in the Najd region.

The argument towards purity and exclusion among the Wahhabists developed even further. The great-grandson of Muhammad ibn 'Abd al-Wahhab and preeminent religious authority under the second emirate, Shaikh 'Abd al-Latif (d. 1876), argued that the Wahhabis had to hate the idolaters (non-Wahhabis in general but the Ottomans and the Egyptians specifically), since this was what God demanded, and that any allegiance to them was a clear act of apostasy. In their exile from Ottoman and Saudi lands, some of the most vocal Wahhabi scholars argued that the "abode of Islam" (*dar al-Islam*) had become polluted by the presence of idolatry, and this xenophobic streak within Wahhabism would be continuously exacerbated throughout the 19th century as they failed to regain their previous ascendency in the region.

The infighting between Wahhabis, and indeed between rival descendants of Ibn Saud, eventually allowed the competing Rashidi dynasty to rise to prominence and dominate the area. By 1891, the Rashidis governed most, if not all, of the central Najd region, and the Saudi emirate collapsed. Unlike the Ottomans, the Rashidis opted to tolerate the Wahhabis (despite the latter deeming them to also be "enemies of monotheism"), mainly as destroying the sect would have been nearly impossible. So Wahhabism continued to be taught, practiced, and lived by, firmly anchoring itself within the culture and religious life of the people of the central Najd region. But what it could no longer do during this period was impose, with violence, a unified Wahhabi vision upon non-Wahhabis in central Arabia and its environs. The uneasy alliances required by this period of turmoil and infighting also required some theological compromises to be made and thus some of the triumphalist, intransigent tones of the earlier period had to be watered down.

THE THIRD WAHHABI EMIRATE: MATURITY AND ORTHODOXY (1902-1953)

After the Rashidis destroyed the second Saudi emirate, the remaining members of the House of Saud found refuge with their previous enemies, the Ottomans, mostly settling in Iraq. But the Rashidis did not manage to pacify the Najd, and their rule was continuously challenged by tribal revolts. In 1901, 'Abd al-'Aziz ibn Saud (d. 1953), the son of the last emir of the second Saudi state, sought to exploit this situation to stake his claim to his family's ancestral lands. With help from the emir of Kuwait, who was also at war with the Rashidis, 'Abd al-'Aziz marched on Riyadh and, against very long odds and severely outnumbered, managed to take the city and rebuild it as a Saudi stronghold.

Over the next thirty years, Ibn Saud would manage to wrest control of Najd and capture most of what would become modern Saudi Arabia. His ascension to dominance during this period was aided and sanctioned by the British, with whom Ibn Saud had formed a strategic alliance in 1914. Ibn Saud found little difficulty in abandoning the Ottomans who had supported his original bid for power when the British offered him independence from Ottoman rule and the prospect of a larger kingdom carved out of Ottoman lands.

The Ottomans were still the major obstacle to Saudi power in Arabia in 1914 and a major barrier for any ambitious king. But with the onset of World War I, allied with Germany and Austria, the Ottomans called for a jihad against Britain, France, and Russia. Subsequently, Britain sought allies. In addition to supplying arms, advisors, and a monthly stipend, Britain vowed to acknowledge Ibn Saud's independence and provided a guarantee to defend him against any external aggression. After the war, the defeated Ottoman Empire collapsed and was partitioned between various mandates and states, with varying degrees of independence. This created a power vacuum in the Arabian Peninsula in which Ibn Saud could move with impunity—the only real limit to his expansion were the territories and interests controlled by Britain in the area. His British alliance in many ways pointed to both the pragmatism of Ibn Saud and the limits of the Wahhabist clergy. Not only was he careful to expand his power in a manner that avoided conflict with the British but when it came to conflict with the ultra-hard-line elements in the Wahhabist movement he was also perfectly content to accept their military aid.

This allowed not only the expansion of Saudi domains but also the aggressive resurgence of an expansionist Wahhabism. Between 1924 and 1925, the Hijaz fell to Ibn Saud's forces (Mecca in 1924, and Jeddah and Medina in 1925). The pluralistic religious practices and cosmopolitan culture of the Hijaz soon gave way to conformity and uniformity of the Wahhabi doctrine. And control of "the Two Mosques" also gave the movement a new claim to legitimacy over all Muslims, especially as the Turks had overthrown their sultan and dissolved the title of (Sunni) caliph.

In 1932, after expanding his holdings as far as he could without incurring the wrath of the global imperial powers, Ibn Saud declared the establishment of the Kingdom of Saudi Arabia. However, while allied with the Wahhabi establishment, Ibn Saud was not himself a Wahhabi zealot. Rather than seeking to purge and annihilate infidels from his new Wahhabi kingdom, as a rule Ibn Saud sought loyalty and allegiance from his subjects. Ibn Saud was a politician above all else, and what he needed now was political stability in his new, and still fragile, kingdom. Wahhabis still constituted less than half of his kingdom (and some 20 percent of his new subjects were Shi'a in any case, and these mostly lived in the eastern regions where the major oil reserves were discovered). Pragmatically, Ibn Saud was prepared to let the Wahhabi establishment have their way in some respects while he set firm limits in other areas of policy—including allowing divergent strands of Islam to be practiced in the new kingdom.[13] Thus he tolerated the substantial Shi'a population that lived along the eastern regions of his new kingdom.

This tension still lies at the heart of Wahhabism today. On the one hand we have a resurgent, reassured Wahhabism led by an

13   Said K. Aburish, *The Rise, Corruption and Coming Fall of the House of Saud*, 2nd ed. (London: Bloomsbury, 2005).

establishment, the Saudis, that controls "the Two Mosques" and thus has considerable prestige within the Islamic world. On the other hand, that establishmnet is still dependent on the Saudi political apparatus, which, despite its alliance with the Wahhabis, has interests and responsibilities well beyond those of Wahhabism and is often in a position of having to reign in some of its excesses. For its own part, the majority of the Wahhabi establishment has, begrudgingly, acquiesced to this political reality. It continues to fulfill its part of the bargain and supports the House of Saud's temporal supremacy, submitting to its political diktats when it has no other choice.[14] The large Shi'a population in the east is a particular source of tension. Both the regime and the Wahhabi establishment intensely dislike the doctrinal implications of Shi'a Islam, but the regime is now fully aware that Iran will intervene to protect its coreligionists if the persecution is taken too far.[15]

These tensions run deep in contemporary Saudi Arabia, especially given the fact that while the majority of the Wahhabi establishment accepts the need for some compromises, this leaves a minority with new grievances to add to their past list of complaints against the Saudi state. And when violent, radical dogmatists raise questions about the relationship between the religious establishment and the House of Saud, they tend to do so violently.

THE IKHWAN: THE ORIGINAL WAHHABI ULTRA-RADICALS

The Ikhwan, or "messengers of death," as a onetime advisor to Ibn Saud and minister for education called them, were a group of fearsome Bedouins who had emerged in Abd al-Aziz Ibn Saud's emirate just before World War I and fought the Wahhabi jihad with zeal and

---

14 James Wynabrandt, *A Brief History of Saudi Arabia*, 2nd ed. (New York: Infobase Publishing, 2010).

15 Jakob Reinmann, "Saudi Arabia vs. Iran: Predominance in the Middle East," (Washington: Foreign Policy Journal, 2016).

uncompromising brutality. They received specific education in the doctrines of Wahhabism from senior scholars who used to visit their settlements, and their chieftains and elders were required to travel to Riyadh and 'Uyayna to receive specific instruction from the Wahhabi epicenters of learning. They were immersed in the style of Wahhabism originally espoused by Sulayman ibn 'Abd Allah ibn Muhammad in the 18th century, driven by the doctrines of clan loyalty and enmity to those who did not share their sectarian beliefs. By their existence, they left open the possibility that the Saudi-Wahhabist conflicts of the 1840s and 1850s would flare up again.

There is some debate as to whether Ibn Saud created this force deliberately to help him expand his state in the early days. Alternatively, he might simply have found it to be a useful tool in his wars with the fading Ottoman Empire and other tribes in the Arabian Peninsula. Regardless of the truth, however, they were to cause him a lot of headaches as he tried to impose some notion of internal coherence on his new, emerging state later in his rule. For example, the Ikhwan often clashed with governors appointed by Ibn Saud. They insisted that Shi'as be forcibly converted to the Wahhabi faith (which some did) and be taxed. And they unleashed brutal repression against non-Wahhabis, often attacking and raiding unsuspecting caravans, pilgrims, and villages.

Ibn Saud's repeated attempts to pacify their zeal were unsuccessful. In 1919, Ibn Saud convened senior Wahhabi scholars to address the problem of the Ikhwan. During their deliberations, it was concluded that absolute authority rested with Ibn Saud: he had the sole legitimate authority to announce jihad, and to determine who was and was not an ally. Any who opposed him were declared to have gone against the faith. This understanding represented a pivotal junction in the coevolution of the dynastic rule of Ibn Saud in Arabia and what would become the *mainstream* Wahhabi religious establishment. It defines the relationship between the temporal and spiritual authority of the kingdom to this day. In effect, the mainstream Wahhabists reinterpreted their historical deal with the House of Saud—and acknowledged that the House of Saud was the dominant partner.

However, the Ikhwan were unrelenting. Despite their continued transgressions, Ibn Saud also continued to make use of their military prowess. It was the Ikhwan who led the attack on the Hijaz in 1924, where they repeated the massacre previously carried out at Ta'if. Consequently, Mecca fell without resistance. The inhabitants feared a repeat massacre. Following the capture of Mecca and Medina, it was the Ikhwan who led another destruction of tombs and irreplaceable relics. They destroyed ornaments that were in place at the birthplace of the Prophet Muhammad in Mecca, while in their wake Medina was left resembling the "remains of a town which had been demolished by an earthquake," according to one eyewitness. To calm fears of further destruction, Ibn Saud prohibited the Ikhwan from entering the Holy Sanctuaries of Mecca and Medina at any time in the future. In an attempt to curb their zealotry, he discharged several of the Wahhabi scholars who had been instructing the Ikhwan. He even tried negotiating with them, but their attacks against Ibn Saud's subjects did not desist. In the face of increasing defiance of his authority, it was inevitable that Ibn Saud had to put an end to what had become open rebellion.

The resulting Ikhwan revolt of 1928–29 was put down at the Battle of Sabalah, but only with the aid of the British Royal Air Force and troops from the British-controlled army in Iraq and Transjordan. After quelling the Ikhwan rebellion, Ibn Saud tried to continue developing his kingdom into a sustainable state that could survive in the modern world. However, he still had to deal with the consequences of his earlier pact with the Wahhabist establishment. Equally there remained an element of Wahhabism that would resist Ibn Saud's authority and the various pragmatic moves towards modernity taken by the Saudis and their often reluctant allies in the mainstream Wahhabi establishment.

This rejection of any compromise is a logical conclusion of a reactionary, xenophobic, violent ideology. It is difficult to imagine, after all, that Al-Wahhab himself would be happy with the compromises that the mainstream Wahhabi establishment has been forced into due to their relationship with the Saudi regime. The Wahhabists have always had to choose between adapting to the demands of the House of Saud (and some compromises with their own doctrine) or religious purity (on their own terms). It is not clear if Al-Wahhab would have prioritized the maintenance of the original Wahhabi dogmas, unmodi-fied, or the compromises of the centuries-old pact with the House of Saud. In effect, the extremists, within an already extreme theology, at least have the logic of their beliefs on their side. The result is that the Ikhwan were only the first of many outbursts of Wahhabi zeal to pose a threat to the political order of the region in the 20th century. Most often, the first target of these outbursts would be the House of Saud. But soon enough, things were to take on an entirely different dimension.

WAHHABISM BECOMES SALAFISM

Bolstered by Saudi oil revenues since the 1970s, Wahhabism has been aggressively exported throughout the world in the more pal-atable guise of Salafism. This term does not invoke Al-Wahhab or his teaching specifically as the Saudis try to break the link between the modern movement and its roots; rather it invokes the *salaf*, the term for the first few generations of "rightly guided" Muslims. It is thus an attempt at rooting the ideology of Wahhabism into the fundamentals of early Islam. It is an explicit reference to fundamentalism, but funda-mentalism in the sense of being associated with something authentic and authoritative—a move that mainstream Islam allows, and would be sympathetic to; after all, precedent is a cornerstone of Islamic cul-ture and civilization. Today, even the most hard-core Wahhabi scholars refer to themselves with the more sympathetic label "Salafi."

But Salafism is not simply a desire to live and worship according to the original form of Islam while tolerating the choices of others and valuing intellectual curiosity. It remains true to its Wahhabi dogmatic roots. It seeks to "cleanse" all Islam from what it views as condemnable religious innovations, and it continues the tradition of accusing the vast majority of Muslims of deviance, being astray from an "authentic" Islam and the gravest of all sins, polytheism (*shirk*).

Conforming to the Wahhabi global attitude, Salafism does not view itself as one of the competing schools of thought within Islam. It claims to represent "true" Islam in its entirety, and explicitly precludes any possibility of pluralism. In this respect, it is totalitarian—no true Muslim can disagree or diverge from its tenets. This matters, as it shows that we are not dealing with an austere interpretation of personal beliefs that acknowledges the legitimate choices of others[16]—we are dealing with something that treats those who do not agree with its beliefs as no longer being really Muslims. This is an important distinction: not all Muslims who opt to live by a strict interpretation of their faith are Salafists, however, all Salafists start from the assumption that they should have as little to do with the rest of society (both Muslim and non-Muslim) as possible in order to safeguard their own purity.

However, unlike historical Wahhabism, the "mainstream" Salafism packaged for export—as promulgated by the Saudi state, articulated by state-employed Saudi scholars, and perpetuated through state-funded institutions—does not advocate violence.[17] Indeed, that may be the only significant change that has resulted from the adoption of the "Salafi" label. Effectively whitewashing the very bloody history of Wahhabism, the current grand mufti of Saudi Arabia, 'Abd al-'Aziz bin 'Abd Allah Al al-Shaikh, urged the faithful to "understand that the path of reform never comes through violence. Islam is not a religion of violence. Islam is a religion of mercy for everyone." From the advent of its modern manifestation, mainstream Salafism has eschewed violence, with Salafi scholars consistently condemning terrorism generally, and bin Laden specifically.

This makes a lot of sense as a tactical move for Wahhabis for a diverse array of reasons. First of all, the compact between the Saudi state establishment and the mainstream Wahhabi religious establishment can only work if that Wahhabi establishment delegitimizes violent insurrection against the Saudi regime from the more radical Wahhabi elements. As with the Ikhwan, and as we will see below, this is a constantly recurring threat for the House of Saud.

16   Al-Arian, "Why Western attempts to moderate Islam are dangerous".

17   Mohammed, *Caliphate Reloaded: Past, present and future Muslim discourse on Power*.

Secondly, if Wahhabism is to be successfully exported abroad, it needs to be more palatable to those Muslims raised in mainstream traditions—all of which emphasize the nature of Islam as a religion of peace. Taking this step of departure from Wahhabism's militant roots was perhaps the single most effective marketing ploy for the Wahhabi establishment, as it has allowed them to further the expansion of their creed.

But despite Salafism's marketing pitch purporting to offer a coherent, monolithic, global idea of Islam with clear, distinguishable boundaries and definitions, none of the internal debates and divisions of Wahhabism have actually been resolved. Even under the new label, Salafism/Wahhabism continues to have the same moderate and extreme factions, and they continue to be at loggerheads with one another. These tensions have boiled over in the past, and in these times, the preached eschewing of violence is also often forgotten. We are seeing the reemergence of the true Wahhabi tradition.

INTERACTION WITH THE MUSLIM BROTHERHOOD

The Salafi tendency to descend into Wahhabi-style violence was not helped by the vagaries of history, such as the curious relationship that the kingdom would develop with the Muslim Brotherhood (al-Ikhwan al-Muslimin). In the early years of the 20th century this became active in many Arab states—including, post–World War II, the then largely secular regimes such as Nasser's Egypt.[18] In this conflict, the Brotherhood found willing allies in the Saudis. They were opposed to Nasser in Egypt both on nationalist grounds (in effect they were rivals for leadership in the Arab world) and his secular policies, and the two countries came close to open warfare after clashes between their proxies in the Yemen in the mid-1960s.

---

18   James P. Jankowski, *Nasser's Egypt, Arab Nationalism and the United Arab Republic* (Boulder, Co: Lynne Rienner, 2001).

Throughout the 1950s and 1960s, both kings Saʻud bin ʻAbd al-ʻAziz (r. 1953–64) and his successor, Faisal bin ʻAbd al-ʻAziz (r. 1964–75), provided sanctuary for members of the Muslim Brotherhood, despite its doctrinal differences with Salafism, in the idea that this loose alliance could foster the formation of a bulwark against increasingly popular atheist and socialist movements in the Muslim world. Brotherhood members fled the oppression they faced in socialist and secular Syria and Egypt and found refuge in Saudi Arabia.

At the same time, the Saudi economy was expanding and suffering for a lack of domestic skilled labor. Many Brotherhood members were academics or were from professional backgrounds, and they could contribute to the new growth sectors in the economy. Crucially, among the most important sectors in need of specialists were education, media, and health. Of particular significance, some Brotherhood members were offered prominent teaching positions at the new Saudi universities. Among such individuals was Mohammed, the brother of Sayyid Qutb, who was to be executed for trying to assassinate Egypt's socialist president Nasser, and who today is recognized as a key originator of the modern form of violent Islamism.

Mohammed continued to preach his brother's work and taught Osama bin Laden along with Safar al-Hawali, who was to later become one of the leading shaykhs of the "Sahwa," or "awakening" movement in the 1990s. No one could suspect it at the time, but the presence of the Muslim Brotherhood would amount to an "infiltration of modern Islamic revivalism into the kingdom" with profound consequences for the country's religious makeup. Eventually, it was to "shake the Wahhabi hegemony in the later decades of the 20th century." Indeed, in 2002, the Saudi interior minister, Prince Nayef bin ʻAbdul ʻAziz, publicly lamented how his country had supported the Muslim Brotherhood, while they were oppressed elsewhere, only for them to stir up trouble within the kingdom,[19] and indeed throughout the entire Muslim world.

---

19 Mohammed, *Caliphate Reloaded: Past, present and future Muslim discourse on Power.*

OIL–SAUDI ARABIA BECOMES RICH

Fascinating as the story so far is, none of this would have even made the history books of the wider region, never mind the world, were it not for a momentous event in the history of the region, and indeed, of the world—the discovery of the largest reserves of oil and gas in the world under the kingdom in 1938. At that stage an essentially tribal nation, riven by religious disputes, commenced its journey to becoming one of the richest states in the Arab world.

By 1950 Saudi Arabia was producing around 500,000 barrels a day, and the state was receiving revenues of $50 million per annum.[20] By 1960, 80 percent of all government revenues came from the oil industry. On one hand, this was an incredible source of wealth for a state that in the early 1930s was largely dependent on subsistence farming and the income generated by Muslims undertaking pilgrimages to the holy cities. However, this wealth has created a number of problems which feed into the core themes in this book. The result was that the Saudi state was able to accept high underemployment of its own nationals and transfer a substantial amount of the oil wealth to the population via employment in the public sector[21] (which includes the oil sector) or relatively generous social welfare provisions.[22]

As discussed earlier, this wealth was also partly used in funding a large number of mosques and madrassas across the globe, which were then used to export Wahhabism under its more friendly guise of Salafism. However, this was not the only external adventure of the Saudi regime in the 1950s and 1960s. Both its own rulers and its external backers in the United States and the UK felt threatened by the various strands of Arab nationalist and socialist movements such

---

20 Wayne H. Bowen, *The History of Saudi Arabia* (Westport, CT: Greenwood Press, 2008).

21 Patrice Flynn, "The Saudi Arabian Labor Force: A Comprehensive Statistical Portrait," *The Middle East Journal* 65, no. 4 (2011); M Ramady, *The Saudi Arabian Economy: Policies, Achievements and Challenges*, 2nd ed. (London: Springer, 2010).

22 Andy Sambidge, "Saudi king approves $312m payout to poor," ArabianBusiness.com, 2010 http://www.arabianbusiness.com/567647-saudi-king-approves-312m-payout-to-poor.

as the Ba'ath in Iraq and Syria and Nasser's Egypt.[23] All of these were to some extent pro-Soviet—or perhaps more strictly anti-American—with Assad's Syria becoming increasingly close to the Soviets[24] in the 1960s. In turn, Saudi Arabia took the side of the West in this regional variant of the global cold war. Its contribution fundamentally was to fund hard-line Sunni movements (such as the Muslim Brotherhood) as well as those more closely aligned to its own Wahhabist faith as a counterbalance.

Such funding led to the growth of Islamist movements across the region; by the early 1980s this had seen the assassination of Egypt's Anwar Sadat (in part due to his willingness to compromise with the Israelis) and the revolt of the Muslim Brotherhood in the Syrian city of Homs.[25] These acts of violence led to repression of Sunni extremists in both countries, with some fleeing to Saudi Arabia and others organizing what were to become long-running insurgencies against their own regimes. Equally the funding of Wahhabist extremists started to have direct consequences for the Saudis at home. The storming of the Grand Mosque in Mecca in 1979 threatened the core of the kingdom, especially as the militants made it clear they were acting due to their belief that the Saudis had diverged from the true path.[26]

However, 1979 also brought two other events that have had long-term consequences for both the Saudis and the religious tradition they have sponsored.

The Shah of Iran fled in the face of massive popular revolts. Having been put in place by the British and Americans in 1953, he sponsored his version of "Westernization" of the country. However, for many Iranians this meant increasing poverty and hardship, and the hard-line Shi'a leadership sought to exploit the religious element to this discontent. After the 1979 revolution, originally the Shi'a religious

---

23 Michael Skells, "Wahhabist Ideology: What it is and why it's a problem," Huffington Post, 2016 http://www.huffingtonpost.com/entry/585991fce4b014e7c72ed86e?times tamp=1482266088767.

24 Derek Hopwood, *Syria 1945–1986* (London: Routledge, 2013).

25 Robert Fisk, *Pity the Nation: Lebanon at War*, 3rd ed. (Oxford: Oxford University Press, 2001).

26 Skells, "Wahhabist Ideology: What it is and why it's a problem".

and political leadership had to rule with both secular liberal parties and the pro-Soviet *Tudeh*. By 1981 Khomeini had eliminated all the other factions—in part using the excuse of Saddam Hussein's invasion—and instituted an "Islamic Republic."[27] Of concern to the Saudis was not the claimed religious nature of this regime but the fact that it represented a return of the Shi'a to political power (something that had not been the case since the fall of the Iranian Safavid Empire in the mid-18th century).[28]

The new Iranian regime started to sponsor Shi'a groups across the Middle East. By the mid-1980s, the Amal[29] had emerged as a domestic Lebanese opposition to Israeli occupation of southern Lebanon (and later morphed into Hizbollah). By the early 1990s it became increasingly clear that Shi'a communities spread across the Gulf region, Iraq, Syria, and Lebanon were becoming increasingly well organized and self-identifying as Shi'a rather than as part of wider confessional or political groupings. Since the Saudis, along with the other Sunni Gulf kingdoms, have a large Shi'a minority of their own, this represented a growing threat. Equally the Saudis have become engaged in an increasingly bitter struggle with Iran for control of what both see as key client states.[30] This has left the Saudis with a series of proxy wars with Iran on its northern and southern[31] borders, as well as a potentially major security problem in its eastern provinces.

However, a seemingly endless struggle with an emboldened Shi'a polity is not the only bitter consequence of 1979 for the Saudis. Under pressure from the United States, the Soviet Union came to see the latest factional struggle in the Communist regime in Kabul not just

---

27   John Foran, "A Theory of Third World Social Revolutions: Iran, Nicaragua, and El Salvador Compared," *Critical Sociology* 19, no. 2 (1992).

28   Reinmann, "Saudi Arabia vs. Iran: Predominance in the Middle East."

29   Fisk, *Pity the Nation: Lebanon at War.*

30   Marcus George, "Iran's Revolutionary Guards commander says its troops in Syria," Reuters, 2012 http://www.reuters.com/article/us-iran-syria-presence-idUSBRE88F0 4C20120916?feedType=RSS&feedName=Iran&virtualBrandChannel=10209&utm_ source=dlvr.it&utm_medium=twitter&dlvrit=59365.

31   Noel Brehony, *Yemen Divided: The Story of a Failed State in South Arabia* (New York: IB Taurus, 2011).

as infighting but as an attempt to end Afghanistan's alliance with the USSR.[32] The socialist regime that had taken power in the early 1970s had always been opposed by an incoherent religious opposition, but once the Soviet army invaded, the logic of rebellion changed. Within Afghanistan a previously religiously inspired opposition quickly became a nationalist revolt against the invader. Externally, the United States was keen to ensure the Soviets suffered financial and material costs in Afghanistan, and one key to achieving this was to fund the various opposition groups. Finally, the Saudis had funds and a particular manpower problem. By 1979 some of the keener Wahhabists had turned on the regime, and sending them to fight jihad in Afghanistan was an attractive alternative for the Saudis. If they won, it would weaken the secular, nationalist, and socialist regimes that Saudi Arabia was already struggling against across the Middle East. If they died, at least they could cause no more trouble in Saudi Arabia.

The Soviets made several attempts to pull out, only to find the opposition had no interest in a negotiated settlement. Even so, by 1985, Soviet troops were mostly no longer engaged in combat, and from 1987 the Soviets started to withdraw. This was completed by early 1989, and their proxy regime was to cling to some degree of territorial control until 1992. As we will see, many jihadists then returned to their host countries, emboldened by victory and convinced they had uncovered a combination of religious beliefs, political organization, and military tactics capable of bringing down a global superpower. Unfortunately, after 1992 their target was no longer the now dissolved Soviet Union: it was the United States and the states it supported across the Islamic world.

These two problems quickly morphed into a major foreign and domestic policy challenge to the Saudis as the Cold War drew to a close. Their approach to dealing with the arrival of a more confident Shi'a movement was, and continues to be, to fund radical Sunni groups that share the Saudis' Salafist outlook. However, these groups often overlap those directly aligned to AQ or ISIS, and the ideological differences are minimal—often, as in Syria, the difference is about the scope,

---

32   Thomas G. Paterson et al., *American Foreign Relations: Since 1895*, vol. 2 (Belmont CA: Wadsworth, 2009).

not the nature, of the planned revolution (where most Salafist groups wish to impose an Islamic republic on Syria but have no interest in establishing a wider caliphate or waging war directly on the West).[33] In Yemen, their search for allies in their attack on the Shi'a Houthis has led them back into a direct alliance with the local AQ faction. Equally while many Salafist groups are quite prepared to wage sectarian war against the Shi'a, they actually aim for a regime akin to that in Iran, with a very limited form of democracy constrained and controlled by a dominant and entrenched religious elite. Domestically, the Saudis now fear both their own Shi'a minority and the returning Salafists even as they face a major economic crisis as oil revenues decline.

THE DOMESTIC CHALLENGES OF CONTEMPORARY SAUDI ARABIA

T oday, all this escalating international tension, disputes within the Wahhabist community, and problems with the large Shi'a population in the east have come to a head just as the Saudi economy has started to weaken. As a state, it became dependent on high oil prices, and today, the oil wealth is rapidly diminishing, and not just as a source of current income. The large Saudi financial reserves are being drawn on to maintain social welfare systems, support wages, pay for a large army and the religious infrastructure. Their reserves dropped from around $737 billion in August 2014 to $636 billion in November 2015—a decline of $7 billion a month[34]—and there is no reason to believe this will change until world oil prices recover.[35] With the recent trend towards falling oil revenues (and the need to use the

---

33   Ibrahim, "The Resurgence of Al-Qaeda in Syria and Iraq."

34   John Kemp, "Saudi Arabia's dwindling oil revenues and the challenge of reform," Reuters, 2016 http://www.reuters.com/article/saudi-oil-kemp-idUSL8N1553PO.

35   Ironically one reason the Saudis are keeping production high and prices low is to limit the scope for the Iranians to invest in their own oil industry—in effect the Saudis are undermining their own source of wealth in order to weaken their main rival.

accumulated wealth of earlier years to pay for current expenditure), the Saudis need to modernize their economy.

Some commentators treat the idea of the Saudis being serious about modernization as deeply implausible. However, in their own terms they are very serious. Nonetheless, it is useful to understand what they are aiming for. They are looking for a diversified economy that is no longer reliant on oil, will be able to employ their relatively large domestic population, and can take advantage of the purchasing power of both their own people and others in neighboring states. This has been their notional goal since the early 1970s,[36] even if they have been able to put off any hard decisions for many years. They also want to improve the administrative efficiency of their state[37] to provide a basis for economic prosperity, reduce the costs of their bureaucracy, and minimize discontent due to inefficiently delivered systems.[38] Equally they are aware of the advantages of making high-quality Internet services relatively easy to access even if they are also very aware of the risk that their population might start to challenge the worldview of the Saudi state.[39] At the moment Saudi censorship is relatively broad-brush—sites deemed to be pornographic, hosted in Iran or Israel, are all banned, but social media is relatively easy for an increasingly technologically aware population to access. Though it might surprise Westerners, the Saudis are also serious about wanting to increase the number of women in the workforce,[40] especially as women are increasingly completing tertiary education in a range of technical subjects.

---

36 WA Beling, *King Faisal and the Modernisation of Saudi Arabia* (London: Croon Helm, 1979).

37 Jamil E. Jreisat, "Administrative Reform and the Arab World: Economic Growth," *Review of Policy Research* 16, no. 2 (1999).

38 MO Al-Fakhri et al., "E-Government in Saudi Arabia: Between Promise and Reality," *International Journal of Electronic Government Research* 4, no. 2 (2008); BA Alsheha, "The e-government program of Saudi Arabia: Advantages and challenges," (Riyadh: King Fahd University of Petroleum and minerals, 2007).

39 Barney Warf and Peter Vincent, "Multiple geographies of the Arab Internet," *Area* 39, no. 1 (2007).

40 Mohammed Abdullah Aljebrin, "Labor Demand and Economic Growth in Saudi Arabia," *American Journal of Business and Management* 1, no. 4 (2012); Flynn, "The Saudi Arabian Labor Force: A Comprehensive Statistical Portrait."

However, this does not mean that the Saudi policy makers are aiming for a conventional liberal market economy. In part, they have no intention of compromising their own religious norms. They may be prepared to challenge the more hard-line sections of the Wahhabist religious hierarchy, but this is not to say they wish for anything other than a state, society, and economy that are compatible with their own ideology. They simply wish for all these things to be effective and efficient. They know they cannot sustain an economy with over 20 percent unemployment among their own nationals while the work-force is mostly made up of foreign workers (many without legal work permits and most recruited either elsewhere in the Middle East or in India and East Asia). However, while young Saudis have traditionally prized jobs in the public sector (and this includes the petrochemical industry), they have shunned jobs in the service sector and the wider private sector.[41] State control over labor allocation and recent reforms in terms of forcing firms to employ more Saudis have made some progress in this respect, but the Saudi regime faces considerable resistance from both their own population and employers in trying to normalize their economy. But they no longer have much choice—falling oil revenues make it essential that they deal with these problems, including how to bring women into the workforce while retaining both social constraints on the mixing of genders and Wahhabist/Salafist religious demands.[42]

This highlights a key problem with their modernization program. They face resistance not only from a population that has become used to a lifestyle fuelled by oil revenues but also from the religious

41 Muhammad Asad Sadi, "The Implementation Process of Nationalization of Workforce in Saudi Arabian Private Sector: A Review of "Nitaqat Scheme"," *American Journal of Business and Management* 2, no. 1 (2013).

42 The employment of women is perhaps the most obvious issue where Saudi religious preferences directly clash with the desire to have a modern efficient economy. For the most part, Saudi employers tend to opt for gender segregation (so, for example, they will staff call centers just with women), which brings some women into the workforce but also limits their opportunities. On the other hand, in the state-controlled banking and health sectors it is increasingly common for men and women to work side by side, and this is slowly being adopted in the private sector. Both solutions have been criticized by elements within the religious establishment.

fundamentalists. For years, the regime has been able to deal with the pressure from the Wahhabist establishment by running a distorted economy. This has allowed them to bow to demands that women are mostly excluded from the labor force while at the same time allowing them access to higher education. It has also created the wealth that has been used to build mosques around the world and to sponsor Wahhabist clerics to run them—a theme we will return to. However, the flawed economy has also created a problem of many bored, underemployed young men. These young men are now facing substantial pressure to take up jobs in sectors of the economy they have avoided for decades and see as only offering low-prestige work. A volatile mix of lower incomes, continuing high domestic unemployment, and young Saudis facing the tedium of working in the service sector compared to the apparent glamor of jihad are all likely causes of unrest. And—again as we will see—there are plenty of groups eager to make use of domestic dissent.

THE MUSLIM BROTHERHOOD AND THE DEVELOPMENT OF ISLAMIST SALAFISM

As we have noted, the fusion between the Muslim Brotherhood's militancy and Salafi dogmatism has been important in creating the intellectual basis for modern jihadi terrorism. This developed into first Al-Qaeda and then ISIS primarily due to the Saudi response to the Iraqi invasion of Kuwait in 1990.

Following this invasion, bin Laden, recently returned victorious from the campaign to drive the Soviets out of Afghanistan, made an offer to King Fahd to defend the kingdom's borders. He urged the monarch not to bring foreign troops into Saudi Arabia, into the *dar al-Islam*, home to Islam's most holy and sacred sanctuaries. His concerns for the religious purity of the land were but a modern incarnation of the concerns raised by Sulayman ibn 'Abd Allah ibn Muhammad in his anti-Ottoman fatwas, and those of the extremist Wahhabis from the second emirate.

Fearing a possible invasion of the kingdom from Saddam Hussein, Fahd rejected bin Laden's concerns and declined his offer of military support. Realistically, bin Laden and his meager forces had no chance of stopping Saddam's army in open confrontation. Instead, Fahd allowed some 750,000 non-Muslim troops, mostly American, to be stationed in Saudi Arabia. This move, though contentious among the Salafis, was nonetheless religiously sanctioned by the mainstream Salafi religious elite, headed by Shaykh 'Abd al-'Aziz bin Baz (d. 1999), then chairman of the Supreme Council of Ulema (grouping of Wahhabi religious scholars). Inflamed, bin Laden condemned the actions of the royal ruling family and rejected the reasoning of mainstream Salafism. Many radicals of bin Laden's generation followed his lead.

Because they had allowed foreign, non-Muslim troops to be stationed in the Holy Land, both the House of Saud and the Salafi establishment had opened themselves to challenges against their religious legitimacy and authority from both Wahhabi-dogmatic and Brotherhood-militant elements. The growing criticism eventually developed into a full-blown crisis, which created a deep schism within Salafism that continues to this day. On the one hand you have the House of Saud and mainstream Salafi establishment, in control of the state and oil revenues. On the other, you have Saudi jihadi-Salafis and hard-line Wahhabi scholars seeking to delegitimize and depose the comfortable Saudi-Shaykh alliance and undo the Saudi state as we know it today. Equally as the petro-economy continues to fall apart, the Saudi state is also coming under more criticism from the liberal technocratic elements in Saudi society.

This fusion is deeply challenging, and many systematic critiques of the regime have come from among the nonviolent political Salafis, who have nevertheless been influenced by the Muslim Brotherhood. This movement was primarily comprised of professionals, engineers, doctors, and professors. Their most notable and unusual angle of attack was to challenge the governing elites competence to govern: they argued that the Saudi-Shaikh establishment was failing to govern effectively and that there was an urgent need for administrative reform, reducing political corruption, and challenging the poor economic management of the country.

From the other end, a number of the Sahwa shaykhs publicly con-demned the decision to allow non-Muslims into the Holy Land and rejected both Bin Baz's fatwa and the judgments and reasoning of the other mainstream Saudi Salafis. While holding the senior Salafi scholars in deference, they nonetheless believed that they were out of touch and ill equipped to deal with, and understand, the "deeper" geopolitical realities of the region.[43]

The Islamist Salafis believed that by inviting non-Muslims (pri-marily Americans) into the Holy Land, mainstream Salafis had created the means by which the kingdom would be colonized—not to mention their traditional concerns over the Islamic purity of the land. They argued that while mainstream Salafi scholars obsessed over the evils of saint worship, innovation, *shirk*, and the intricate details of ritual purification and prayer, the Muslim world was under siege; it was being occupied and dominated by non-Muslims while other Muslim countries were left to the tyrannical rule of "Muslim" puppets rulers, like the Egyptian secular dictators allied with the United States.

The two most influential Sahwa shaykhs were Safar al-Hawali (b. 1954) and Salman al-Awda (b. 1955), who, as a consequence of their public denunciations of the government and ruling religious elite, both ended up in prison in 1994. The Sahwa shaykhs were not the first to break with the mainstream Salafi establishment to rebuke the monarchy openly for its alliance with Washington, or to condemn it for its apparent lack of religiosity. But their open revolt brought back uncomfortable memories for the Saudis, and the resulting heavy-handed response was only to be expected. Of course, once the state resorted to violence, arbitrary arrest, and torture, it naturally exacer-bated the schism between the two sides even further. In a movement already obsessed with purity of doctrine, ready to condemn those who disagreed as heretics (or worse), an intra-Saudi bloodbath became inevitable.

---

43   Mary Ann Tétreault, "Globalisation and Islamic Radicalism in the Arab Gulf Region," in *The Transformation of Politicised Religion: From Zealots Into Leaders,* ed. Hartmut Elsenhans, et al. (London: Routledge, 2015).

THE EMERGENCE OF JIHADI-SALAFISM IN SAUDI ARABIA

Jihad came to Saudi Arabia on November 13, 1995, when a powerful bomb exploded outside the American training mission for the Saudi National Guard in Riyadh, killing five Americans and two Indians. Shortly afterwards, the Saudi government received demands for the withdrawal of American forces from the Holy Land.

The perpetrators were soon caught and executed. But what did worry the House of Saud was that they turned out to be veteran jihadis, returned from Afghanistan, just like bin Laden. This was a bad omen—there were thousands of such individuals whom the Saudis had exported to Afghanistan in the 1980s, who had now returned to the country. Sure enough, there have been subsequent attacks virtually every year since, and especially in 2003 and 2005, when Saudi Arabia suffered the worst terrorist attacks in its modern history.

This dispute was not just about dogmatically extreme Islamist Salafis feeling that the House of Saud had made a compromise too far. This was something else. It looked as if the strain of Salafism that Saudi Salafis took with them to Afghanistan to fight jihad against the Soviets had mutated. When Arab mujahedeen returned from Afghanistan, hardened by war and emboldened by victory, they entered into bitter disputes with the soft, complacent, and "compromised" mainstream Salafi establishment. Although they shared the same Salafi dogmas and creed as the religious establishment, they had seen violent jihad in action, and they had seen it succeed. The Soviet defeat in Afghanistan had been, after all, a remarkable achievement and one that stood out in recent history as a boost to Muslim pride.

Taking a cue from what had "worked," they called for action in the guise of a renewed jihad against all ills and injustices that they thought beset the Muslim world as they saw it, especially in its Arab heartland—whether they were "corrupt" or compromised Muslim leaders, like the House of Saud, or foreign occupying forces, like the Americans stationed in the country.

These jihadist Salafis had initially tried to engage positively with the religious mainstream establishment, and many still respected Bin

Baz. They were happy to grant that the Ulema had been deceived and misled by the Saudi government. But when the Salafi establishment refused to respond to these overtures, the jihadists turned against them as well. They had concluded that the ruling religious elite too were active agents of the Saudi regime, which, in turn, were puppets of the Americans and Zionists. And then their position hardened even more. Now, the jihadi-Salafis and mainstream Salafis diverged over four fundamental questions:

1. Whether ordinary Muslims can call their leaders apostates and wage jihad against them for their lack of religiosity.

2. The nature of "defensive" and "offensive" jihad.

3. The legitimacy of "martyrdom operations."

4. The legitimacy of targeting civilians.

These questions haunt Saudi Arabia to this day. And since 9/11, they haunt us in the West as well.

SUMMARY

'Abd al-'Aziz ibn Saud built a kingdom that lasts to this day and is wealthy beyond the wildest dreams of his predecessors. Much of that success has had to do with having the good luck to discover massive oil reserves, but Ibn Saud also proved to be an effective, pragmatic leader. Unlike his zealot predecessors of the 18th and, to some extent, the 19th century, he showed great political acumen, often opposing the Wahhabi elite he relied on, in the interests of establishing an enduring modern state. He challenged mainstream Wahhabi doctrine by entering into an alliance with the infidel British, surrounded himself with non-Wahhabi advisors, sent his sons to infidel lands for education. He initiated a process for modern schooling within Saudi

Arabia, and introduced necessary new technologies, even as some Wahhabi scholars denounced the Internet as tools of the devil.[44]

He crushed dissent, especially when he could isolate the dissenters from the mainstream Wahhabi establishment, and while Wahhabi scholars would often privately disapprove of his decisions, he kept them onside and convinced them to continue to recognize him and his heirs as rightful and legitimate leaders. Above all, he made them see that it was in their best interest that the House of Saud maintain their prerogative to rule absolutely—and in this he was aided by having access to the sudden influx of wealth in the years after 1940, which allowed the regime to carry out a degree of modernization while still meeting the key demands of the Wahhabis. In return for their support, Ibn Saud allowed the Wahhabis to take charge of religious education and institutions, and to establish Wahhabism as the official faith of the Kingdom of Saudi Arabia. The continued stability of this pact between the House of Saud and the Wahhabis is the fundamental cornerstone of the continued stability, even survival, of the kingdom.

But make no mistake about it. This political order came at a huge blood cost. By the time the Saudi-Wahhabi state consolidated power in 1932, there had been many massacres in Arabia in which Muslim women and children had been slaughtered, and thousands of public executions and hundreds of thousands of amputations had taken place. The death toll is estimated to be around a quarter of a million—a significant proportion of the sparsely populated central Arabian region.

But his most lasting legacy may well be the establishment of the Saudi-Wahhabi-oil compact, which became a dynamo of political instability in which the Kingdom of Saudi Arabia can only survive as long as it successfully exports its internal tensions and contradictions.[45] And, as we shall see, the death toll of this alliance will continue to grow for the foreseeable future.

---

44   A. Pons, "E-Government for Arab countries," *Journal of Global Information Technology Management* 7, no. 1 (2004).

45   Nicholas Kristof, "The Terrorists the Saudis Cultivate in Peaceful Countries," *The New York Times*, 2016 http://mobile.nytimes.com/2016/07/03/opinion/sunday/the-terrorists-the-saudis-cultivate-in-peaceful-countries.html?_r=1&referer=http://m.facebook.com/.

PART THREE
MODERN JIHADISM

Modern jihadism is the current offshoot of jihadi ideology from mainstream Salafism. The primary body of belief and doctrine for these modern jihadists overlaps with those of quiet Salafis and classical Wahhabism. Wahhabism was, in turn, a violent, iconoclastic, exclusivist offshoot of Sunni Islam. Modern Salafism is a development of Wahhabism that has toned down its radicalism and violent tendencies due to a historical power-political compromise between the Wahhabi establishment and the House of Saud during the evolution of the Kingdom of Saudi Arabia in the last century; nevertheless, it still evolved from Wahhabism. Jihadi Salafism rejects the doctrinal and political compromises made by the Salafi elite to facilitate their alliance with the House of Saud over the decades, and thus it revives both the radicalism and the violent tendencies of Al-Wahhab's immediate followers. Though it would be an oversimplification to say that today's jihadism is the same as the original Wahhabism, not least because modern jihadis embrace Western, non-Islamic technology in their fight and have also been influenced by a long and diverse tradition of radical Islamic and anti-Western/anti-imperialist thinking, in many respects one could say that modern jihadism is closer to the Wahhabism of the first Saudi emirate both in letter and in spirit than it is to modern Salafism.

THE LOGIC OF TERRORISM

Before looking at the underlying logic for violent Salafism it is useful to consider the wider question of why, and when, people come to carry out acts of violence for any cause.[1] In terms of framing our response to the current form of violent dissent, we can learn much

---

1   James D. Fearon and David D. Laitin, "Violence and the Social Construction of Ethnic Identity," *International Organization* 54, no. 4 (2000).

from the wider motivation towards violence and how this has been handled in other situations. Most political[2] and psychological[3] studies are consistent in arguing that the fundamental cause is a belief that the existing state of affairs has no legitimacy;[4] that the excluded have no part in other forms of debate (not simply that their views are those of a minority but that there is no peaceful means to further their goals); and that it is necessary to replace the existing state of affairs. Exclusion from other forms of political participation and a belief that the status quo is inherently unfair are the key aspects of the process.[5]

Given these two issues it is no surprise that violent dissent is often associated with authoritarian regimes.[6] Whether the regime is a product of domestic political change or imposed by external conquest, many will see it as lacking legitimacy. For the most part peaceful protest is not a valid option, but many people would like to see such a regime replaced by something more humane. However, even so, not everyone who would wish to see radical regime change will engage in, or even actively support, acts of terrorism. This of course raises a further question as to who labels which movement as terrorist.[7] Opening this debate can lead to taking the view that acts of violence are perfectly acceptable when we agree with the motives or share a common

---

2   Ted Robert Gurr, *Why Men Rebel* (Princeton, NJ: Princeton University Press, 1970).

3   Jeff Victoroff, "The Mind of the Terrorist," *Journal of Conflict Resolution* 49, no. 1 (2005).

4   Wider psychological theories of conflict all point to a belief in the lack of legitimacy to the current arrangements as an essential precondition for dissent and disagreement becoming outright conflict. For the natural human and political process of disagreement to be managed, both sides have to accept that the wider framework is acceptable and, even if only very roughly, "fair." See for example, Roger Brown, *Social Psychology*, 2nd ed. (New York: Free Press, 1986).

5   Alberto Abadie, "Poverty, Political Freedom, And The Roots Of Terrorism," *American Economic Review* 95, no. 4 (2005).

6   In genuinely totalitarian regimes (such as the USSR or Nazi Germany) dissent tends to take on three forms. It can be diverted into simple criminality (a common factor in the old Soviet Union), it can manifest itself as conflicts within the ruling elite, or in people seeking to escape the regime. Conventional terrorism is less commonly a feature of such regimes due to the repressive nature of the state.

7   Martha Crenshaw, "The Causes of Terrorism," *Comparative Politics* 13, no. 4 (1981); Colin Wight, "Theorising Terrorism: The State, Structure and History," *International Relations* 23, no. 1 (2009).

enemy. However, it is easier, and more appropriate, to use the concept of terrorism to capture a particular form of political action—the use of violence by groups operating outside the state to achieve particular ends—which allows us to ignore the wider ethical question of whether or not we agree with the motivations of those carrying out such acts.

We must return to the original question: Why, even in repressive regimes, do few people engage in acts of terror? In part, many are scared of reprisals, and others are simply trying to live their own lives as invisibly as possible. To place the issue into context, by mid-1944 northern and central Italy were occupied by the German troops and ruled by Mussolini's Salo Republic.[8] Neither had popular appeal, and of course the south of the country was firmly under the control of the Anglo-American armies. In these circumstances, Italy produced a large and effective resistance movement grouped together under the political body of the Committee for National Liberation. This brought together a wider peaceful resistance and provided support for those actively fighting (it also tried to form an embryonic government for postliberation Italy). Within this wider organization it was estimated that the armed resistance was some seventy to eighty thousand strong, and of these most only took part in essentially defensive actions such as protecting rural areas that the partisans dominated. (In such regions almost all adults would carry guns, classifying themselves as partisans even if they did not take part in combat except in self-defense.) In urban areas, small armed groups were formed that carried out assassinations of German officials and Italian collaborators. These were limited to a few people, in part as the work was very dangerous, in part due to a fear of spies, and in part as few were prepared to undertake such killings. In effect, even in the situation of a despised regime, a wider mass resistance movement, and the clear prospect of overall victory (there was little doubt by this point that in the end the Allies would clear the Germans out of Italy), few people will actually take part in killing for political ends.

So this raises the question: what shifts someone from dissent against the status quo to violence? In this chapter we will look at the logic

---

8   Paul Ginsborg, *A History of Contemporary Italy: 1943-1980* (London: Penguin, 1990).

of this process specifically in the context of modern Salafism, and compare it against the wider historical context.

First, ignoring the issue of motivation, is there a "type" of person who is most likely to engage in terrorism? Studies of the membership of left-wing and nationalist terrorist groups active in the United States and Western Europe in the 1960s and 1970s found that members were often well educated, often professionals, and the groups had a relatively high number of female participants. By contrast, those drawn into right-wing terrorism were often socially marginalized, less well educated, and more likely to be men. A similar trend was found in the Palestinian and Middle Eastern terrorist groups that dominated the 1980s with fighters who were often from poor backgrounds (both in terms of wealth and education) and overwhelmingly male. This was still the case among the Palestinian terrorist groups all through the 1990s, but by 2000 these groups had mostly ceased their earlier actions and had been replaced by Hamas acting as a quasi state entity with the goal of attacking Israel. Conversely, members of Hizbollah in Lebanon were more likely to have secondary education than the average Lebanese.[9]

In effect, the socioeconomic background of likely involvement in terrorist groups varies. Some terrorist movements have drawn their members from the more affluent (and better educated), while others have relied on those who are deprived and poorly educated. This may appear to call into question the common assumption that material deprivation is a common trigger for the evolution of violent terrorism. However, the related question of what conditions make the *formation* of a violent terrorist group more likely is a valuable one. Equally, as we will see, terrorist groups need far more support than just their active members. Thus the existence of poor governance, combined with poverty, can create this wider group of sympathizers needed for active terrorists to operate.

If we cannot use socioeconomic background and education as likely indicators, can more personal issues such as family background or psychological traits inform us? A German study of left-wing terrorists in the early 1980s found that 25 percent had lost one parent by

---

9   Victoroff, "The Mind of the Terrorist."

the age of fourteen, 33 percent had had serious conflict with their parents, and 33 percent had been convicted by a juvenile court.[10] At a more psychological level, an Italian study of right-wing terrorists found that common characteristics were: "(1) ambivalence toward authority, (2) lack of self-awareness and a tendency towards narcissism, (3) adherence to convention, (4) emotional detachment from the consequences of their actions, (5) sexual uncertainty, (6) magical thinking, (7) destructiveness, (8) low education, and (9) adherence to violent subculture norms and weapons fetishes."[11] Other studies suggest that people who join such groups do so out of a desire to belong to some larger entity; can be narcissistic (drawing importance from the perceived centrality of their acts); tend to see the world in black-and-white terms (which provides a ready justification for extreme violence); may wish to take revenge for some (real or imagined) personal slight (or a slight against a group they identify with).

Another enduring question is whether or not members of such groups can be properly described as psychopaths. It is clear that the deliberate dismissal of their victims' humanity, and a very self-serving set of justifications, have much in common with sociopathy (and narcissism[12]), but we need to use labels such as *psychopath* carefully, as most members do not meet this criteria—they manage to justify their brutality to themselves, but they may not actually derive much personal pleasure from hurting other people. Of note, once such groups do collapse, many former members suffer sustained psychological problems as they seek to reconcile their previous acts with the failure of their cause,[13] displaying a emotional response not indicative of true

---

10   Ibid.

11   F. Ferracuti and F. Bruno, "Psychiatric aspects of terrorism in Italy," in *The mad, the bad and the different: Essays in honor of Simon Dinitz*, ed. I. L. Barak-Glantz and C. R. Huff (Lexington, MA: Lexington Books, 1981).

12   Tori DeAngelis, "Understanding terrorism," *American Psychological Association* 40, no. 10 (2009); Victoroff, "The Mind of the Terrorist."

13   As an example, this is becoming noticeable in Northern Ireland as former members of various terrorist groups are themselves seeking psychological help to deal with the memories of their own actions.

psychopathy. Having said that, if someone really is a psychopath, then joining a violent terrorist group can provide a means to carry out acts of violence, but to attribute membership in a terrorist group to psychopathy is simply not a good personality marker for potential members.

Thus, we are still left with an unclear picture of how someone moves from identifying a situation that they feel needs to change to using violence.[14] It would appear at the level of personal characteristics that different types of terrorist groups (perhaps drawing from very different cultures) attract different types of people.[15] Some of the above might indicate that those drawn into left-wing terrorism in Europe in the 1960s and 1970s were better educated than most in society. This may be true, but it is doubtful that those who joined various third world liberation struggles, notionally in support of Marxism, would fit such a description. So, it is not the notional goals of a group that determine who is drawn into violence. If John Horgan is correct,[16] we need to understand entry into terrorism as a combination of "push" factors (i.e., what motivated them to consider a violent response) and "pull" factors (i.e., what attracted them to a particular group). Of importance in regard to the push factors is the fact that they are often unaware of the grim realities of life as a terrorist; for the pull factors, the perception that their chosen group will be successful. This, in turn, may explain why in some places terrorist groups arise very briefly only to collapse soon after,[17] as they can offer no feasible route to success for their putative members.

What is better known is what happens once someone joins such a group. All the evidence is that in-group indoctrination is substantial

---

14 Charles Tilly, *The Politics of Collective Violence* (Cambridge: Cambridge University Press, 2003).

15 John Horgan, "From Profiles to Pathways and Roots to Routes: Perspectives from Psychology on Radicalization into Terrorism," *The Annals of the American Academy of Political and Social Science* 618, no. 1 (2008).

16 Ibid.

17 Examples of this ephemeral terrorism could include movements within Quebec nationalism, left-wing terrorism in France in the 1970s, and the episodic nature of far-right terrorism in many Western European countries.

and powerful.[18] In part to justify both their decision to join, as well as any acts they may have carried out, members tend to adopt an even more extreme black-and-white worldview—this is essential for them to both function as terrorists and self-justify their actions.[19] At that stage breaking their attachment to their new group identity becomes increasingly hard. Ideologically, at this stage, groups and individuals can remain committed to terrorism even if they have notionally achieved their initial goals.[20] This suggests that while such groups may appear to have a very rigid ideology (Marxism, nationalism, fascism, Salafism), in reality this is less important than group maintenance, which then becomes the key goal—along with belief in an infallible leader who is always right regardless of short-term lack of success. In effect, strengthening in-group ties can become far more important than the notional goals of the organization. In combination this strongly suggests that it is far easier to prevent someone entering into terrorism than to convince them to give it up.

Throughout history, if such groups eventually abandon violence, it is often in the face of no longer being able to see how they might realize their goals. Some of this blockage can come from effective counterterrorism work (the IRA in Northern Ireland moved towards a political solution once it was clear they no longer could function as a structured terrorist group), but also loss of their wider base can be important (one reason the Red Brigades in Italy fell apart was widespread disgust with the group after their murder of the former prime minister, Aldo Moro,[21] which stopped the flow of new members and led many who had provided nonviolent support to break away). Linked to this can be a strategy of offering reduced prison sentences for any who wish to testify against their former comrades. This directly undermines

---

18   Thomas Hegghammer, "Should I Stay or Should I Go? Explaining Variation in Western Jihadists' Choice between Domestic and Foreign Fighting," *American Political Science Review* 107, no. 1 (2013).

19   Carole Beebe Tarantelli, "The Italian Red Brigades and the structure and dynamics of terrorist groups," *The International Journal of Psychoanalysis* 91, no. 3 (2010).

20   Max Abrahms, "What Terrorists Really Want: Terrorist Motives and Counterterrorism Strategy," *International Security* 32, no. 4 (2008).

21   Paul Ginsborg, *Italy and Its Discontents: 1980-2001* (London: Penguin, 2001).

the importance of social networks within the group,[22] which are, in practice, so important to these groups' survival.

THE LOGIC OF SALAFIST TERRORISM

As we have seen in section 2, the intellectual roots of modern Salafism are complex. It is a fusion of the Saudi-led reinterpretation of Wahhabism, heavily influenced by the non-Wahhabist Muslim Brotherhood and drawing substantially on the history of what is now Saudi Arabia since the late 17th century. Not surprisingly, with such disparate roots, there is substantial disagreement among even militant Salafists, but there are a number of common themes that set Salafism apart from traditional Islam. To this should be added that the movement has evolved according to its own recent histories and its various adherents have drawn very different lessons from key events such as the defeat of AQ in Iraq and events since 2007. In this section, I seek to set out the main common issues.

FRIEND AND FOE

The broader material presented in the first half of this section is helpful when trying to understand modern-day jihadi terrorism. Such movements share many of the same characteristics (including that of goals[23] expressed in terms of purity and simplicity), and they too make use of a wider discontent with the modern world. However, jihadi terrorism is not simply the latest incarnation of a long-standing

---

22 Abrahms, "What Terrorists Really Want: Terrorist Motives and Counterterrorism Strategy."

23 Ibid.

problem. It has its own logic and its own (professed) goals. So if we are to understand how it has become a powerful movement, we need to understand just what they claim to be fighting for and what their justifications are for the violence they use.

One of the pillars of the modern jihadist movement is the Mardin Fatwa and its contemporary iterations. A fatwa is a ruling by an accepted Islamic jurist. The Mardin Fatwa was issued by the jurist Taqi al-Din Ahmad almost seven hundred years ago, in response to a question concerning whether or not the Muslim inhabitants of Mardin should immigrate to Muslim lands. The question arose because Mardin had recently been occupied by Mongols who, while professing the Islamic faith, only a few years before had killed huge numbers of Muslims, enslaved their children, and burned down their mosques. The Mongols neither ruled fully by Islamic law (it was a mixture of Sharia and the Yasa, the legal code of Genghis Khan) nor made any excuses for their lack of adherence to some Islamic norms. Not to mention the fact that the mass killings they had carried out as they had conquered the region left a deep legacy of bitterness towards their rule.

This fatwa described the world in a bipolar manner, divided into an abode of peace/Islam (*dar al-Islam*) and an abode of war/heresy (*dar al-harb*), and Ibn Taymiyya declared the lands occupied by the Mongols to be in the *dar al-harb*, the abode of war. This is, of course, the argument that the Wahhabis would later use in order to urge insurrection against Ottoman rule when they rejected the authority of the Ottoman Sultan due to the supposed polytheism of the Turks. Such a revolt, according to the Mardin Fatwa, is not only permitted but actively required, and resistance by the local Muslims to Mongol rule, even if the Mongols themselves would now have regarded themselves as Muslims, was essential. This judgment, this fatwa, has formed the key reference for those who both excommunicate fellow Muslims and seek to take up armed rebellion against Muslim rulers and governments that are deemed to be insufficiently "Muslim." It created the precedent by which any Muslim individual or group could decide of their own accord that their rulers or the governing authority ruling over them are not true Muslims, and thus have no legitimacy to rule at all.[24] It also allows such individuals or groups to engage in violence and call others to join them in perpetual jihad against any authority in any territory that they perceive to be outside of the *dar al-Islam*, the abode of peace. In other words, this fatwa created an ideology in Islam that allows any group of Muslims to see themselves as an oppressed minority, ruled over by illegitimate rulers. In consequence, such a group will find itself in a state of perpetual war with the entire world outside their own group and able to designate its own definition of the "enemy." This mind-set informed the Wahhabi ideology four centuries later—and it continues to form the foundation of jihadism today.

In particular, Muhammad 'Abd al-Salam Faraj (d. 1982), the author of one of the founding texts of modern radical Islamism, *The Neglected Duty*, drew comparisons between contemporary Muslim rulers and the medieval Mongol rulers who were the targets of Ibn Taymiyya's attacks. Faraj cited the Mardin Fatwa, arguing that a Muslim country can cease to be the abode of peace and become an abode of war, even though its inhabitants are Muslims and it is for all other intents and purposes a Muslim country. He did so in relation to the socialist secular administrations of Gamal Nasser and Anwar Sadat in his native Egypt. He did not stop at providing an intellectual justification for jihad but took part in organizing the assassination of President Sadat—for which he was subsequently executed. However, his intellectual legacy has proved to be enduring. His use of the Mardin Fatwa to define friend and foe and to urge violent action against "the enemies of Islam," both at home (*the near enemy*) and abroad (*the far enemy*, usually in the form of foreign, non-Muslim powers—most often, of course, the USA), would prove fundamental to the development of the modern jihadi worldview.

However, while people like Faraj created the intellectual arguments behind modern jihadism, the movement remained weak and mainly centered around Islamist oppositions to secular Arab regimes in Egypt, Syria, and Yemen. The catalyst for the expansion of modern jihadism into a global movement was the Soviet invasion of Afghanistan in 1979.

---

24 And, to link back to the discussion at the start of this section, a perception that the status quo is illegitimate or unfair is critical to allowing people to believe that violence is an appropriate response.

This enabled the worldview of the Muslim Brotherhood to reach a wider audience than those struggling against the authoritarian, notionally socialist, regimes in countries such as Syria, Egypt, and Iraq.

In 1973 a group of progressive, leftist, and communist elements staged a coup d'état in Afghanistan, overthrowing the shah and establishing a secular government. However, the ruling People's Democratic Party of Afghanistan descended into factionalism and infighting, which culminated in the 1978 Saur Revolution. This change did not resolve the political instability, and the country was teetering on the edge of civil war. In these circumstances, the US National Security Advisor, Zbigniew Brzezinski, was able to convince the Soviets that the country was likely to shift away from its alliance with the USSR.[25] In response, and in a move that was to inflict massive suffering on the Afghan people, the Soviet Union intervened in the country to support its favored faction in December 1979. They brought a large force into the country to try and aid the government in maintaining its grip on power. They would be there for ten years.

The initial opposition to the Soviet invasion was led by the conservative Islamist elements of the country, the rural tribes, and the local religious authorities. The brutal Soviet crackdown on these people quickly invited comparisons with Ibn Taymiyya's Mongols. The tracts of a local Islamist, 'Abdallah Yusuf 'Azzam (d. 1989), explicitly cited the Mardin Fatwa as a reason for Afghans to resist the Soviet occupation. This local resistance was sufficient to bring about the involvement of many regional Islamic powers, not least Saudi Arabia and Egypt, and indeed the United States, as the fighting gave the Americans the chance to bring about Brzezinski's promise that "now we can give the USSR its Vietnam War."[26]

As we have seen with today's hindsight, with American encouragement and logistical support, Afghanistan quickly became the global dumping ground for jihadists and radical Islamists, who would travel from every corner of the Muslim world to repel the Communist invasion of Afghanistan. For example, Egyptian president Hosni Mubarak

---

25   Paterson et al., *American Foreign Relations: Since 1895*, 2.

26   Ibid. p. 436

released many radical Islamists from prison on condition that they "leave Egypt and go to Afghanistan."[27] Ayman al-Zawahiri, who was to lead Al-Qaeda after the death of bin Laden, was among those radical Islamists who were released by Egypt. For their own part, the Saudis appeased the clamoring religious establishment by encouraging the most radical and troublesome elements of the country's religious zealots to go to the Afghani jihad, most notable among them Osama bin Laden.

Afghanistan quickly became a melting pot of violent ideas: those who were disciples of Sayyid Qutb, the 20th-century ideologue and chief architect of radical Islamist thought, introduced Takfirism to the transnational ensemble of jihadis, while the Salafis inspired all with their puritan zeal. This development can be seen most clearly through the prism of the personal relationships of the individuals in the mujahedeen leadership. Montasser al-Zayat, former friend and colleague of al-Zawahiri, who had also been imprisoned with him in Egypt, noted that it was in Afghanistan that the strong friendship between bin Laden and al-Zawahiri grew, and it was al-Zawahiri who introduced substantial changes in Osama bin Laden's interpretation of Salafist ideology.

While not using the Mardin Fatwa specifically, bin Laden frequently cited other fatwas of Ibn Taymiyya to justify indiscriminate violence. All the while, Ayman al-Zawahiri, second in command and later bin Laden's successor in what would become Al-Qaeda, went to great lengths in arguing that the circumstances of Muslims were, and continued to be, identical with those of Ibn Taymiyya in Mardin centuries ago. It was in the mountains of Afghanistan that Islamists, radicals, and jihadis from around the world came together to forge modern jihadism, and it was there that they decided who was friend and who was foe. The crucible of the Afghan war brought together the disparate strands of radical Islam with those committed to using violence in what they saw as the defense of their faith. Taking the concepts of the

---

27 As we will see, this mistake is still being repeated. The Saudis sent convicted jihadists to Syria on the promise that they would fight for those Salafist groups that had Saudi approval.

Mardin Fatwa to heart, these men quite predictably concluded that most of the world was in the abode of war.

But Afghanistan did much more than synthesize this ideology. It was also the battleground on which the foot soldiers of jihad trained, with much support from the United States, UK, Saudi Arabia, and other future targets of the jihadis. It was where they gained a sense of purpose and an idea of how they could achieve their aims—for the fact is that the jihadis, or the "mujahedeen," as they called themselves at the time, won the war with the Soviet Empire. The Soviets had started looking for a negotiated exit by 1983, but, backed by the United States, no rebel group would give in. In response, the Soviets undertook the classic response of trying to use local forces to wage the war so as to limit their own casualties. Finally after the death of around fifteen thousand of their soldiers, the Soviets pulled out in 1988. Whether the resistance had beaten the Soviets is debatable, but it had certainly forced the Soviets to shift from seeking a negotiated exit to announcing a unilateral withdrawal by 1988. But once the Soviet threat to Afghanistan was repelled, it was not long before other political regimes and even whole countries came into view for the jihadis as threats to the *abode of Islam*. And to them it was only too clear how they should tackle these threats.

ENEMIES NEAR AND FAR

After the success against the Soviets in Afghanistan, bin Laden returned to Saudi Arabia in 1989 and shifted his approach to preach about the liberation of Jerusalem. He turned his focus on new enemies: America and Israel. However, both, mainly due to the long-standing Israeli-Palestinian dispute, could be seen as the traditional target of many political and religious movements within the wider Arab world. As such, in identifying America and Israel as his primary enemies, bin Laden was doing little that stood outside a wider worldview of many in the Arab world.

But then something unprecedented happened. In 1990, Saddam Hussein invaded Kuwait, principally in order to secure access to its oil fields. The Saudis immediately started to panic that they might be next—and for good reason. The majority of the Saudi reserves are found in the al-Ahsa, just south of Kuwait, on their eastern coast. The Saudis were in control of the world's largest proven reserves of oil, but, despite having stockpiled modern weaponry for many years, their untrained, untested army was no match militarily for the well-trained, well-equipped, and battle-hardened Iraqi army.

In these circumstances, bin Laden was quick to offer King Fahd his help in defending the kingdom's borders. But King Fahd was not about to put the fate of his kingdom in the hands of a small band of muja-hedeen, so he declined bin Laden's offer and instead agreed that the United States could station some 750,000 non-Muslim troops in Saudi Arabia. This move was then religiously sanctioned by the mainstream Salafi religious elite, headed by Shaykh 'Abd al-'Aziz bin Baz (d. 1999), then chairman of the Supreme Council of Ulema (religious scholars). This deepened the split in the Wahhabist community, as the issue of foreign troops being in Saudi Arabia, which is home to Islam's most holy and sacred sanctuaries, was to become an early area of contention between those attracted to jihad and the Wahhabist establishment. That the troops were principally drawn from the United States, as opposed to forces drawn from parts of the former Ottoman Empire, only made things worse.

At this stage the identification of Israel and America as the enemies (a view probably widely shared across the Arab world) morphed into something very different. The Saudis suddenly became seen as not just doctrinally dubious; they became illegitimate rulers and one of the prime targets of a movement they had spawned. Picking up the lan-guage of the Mardin Fatwa, the Saudi regime was identified as having lost legitimacy and became a target in its own right. Bin Laden thus rejected the sanction of the Ulema and the reasoning of mainstream Salafi establishment and condemned the actions of the royal ruling family. To him, this desecration of the Holy Land rendered the Saudi state as *dar al-harb*, abode of war, just like the Ottoman state during the early days of Wahhabism. This fitted into the Taymiyya-inspired binary worldview of the jihadis, and the Saudi regime was thus designated as a "near enemy," yet another oppressor of "true" Islam in ostensibly Muslim lands.

After a couple of feeble attempts urging the Saudi and Salafi establishment to reconsider their position on the issue in letters sent from exile in Sudan, Osama bin Laden, his followers, in what was now becoming known as Al-Qaeda, and other jihadi elements effectively declared jihad on the House of Saud, Israel, the United States, and the West. The 1995 attack on the American training mission in Riyadh followed and led to a concerted campaign of terror attacks on the Saudi state, on US and Western interests, and diplomatic missions and military bases in the Islamic world and eventually in the United States and Europe, as seen in attacks in Paris and New York. Bin Laden's formal announcement, the *Declaration of War against the Americans Occupying the Land of the Two Holy Places*, came in 1996, after he had moved back to Afghanistan, where he received sanctuary from the new Islamist Taliban regime. At this stage he also explicitly declared his belief that the Saudi monarchy had committed apostasy for allowing non-Muslim troops to be stationed in Saudi Arabia. The theological authority whom he cited to justify this declaration of apostasy came from none other than Muhammad ibn 'Abd al-Wahhab (d. 1791), the founder of Saudi Arabia's own official religious doctrine—again drawing on the original Wahhabist focus on driving out the Ottoman forces from the region.

The jihad turned global in 1998, when the two old jihadi friends, bin Laden and al-Zawahiri, merged their respective jihadist and *takfiri* organizations and jointly released the infamous call to a global jihad under the *Declaration of Jihad on the Jews and Crusaders*, which called for killing of "the Americans and their allies—civilian and military." Bin Laden had convinced al-Zawahiri to drop his focus on fighting the "near enemy" (in al-Zawahiri's case, the immediate target was the Egyptian government and its officials) and to prioritize fighting the "far enemy," the United States and her allies, who supported and sustained both the Egyptian and the Saudi regime, as well as that other permanent enemy, Israel. His stated reasons for war were the continued presence of American troops in Saudi Arabia, the imposition of US and UN sanctions on Iraq, and America's continued support of Israel. Just three years later, the old mujahedeen and their band of followers would go on to commit the worst attack on US soil since Pearl Harbor, on September 11, 2001.[28]

THE "JUST" WAR

The worldview of the jihadis, from bin Laden and al-Zawahiri, through Al-Qaeda and up to ISIS today, can be summarized, somewhat simplistically, as follows:

The Current World Order

- Muslims are the victims of a global conspiracy to destroy Islam, led by the Christian Crusaders of the West and their Zionist allies in Israel.

- This divides the world into a starkly bipolar perpetual struggle between the abode of war/heresy (*dar al-harb*) and the abode of peace/Islam (*dar al-Islam*) of the true believers.

Doctrines

- The *al-wala' wa al-bara'* dogma: It is a religious duty to hate and to fight violent war against non-Muslims, apostates, and hypocrites.

- *Takfirism*: Muslim leaders who are tacit in supporting the Crusader-Zionist alliance and the people who aid them or who exhibit incorrect creed should be excommunicated and thus become "apostates"—this makes them legitimate

---

28 Ruthven, *A Fury for God: The Islamist Attack on America.*

targets of jihad, and, under Sharia law, liable to lawful execution.

- *Jihadism*: There is an indiscriminate right and duty to use violence for "rightful" political ends (i.e., to "repel foreign occupiers from Muslim lands to emancipate and liberate Muslims"). This means that when attacking both the "near" and the "far enemy," it is legitimate to attack both combatants and civilians. It is especially legitimate to attack the civilians of democratically elected "aggressors," as these civilians "have blood on their hands" by voting for their governments who oppress Muslims.

- *Salafism*: For all other practical intents and purposes, jihadis adhere to the same beliefs and doctrines as mainstream Salafis—a fundamentalist, literalist reading of the Qur'an and the Sunni *hadiths*, intolerance of any interpretations or readings of these texts outside of the interpretation of the Wahhabi/Salafi tradition, and outright hostility towards any dogmas or practices not mentioned in the fundamental texts (except those favored by the Salafis and the jihadis themselves, of course).

End Goal

- The *Islamic state*: The end goal of the jihadist ideology is nothing less than the establishment of a new, righteous Islamic state to serve as the *dar al-Islam* for all "true" Muslims. This state should be global and all encompassing—that is, totalitarian in its character—and the current so-called Islamic State in Iraq and Syria is but the embryonic core of this state to come. The ideology is *millenarian*—it believes that the end of the world is at hand, and many jihadis believe that on its way to becoming the global caliphate, ISIS will also be fighting the final battle between good and evil, which will prompt

the return to earth of all the prophets and the days of the
Final Judgment as described in Islamic eschatology.

Once all these beliefs are understood, both the original concepts
and how these ideas have fused and evolved in the last three to four
decades, we have most of what we need to understand the modern jihadi
ideology, and, to a large extent, the day-to-day behavior of most of the
rank-and-file jihadis, both in ISIS-controlled territory and across the
world. This provides one explanation for the extraordinary brutality of
the ISIS fighters, their uncompromising zeal with regards to the actual
fighting, concomitant with their rather more relaxed attitudes towards
the Islamic injunctions towards probity, justice, fairness, tolerance, and
peace, and simply the extraordinary fact that so many young people
with reasonably comfortable lives in developed countries are so eager
to throw themselves right into the middle of the horrors of war.

However, despite these similarities, we will go on to explore how
more significant differences in practice among violent jihadists have
grown up than their shared ideological roots might imply. As of now,
ISIS is focused on state building and the "near" enemy. Conversely,
all that is left of Al-Qaeda is still focused on the "far" enemy and now
stresses alliance building across the wider Salafist community (and in
consequence is toning down its calls for the deaths of those defined
as *takfir*), while many other Salafist groups are focused on fighting to
change the government of their own particular country.

Even within these broad groupings there is a disconnect between
notional aims and practical tactics.[29] Today, the strategies, tactics, and
movements of the ISIS hierarchy are not so neatly captured by this
description of their ideology. And that should come as no surprise.
Not all ISIS fighters, especially higher in the military hierarchy, are
"true believers" in any sense. A significant number of officers and
commanders were high-ranking military and intelligence officers
in Saddam Hussein's Ba'athist regime. These erstwhile secularists of
Sunni background were criminalized by the US and Western occupiers

---

29 Abrahms, "What Terrorists Really Want: Terrorist Motives and Counterterrorism
    Strategy."

of Iraq after the fall of Saddam's regime and persecuted by the Shi'a-dominated civilian regime of Nouri al-Malaki in Baghdad since the withdrawal of Western troops, and ISIS was the only group that would take them in and usefully employ them. So we must be careful about the extent to which we take any description of their ideology as a reliable predictor of how ISIS will fight on the ground in the Levant. But overall, the overwhelming majority of ISIS fighters, as well as the top leadership of the organization, are "true believers." This is what they are fighting for and why—even if their ability to articulate either a logic or consistent approach is limited.

In truth, a significant part of the success of ISIS can be attributed to the fact that this ideology of jihadism seems to appeal to so many, otherwise diverse, groups of willing fighters, or individuals. This ideology appeals to those who have already been involved in various regional conflicts, which is not inherently surprising. But it is this ideology's appeal to the many Muslim individuals who do not have a direct stake in the fighting: Western Muslim young men (and some women) who leave their homes and their families to risk their lives and livelihoods for the goal of an "Islamic State." The reliable influx of recruits not just from the Sunni-dominated areas of Iraq and Syria but from around the world is what gave ISIS the manpower and the energy to emerge into what it is today, and that it is the jihadi ideology which made this influx possible cannot be overemphasized. So more than anything else, it is here, at the level of ideology, that we need to look in order to understand why ISIS has had the successes it has had so far, why it behaves in the way that it does, and how to contain and then counteract its expansion.

THE "TRUE" FAITH

In the first section we looked at how Islam exploded on the world scene and built the largest empire the world had ever seen out of virtually nothing in little more than one generation. The early successes of Islam did rely on the new religion to defeat the imperial powers who would have subdued it—the Sassanids and the Byzantines. In this sense, warfare and military force did play a huge role in the emergence of Islam, and conflict did shape the religion and the ideology of its leaders. But as I have argued, if Islam had simply been a matter of conquest, then it would have been another dramatically appearing, and equally rapidly collapsing, empire in the region. Instead it endured as a political, religious, and social settlement, and, until the collapse of the Abbasid Empire in the 13th century, it was also the intellectual powerhouse of the world.

In effect, the notion that a small band of Arab camel riders with poor equipment could have conquered, let alone hold onto, a territory stretching from Spain to India on the back of military force alone is fanciful. The military victories of the early caliphs were necessary for the spread of Islam, but they could never have been sufficient for its longevity. What was the key to Islam's success is that it was a positive, open, inclusive, and hopeful system of beliefs in an otherwise morally and politically bankrupt world. The Western Roman Empire had imploded two centuries before. The Eastern Roman Empire was in a sustained cultural and moral decline. The moral vision and hopefulness of Christianity had been sucked out of the faith by the way Constantine had refashioned it as an imperial cult two centuries earlier. And the long-lived Sassanid Empire with its elitist Zoroastrian cult was equally on its last legs. These empires still had power, especially military power, but they lacked legitimacy in the eyes of their subjects.

This is where Islam had the edge: ideology. Islam came with a vision of social justice that people bought into and were happy to be part of. Even those people who did not buy into the religion outright and did not convert lived quite happily under Muslim administration once this was in place. There were plenty of local insurrections and rebellions in this period, but all of them were led by competing sects within Islam. Perhaps with the sole exception of the Jewish Banu Qurayza incident in Medina during Muhammad's first Islamic state, Christians, Jews, and others generally strolled along quite happily in the first centuries when Islam was at its height, and for a long time afterwards too. This is why, fourteen centuries after the initial expansion of Islam, all the territories conquered by the first caliphs are still fully committed to Islam—with the notable exception of Spain and Portugal, where the Europeans waged a concerted campaign of ethnic and religious cleansing against all non-Catholics during the Reconquista and the Inquisition. The reason is quite simply that Islam came with an ethos and a legal system that made the societies it governed a better place for everyone.

Ideology matters. And ideology can build on remarkable military and political success—ideologies that can only exist by mistrusting their populations and by sustained violence tend not to last, as they risk either internal collapse (the USSR) or defeat by their inevitable external enemies (Nazi Germany). If you are an impartial observer, you would of course conclude from the early history of Islam that the right ideology at the right time can change the face of the world and the course of human civilization. If you are a religious fundamentalist, however, you would conclude that the reason why an ideology could be so successful is because it is "true" or divinely inspired, or even perhaps demanded by God. And if you are an Islamist jihadist, you would conclude that the success of the first caliphate was down to the fact that the Qur'an is the eternal, inerrant Word of God, and the *salaf*—the first generations of "right-guided Muslims"—had the exactly correct interpretation of the Qur'an and therefore the eternally divinely perfect moral and political ideology. You would then attribute any decline of the relative status of the Islamic world in global affairs not to the ideology losing its relative edge or to the vagaries of history (e.g., the Mongol invasion, the recurrent plagues that repeatedly decimated the global population, the European Renaissance and Age of Enlightenment) but to moral corruption and straying from the "correct" reading of the Qur'an. Naturally, the answer then is not to try and replicate the achievement of Muhammad's message to make the world a better place for everyone according to its condition and its needs today; rather the answer is to return the world to its "perfect" 7th-century state when the Miracle of God, the Qur'an, was gifted to Muslims and most of the known world.

If this was just the belief of a group of fundamentalists (who exist in every religious and secular belief system, convinced that the only reason for past problems has been a lack of zeal), then militant Islam would not be a serious problem. However, this is not just the ideology of a bunch of crazy fringe jihadis. And herein lies the root—and potentially the solution—to this problem of jihadism that we face today. This attitude that the relative stagnation in the Islamic world is a result of a lack of religious rigor is the worldview, the fundamental way of thinking of Wahhabism and its Salafi evolution. This is the religion of state of the wealthiest and most influential Arab and Sunni Muslim state in the world. And this state is committed to proselytizing this worldview and this attitude towards Islam throughout the world, throwing billions upon billions of dollars every year into educational and publishing efforts, lecture tours and theological conventions. And thus, this fundamentalist, reactionary reading of Islam is today the most rapidly expanding in the world, both within the Muslim world and outside of it.[30]

Now this is not to paper over the differences within Salafism. We have spent more than a chapter exploring the complicated and schismatic history of this movement, its internal conflicts, and its essential contradictions. Indeed, when analysts, commentators, and policy makers simply equate Salafism with terrorism, they too often fail to grasp important nuances within Salafism. While we have looked mainly at three strands within Salafism—the mainstream, political, and jihadi strands—one Salafi author has pointed out the existence of eight. Among these strands, attitudes towards democracy and other Western institutions, for example, range from indifference to accommodation to rejection. And jihad is seen as a necessity today for only one strand. But my argument is that the fundamental issues underlying the logic of violent jihad are derived from a fundamentalist attitude to the Qur'an and the life of the Prophet, and the binary worldview divided between friend and foe in which only Salafi Islam is seen as a legitimate reading of the Qur'an and the legacy of the *salaf,* and in which everyone who does not agree has lesser moral importance. This is the "true faith" of this ideology regardless of other subtleties and differences, and it forms a characteristic attitude of even the most pacifist

30   Allen, *God's Terrorists: The Wahhabi Cult and the Hidden Roots of Modern Jihad*; Commins, *The Wahhabi Mission and Saudi Arabia.*

Salafism. And once this worldview is accepted, the step towards violent jihad is a very small one—and one that is easy to make by appealing to Qur'anic verses taken out of context by unqualified commentators and the ignorant young men who read them.

It therefore follows that the core of modern jihadism is not, as is commonly believed, its aspect of violence. Jihadis have not invented the instrumentalization of religion (or ideology) towards political ends through violent means. Nor have they invented political violence or even the idea of making a fetish of violence as a tool to motivate the masses. The "propaganda of the deed" was an invention of 19th-century anarchists and became a staple of left-wing terrorist groups in Europe in the 1970s and 1980s.[31] They have not invented suicide bombings,[32] despite what you will often hear or read in the media from even liberal commentators who should know better. Within the recent Islamic context, it was Shi'a groups resisting Israeli and Western interventions in Lebanon that first made substantive use of suicide attacks, such as those that devastated the US Marine base in Beirut in October 1983.[33] From there, it spread to Sunni groups like Hamas and was adopted by many Palestinian groups during the 2000–2005 Intifada. In this context, the tactic of suicide bombing came to be seen not as a tactical response to a particular situation but as the weapon of choice.[34] Nor is the use of suicide bombing a specifically Islamic tactic. It was the mainstay of the mostly Hindu Tamil Tigers in their long war against the Sri Lankan state from the 1970s to 2010.

Equally groups like AQ and ISIS are not the first terror groups to take over territory and try to establish states. Many previous radical movements have sought to make the transition to control of territory with the goal of consolidating their rule and spreading their ideology.

---

31   Philip Willan, *Puppet Masters: The Political Use of Terrorism in Italy*, 2nd ed. (New York: Authors Choice Press, 2002).

32   Benjamin T. Acosta, "The Suicide Bomber as Sunni-Shi'i Hybrid," Middle East Forum, 2010 http://www.meforum.org/2743/suicide-bomber-sunni-shii-hybrid#.Vw_5u8joaII. twitter.

33   Fisk, *Pity the Nation: Lebanon at War.*

34   Acosta, "The Suicide Bomber as Sunni-Shi'i Hybrid".

These are mere tactics, a set of means to an end. These means, the violent aspects of jihadism, are simply the logical conclusion of the core attitudes, dogmas, and moral attitudes of Salafism.

It is true that most strands of Salafism have repudiated this violent aspect, but this repudiation is very thin on the ideological ground. The fact of the matter is that the core tenets of Salafism imply the same tendency towards violence that was present in both the historical full-blooded Wahhabism of the past, and in the modern jihadism of the present. As we saw in the introductory discussion, one common cause of terrorism is a perception that the "other" has no legitimacy, and, in consequence, there is no option but to use violence to challenge this. This is invariably self-serving. It is true that Northern Ireland before 1968, and the start of what became known as the "Troubles" lasting into the 1990s, was a flawed democracy, but it was still a democratic state. The Italy that the Red Brigades tried to destroy was a functioning democracy with the largest Communist Party outside the Soviet bloc. There are occasions when terrorism can be seen as a response when all other options are closed off, but these have been rare.

So to tackle violent jihadism we need to contest the Manichean worldview of the nonviolent Salafis. We cannot leave the "peaceful" Salafis to go around the world and proselytize their ideology of bigoted moral superiority and reactionary fundamentalism, hoping that all their converts will be happy to leave the House of Saud and the Salafi elite in Riyadh to make all decisions on how to best pursue the Salafi vision of the future of Islam. Once the logic of "us" vs. "them" is firmly implanted, some will easily make the next step to the use of violence.[35]

So when discussing Salafism, the issue is not whether mainstream strands of Salafism condone terrorism. Clearly, they do not. Especially since the mainstream Salafi establishment is a staunch supporter of the House of Saud, whereas the jihadis are now at war with the House of Saud. Indeed, mainstream Salafi scholars urge the faithful to inform the appropriate authorities if they come into any information about potential terrorist plots or have knowledge about individuals that

---

35   This theme of a bridge from peaceful, "quietest" Salafism to violent jihad is the focus
      of the next chapter.

incite terrorist acts—and this is not just inside Saudi Arabia. Rather, the issue is whether mainstream Salafism provides the theological basis and creates an environment that allows people who see themselves as true believers to resort to violent means for ideological ends.

My contention is that it does—beyond any shadow of a doubt. This causation between ideology and violence is not new. Left-wing terrorism in Europe in the 1970s and 1980s survived not just because of a small core of fully committed members but because there was a much larger intellectual worldview that accepted violence, was prepared to condone it, and provided a staging post for radicalized young people before they moved into the orbit of the explicitly terrorist groups.[36] This is not to simply say that modern-day jihadists are little but a continuation of earlier forms of violent dissent—they share some methods and mind-set but have supplemented other violent traditions with their own particular interpretation of Islam.[37] In particular, their embrace of "martyrdom" has taken the traditional willingness of terrorists to take risks with their own lives to a new level—actively seeking death.[38]

Both Salafis and jihadis today harbor an idea of moral superiority over non-Salafi Muslims and are methodically intolerant towards these "misguided" deviants. Both have few qualms about labeling other Muslims as apostates for what they view as unsound doctrine or religious practices, and they agree in almost all other respects on what constitutes such unacceptable practices. In both cases, the Sharia punishment for apostasy is taken to be death, as a matter of course.

Towards non-Muslims, both advocate cultural isolationism and separatism. The dogmatic attachment to al-wala' wa al-bara' (whether in a politicized form or not) has led to pronouncements by mainstream Salafi scholars that are rather difficult to stomach for civilized ears in the West, both Muslim and non-Muslim. Muslims living in the non-Muslim have been urged to immigrate to Muslim lands because

---

36 Tarantelli, "The Italian Red Brigades and the structure and dynamics of terrorist groups."

37 Meijer, *Global Salafism: Islam's New Religious Movement.*

38 Raffaello Pantucci, *"We Love Death As You Love Life": Britain's Suburban Terrorists* (London: C.Hurst & Co, 2015).

"settling in the countries of the unbelievers will lead to loyalty [to them]," while Shaykh 'Abd al-'Aziz bin Baz, grand mufti of Saudi Arabia, casually proclaimed that the Jews "and the polytheists are greatest in enmity to believers." These were not the words of Osama bin Laden but of the leading religious scholar of the Saudi kingdom, the heart of the "peaceful" Salafi establishment.

Meanwhile, books by mainstream Salafis, frequently promoted aggressively in the mosques, which receive Saudi financial support, develop this theme of *al-wala' wa al-bara'* and often warn against taking Jews and Christians as friends, lest "true" Muslims be corrupted by their deviant beliefs.[39] As precautionary measures to insulate against the risks of ideological contamination, mainstream Salafis have developed a list of actions that are discouraged, even prohibited, for "true" Muslims. For example:

- Adopting non-Muslim dress or language

- Helping non-Muslims

- Seeking non-Muslim assistance or trusting them

- Using the non-Muslim calendar or observing their holidays

- Speaking well of non-Muslims

- Supplicating for non-Muslims and being compassionate to them

And whenever the Salafi establishment does do things that smack of tolerance and a willingness to cooperate with non-Salafis, Muslim or otherwise, they feel the need to explain their potentially suspicious behavior. Such interaction is deemed so controversial that mainstream Salafis list a number of "permissible interactions with the disbelievers,"

---

39 For example: Muhammad bin Abdul-Wahhab, Three Fundamentals of Islam, (New York: Al-Ibaanah Book Publishing, 2014), https://abdurrahmanorg.files. wordpress.com/2014/08/the-three-fundamental-principles-shaykh-bin-abdul-wahab-al-ibaanah-com.pdf;—, Explanation of "The Four Rules Regarding Shirk", (New York: Al-Ibaanah Book Publishing, 2003), http://tawheednyc.com/aqeedah/tawheed/Shirk.pdf.

so long as these interactions do not require the Muslim to show either love or allegiance to them in such affairs. Among those listed are business transactions, hiring non-Muslims for their expertise, and even responding in kindness, so long as it is the other who initiates the kindness, since this is "compensation" for being shown kindness and "not from the angle of loving them." Al-Fawzan does note, however, that "it is obligatory to be kind to one's disbelieving parents," though this too must be done "without loving them."

The notion that this is an ideology that can fit in harmoniously in the modern, globalized world (let alone in a functional multicultural society), and that these are the people who we should cooperate with in fighting global jihadi terrorism as an international community, is, or at least should be, patently absurd. These people, our Salafi *allies* in the "War on Terror," share the very same "true" faith as the jihadis themselves. It is their belief that non-Salafis should ideally not exist, and insofar as they do, they should not be regarded as equal human beings, worthy of the same rights, dignity, and treatment. Their very existence is a spiritual burden upon the "true" Muslim, and any interaction with them can never be anything more than a regrettable, necessary evil.

IDEOLOGICAL WAR

It thus follows that what we had suspected all along—that the Bush administration's notion of the "War on Terror" is misguided and ineffective—is in fact true. Terrorism is but a tactic, one that has been employed in relatively similar guises throughout much of the history of civilization, by various actors, for diverse purposes. Our real focus is, or at least should be, a concern with Salafi "true" faith—an ideology that defines itself as in perpetual war with all human beings that do not adhere to it and dictates that the rest of us should, ideally, not exist at all. So if we are going to be "at war" with anything, unhelpful as that terminology may be in this case, we should be at war with this kind of intolerant and expansive kind of reactionary fundamentalism, which inevitably boils over into self-righteous violence irrespective of the judgments and injunctions of the senior Saudi propaganda machine.

This is a difficult argument to make for any liberal, and indeed for any civilization that sees itself as broadly liberal, as we do in the West. The premise of liberalism is that, aside from a minimal set of standard rules of peaceful engagement agreed on in common, everyone should be free to do as they please, believe as they please, and develop whatever cultures and ideologies suit them best. It is thus always somehow intellectually uncomfortable for a liberal to make a case for intolerance even when faced with intolerant, totalitarian ideologies. But for liberalism to work as a framework for a diverse society tolerant of diversity of opinion, ideology, and practice, people do need to agree to that minimal set of standard rules. Liberalism only works when everyone is happy to agree to live within the liberal framework, and concede that it takes precedence over their own particular interests and prejudices. You can choose to live your own life according to an austere interpretation of your personal beliefs (whether derived from any religion or purely secular)—it is when you deny others similar rights in how they make their own choices that problems occur.

And this is exactly what some parts of Wahhabism/Salafism/jihadism most staunchly refuse to accept—the fundamental core requirement of genuine cooperation that we should agree that we all have an equal right to exist and lead our lives in diverse ways. This ideology is not at war with American foreign policy, or its culture of consumerism or Western "sexual decadence." It is at war with the idea that anyone has the right to live in any way that diverges from their reinterpretation of the societal norms of 7th- and 8th-century Arabia. But, as we will see, we still need to be careful in our response. Research in the Netherlands[40] suggests that some Salafist communities amend their behavior when they live in a predominantly non-Muslim country and do accept the legitimacy of the current social arrangements. This

---

40   Ineke Roex, "Should we be Scared of all Salafists in Europe? A Dutch Case Study," *Perspectives on Terrorism* 8, no. 3 (2014).

matters, because conflict does not come from differences of opinion; it comes when people perceive that there is no other way to express a dissenting view.

This leads to a complex argument. At one level, as explored in the first section, the issue with Salafism is not that it is simply the ideological consequence that flows from a personal interpretation of Islam. In fact, it is in many ways the exact opposite of the teachings and practices of Muhammad and the first caliphs. Nor is this kind of attitude, this tendency of putting an ossified, antisocial ideology over concern for other people, specific to Islam. One can draw a very clear and intuitive distinction between decent human beings—human beings who value getting along with each other above ideology, whether because God tells them to or because they find it natural and intuitive without any appeal to religion—and sociopathic zealots who are itching to oppress and kill for the sake of one ideology or another, whether religious or secular, whether "Islamic" or Communist.

Mainstream Muslims (though not mainstream Salafis), moderate Christians and Jews, and casual agnostics and atheists belong to the first group. And my contention remains that Islam was a religion aimed at these people—as was Christianity and most other religions in their early, expanding stages. These are the kinds of people who understand that the point is to make the world a better place for everyone, and that in order for them to be able to do so they need to talk to each other and learn from each other.[41]

Jihadis (and really all flavors of Wahhabis, or other kinds of latter-day Kharijites), the Christian Lord's Resistance Army, the ultra-Hasidic Jewish settlers in the Israeli-occupied territories, Pol Pot, the Stalinist elite, and the Nazis belong to the second category. These become nothing more than glorified death cults—more than willing to kill not only their enemies but also their own supporters, who are seen as expendable in the search for a new, perfect world. The mind-set of such groups has a long and grim history.[42]

---

41 Ramadan, *The Messenger.*

42 Norman Cohn, *The Pursuit of the Millenium*, 3rd ed. (London: Paladin, 1970).

We should therefore have no qualms about "being at war" with this ideology, any more than we would have qualms about being at war with Nazism. But we should be clear—both to ourselves and in the way we conduct our foreign policy—that we are not at war with Islam. We are, and we should be, at war with a death cult that employs some of the symbols and theology of Islam within its own antihuman ideology.[43] This is why it is so important that the Islamic world and Muslims all over the world in general should be engaged and invited to take part in this struggle, especially those Muslims whose religion the jihadis are trying to hijack—the mainstream Sunnis. We should not only ask them to join in this war against this ideology of death but invite them to lead the charge. And in doing so, to reenact the achievement of the Prophet by beating back the dark forces of this modern *Jahiliya*, this deplorable state of ignorant and mindless sectarian violence. In this sense, the struggle is indeed with all forms of Salafism, even if we make sensible distinctions between its quietest and violent forms and note that it can become accepting of wider norms (even if it sees itself as in some way superior).

The main battleground for this will not be Syria or Iraq—much as it is necessary to contain and ultimately defeat the marauding band of violent thugs roaming over that region, if for nothing else than the sake of the civilian populations of the area[44] and the rich cultural history of the region. Rather, the main battleground must be with the heart of the Wahhabi darkness itself—Saudi Arabia. This means we need to talk first to the House of Saud. And second, the elite Salafi establishment which they sponsor. It must by now be evident to both these groups that the ideology that elevated both to their exulted status is indeed a death cult, and one that needs to be beaten before it consumes both of them and everything that they have built. It cannot be lost on either of them that it is in fact entirely predictable that they should have become a prime target of the global jihad, and indeed that this is genuinely justified

---

43 United Nations, "The human rights situation in Iraq in the light of abuses committed by the so-called Islamic State in Iraq and the Levant and associated groups," (Geneva: UNHCR, 2015).

44 Amnesty International, "Absolute Impunity: Militia Rule in Iraq."; Human Rights Watch, "Iraq: Women Suffer Under ISIS".

by the very ideology they spend billions every year in promoting around the world.

THE GOALS OF THE SALAFIST MOVEMENT: SHARIA

T he imposition of Sharia law is often presented as a central goal of various Salafist groups. However, Sharia is not the single form of jurisprudence as promoted by groups such as ISIS but a complex (and competing—it is usually acknowledged there are four main Sunni legal frameworks, and Shi'a Islam had produced its own variant[45]) set of legal frameworks. The word *Sharia* is now understood as 'Islamic law.' And that is how it has been understood for most of Islam's history. But the word means 'the way to know God.' Originally, it was what Muhammad and his followers believed they were trying to achieve in Medina: a way of getting to know God through implementing justice, equality, and freedom in human society.

Later Muslim scholars would come to understand Sharia as 'God's Law,' but this was more a consequence of the fact that they were also jurists and tended to have a legalistic frame of mind. It also came to take the shape of law due to the demands of running the huge empire that the Arabs had built by the 9th century, when what we would now call Islamic law was first codified as law. But of course, this body of jurisprudence can only be derivative to the Qur'an, and also to the precedents of the life of the Prophet. The Qur'an outlines a great many principles that inform Sharia, while Muhammad's life and sayings, the Sunna, can give examples of the practical application of these principles. But neither of those sources can hope to cover and give guidance to everyone in every conceivable situation. These limits were recognized in the 9th century when the first traditions of jurisprudence were established, and they are recognized today by the mainstream strands of Islam. When a Muslim meets new circumstances, he is

---

45   Kamali, *Principles of Islamic Jurisprudence.*

supposed to apply his own reason, and the reason of the centuries of Islamic theological thinking, to find appropriate answers to his own problems.

This matters; proper Islamic jurisprudence is the process of developing case law and its applications for new situations. This was the center of the legal framework developed in the Ottoman Empire in the latter part of the 19th century.[46] This flowering and re-formation of one of the major schools of Sunni jurisprudence originated from Ottoman-controlled Syria—a region that, at the time, suffered severely from raids by the religious fundamentalists inspired by Wahhabism and is now suffering once more.

It is not just that one school produced a remarkably liberal set of interpretations of Islamic strictures while the other turned inwards to a reactionary, almost inhuman, mind-set. What matters is that mainstream Islamic law works both by precedent and context, and this is common across all the main traditions. To the Wahhabists, the modern world is polluted, to others it has simply changed, and laws and customs need to be amended to cope with those changes. Worse, much of what the Wahhabists claim to be the original pure values of Islam are in fact little but later cultural accretions. One simple example might suffice to stress this point.

For example, it is commonly assumed in the West, and indeed is practiced in Iran and Saudi Arabia, that Sharia requires that adulterers be stoned to death. But this is not what the Qur'an requires. Rather, it requires one hundred lashings. And only if there were four Muslim men who witnessed and could attest by oath that penetration had occurred—harsh by our modern eyes but demanding of a significant amount of evidence. If anything, stoning adulterous women to death was something that was commonly done by Arabian tribes before Islam. This practice owes more to the Arab *Jahiliya*, and to Christian and Jewish practice at the time following the Old Testament, than it does to Islam. It is both surprising and perverse to see such a practice upheld today as something fundamental to traditional Islamic law and

---

46   Avi Rubin, "Legal borrowing and its impact on Ottoman legal culture in the late nineteenth century," *Continuity and Change* 22, no. 2 (2007).

practice. Similar examples exist about the use of the veil; this is largely a cultural legacy of other non-Islamic practices (mainly in this case adopted from Eastern Orthodox Christianity), but we see it raised by the Salafists to being a point of fundamental principle.

THE ROLE OF THEOLOGY

This leads to the important question: How religious are those who embrace Salafism? This may seem an odd question; after all, they drape their announcements with quotes from the Qu'ran and other Islamic texts. They cite pronouncements made in the mid-13th century as justification for their acts. They claim to aim to bring about a particularly pure version of an Islamic state as mandated by God. On this basis, surely theology is the core of their belief systems? However, as I have argued, they ignore the bulk of Islamic teachings and debate as well as willfully misread the historical record of Islam. What drives them is not *theology* in any meaningful sense but an *ideology*, one that was originally constructed in Arabia in the late 17th century.

Despite the focus in some parts of the media on the role of theology in driving young Muslims to commit terrorist acts, not one of the 7/7 London bombers had any formal religious training. More widely, Reza Aslan notes that only "13 percent of jihadists have had any kind of religious education."[47] Even the leadership lacks religious credibility: bin Laden had no formal religious training, something that was even acknowledged by Mullah Omar, then Afghanistan's de facto head of state and the spiritual leader of the Taliban. In July 2001, he stated that Osama bin Laden's 1998 fatwa where he directed Muslims to kill American civilians and issued a jihad against America was "null and void" since bin Laden was "not entitled to issue fatawa [pl. of fatwa] as he did not complete the mandatory twelve years of Qur'anic studies

---

47   Aslan, *How to Win*, 143.

to qualify for the position of mufti."[48] Ayman al-Zawahiri (bin Laden's successor) is a qualified medical doctor, while Abu Mus'ab al-Suri, "one of Al-Qaeda's leading military thinkers,"[49] studied mechanical engineering and failed to complete his degree.[50]

Of the 9/11 hijackers, bin Laden declared that they did not belong to any traditional school of Islamic law.[51] The credentials of even ISIS's leader, al-Baghdadi, are not altogether clear. Some sources claim that he does indeed have a PhD in Islamic studies,[52] which is really not the same as the twelve years of the Qur'anic studies necessary to become a mufti and be qualified to issue fatawa, while other sources claim that his doctorate was instead in education.[53] The case seems pretty solid: mainstream theology does not promote terrorism. Indeed, there is research that suggests it actually inoculates against it.[54]

Rather, the problem lies with the warped patchwork of "theology" constructed by illegitimate interpreters of Islamic law and how this has been able to gain ground, especially among young, driven, and

---

48   Richard Bonney, *Jihad*, 358.

49   International Centre, *Recruitment*, 22.

50   Brynjar Lia, "The al-Qaida Strategist Abu Mus'ab al-Suri: A Profile," (London: OMS, 2006).

51   His exacts words were "Those youths who conducted the operations did not accept any *fiqh* in the popular terms [. . .]." Cf, Faisal Devji, *Landscapes of the Jihad*, 13.

52   Aaron Y Zelin, "Abu Bakr al-Baghdadi: Islamic State's driving force," BBC, 2014 http://www.bbc.co.uk/news/world-middle-east-28560449.

53   Peter Beaumont, "Abu Bakr al-Baghdadi: The Isis chief with the ambition to overtake al-Qaida," The Guardian, 2014 http://www.theguardian.com/world/2014/jun/12/baghdadi-abu-bakr-iraq-isis-mosul-jihad.

54   A leaked 2008 MI5 report from its Behavioral Sciences Unit that comprehensively investigated pathways into terrorism stated that "there is evidence that a well-established religious identity actually protects against violent radicalisation." Alan Travis, "MI5 report challenges view on terrorism in Britain," The Guardian, 2008 http://www.guardian.co.uk/uk/2008/aug/20/uksecurity.terrorism1. Of course, as we identified earlier, terrorists rarely come from the mainstream of their claimed tradition. Very few members of the Red Brigades had previously been members of the Italian Communist Party, indicating that those exposed to more conventional interpretations of their religious or political tradition are less likely to be convinced by more extreme messages.

morally outraged Muslims, at the expense of normative Islam. It also lies with those who would cynically encourage young Muslims to engage primarily with this kind of theology, for their own political ends. The long list of "hate preachers" operating in Europe (some of which we will discuss in detail in a later chapter) are chief among them. These are then supplemented by the various Saudi individuals and Saudi "educational charities" that are actively fomenting this kind of ideology and targeting it specifically at young people around the world in the Saudis' grand plan to create buffers and proxies against their enemies, principally Shi'a Iran.[55] These people are not worried about the lack of knowledge of Islam among their recruits—a partial understanding is very satisfactory as far as they are concerned.[56] What matters to them is finding disposable people to help them achieve their self-preserving goals.

Then there are the failures of local Muslim communities. Institutional failures within the Muslim community have prevented their leaders from comprehensively tackling and quashing, in any coherent and systematic manner, these radical preachers and their "theology" from its inception. Radical preachers thus far have been tolerated as mere nuisances. Mosques, far from being the breeding centers of radicalization, are predominantly guilty of employing out-of-touch imams from "back home" who failed to engage with the concerns and spiritual needs of today's young Muslims living in Western societies. An ever-increasing number of young Muslims cannot speak or understand the language of their parents—even though this remains the first language of most imams.[57] The pietistic, apolitical, traditional Islam of their parents has become increasingly viewed by young Muslims as obsolete, anachronistic, and culturally irrelevant. And the hole that this has left has been filled with a "pamphlet-based" Islam that promotes an

---

55   Ben Hubbard and Mayy El Sheikh, "WikiLeaks Shows a Saudi Obsession With Iran," New York Times, 2015 http://mobile.nytimes.com/2015/07/17/world/middleeast/wikileaks-saudi-arabia-iran.html?referrer=&_r=1.

56   Lebovich, "How 'religious' are ISIS fighters? The relationship between religious literacy and religious motivation".

57   Richard Holt, "Only 6pc of Imams are Native English Speakers," The Telegraph, 2007 http://www.telegraph.co.uk/news/main.jhtml?xml=/news/2007/07/06/nislam106.xml.

activism grounded by the groundless opinions and politicized diatribes of unqualified interpreters of Islamic law and theology.[58]

So what these young people are learning is not Islamic theology. It is an Islamist ideology. I think perhaps the best way to describe what I mean by ideology, here and throughout the book, is fundamentally just the *ethos* of Wahhabism. That is what both jihadism and Salafism have in common at root. And, crucially, it is what ultimately gets transmitted when Salafism is proselytized. When you preach about Salafism you start with the distinction between "true" Muslim and apostate (*takfir*) or nonbeliever (*kuffar*). The next thing you talk about is war between *dar al-Islam* and *dar al-harb*. And then it is made clear that the West is *dar al-harb* and that They are oppressing Us, both in Western countries and in "our lands." At this point, no scandalized young man, or group of action-orientated young men, is going to wait for you to elaborate on the finer points of how we should withdraw from society and continue to refrain from any political engagement. They are already on a journey towards a violent response to these ills.

Ideally, the challenge is for Muslim institutions, scholars, and theologians to articulate the genuine theology of Islam in a meaningful manner that engages directly with the lives, the worries, anxieties, and hopes of Muslims today, young and old. Especially for those who were born and/or brought up in the West. This is essential to enable young Muslims to recognize just how radically alien this pop-Islamism they get from pamphlets and the Internet really is to genuine Islam.

But in order to get anyone acquainted with the wonderfully positive and world-affirming theology of mainstream Islam, you cannot begin by introducing them to the ethos of Wahhabism. That will poison their understanding of Islam before they even get off the ground. Young people who identify culturally as Muslims and are already prone to grievance politics may well take this ethos, this ideology, and will re-create the horrible monster of Salafi-Takfirism in their minds and

---

58   Willian McCants, ed. *Militant Ideology Atlas* (West Point: Combating Terrorism Center, 2006); Faisal Devji, *Landscapes of the Jihad: Militancy, Morality, Modernity*, 2nd ed. (London: Hurst, 2017).

within their friendship groups. And non-Muslim casual observers may well become horrified and scandalized (and rightly so), and will likely form an ill-informed and grotesque picture of what Islam is about in general. They may even become explicit opponents of Islam, failing to understand that this ideology does not represent Islam. And one can hardly blame them for being revolted by this ideology of death—every mainstream Muslim would be too! From that position comes a very welcome outcome for the Salafists—individuals and politicians declaring that Islam and Muslims are incompatible with the survival of open, pluralist societies.[59] Their belief that such societies can only be protected by removing Muslims of course fits neatly with the Salafist ideology that engagement with the West, and its citizens, has to be minimized if someone is to live a properly Islamic life. In effect, if Western politicians frame all Muslims as "the other," then they are doing ISIS' recruitment work.[60] Clearly there is now a regular narrative by right-wing commentators to the effect that Islam is the problem,[61] but we need to be clear: this generalized argument is exactly what the Salafists want young Muslims to hear.[62]

Now that the origins of today's jihadist and Salafist ideology and how they form the basis for ISIS and terror attacks today are established, a strategy for addressing them can now be formed. I have offered thoughts and commentary as we have gone through the book so far, but now we can finally draw everything together and start working on concrete recommendations for our policy makers, our leaders in our Muslim communities, and indeed for ordinary citizens, Muslim and non-Muslim alike.

---

59 Rowena Mason, "Nigel Farage: British Muslim 'fifth column' fuels fear of immigration," The Guardian, 2015 http://www.theguardian.com/politics/2015/mar/12/nigel-farage-british-muslim-fifth-column-fuels-immigration-fear-ukip; Winston Ross, "Geert Wilders: The 'Prophet who hates Muhammad'," Newsweek, 2015 http://europe.newsweek.com/geert-wilders-prophet-who-hates-muhammad-300266?rm=eu.

60 Luqman Ali, "Why is ISIL able to find recruits in the West?," The National, 2016 http://www.thenational.ae/opinion/comment/why-is-isil-able-to-find-recruits-in-the-west.

61 Douglas Murray, "'Religion of peace' is not a harmless platitude," The Spectator, 2015 http://www.spectator.co.uk/2015/01/religion-of-peace-is-not-a-harmless-platitude/.

62 Al-Arian, "Why Western attempts to moderate Islam are dangerous".

"WE LOVE DEATH AS YOU LOVE LIFE"

One thing that should be immediately obvious about the picture of radicalization presented in this chapter is that there is nothing peculiar about the psychological and social dynamics described. Moral outrage among the young, alienation, a sense, real or imagined, of social exclusion, an individual and collective search for meaning in a frustrating and morally bleak world, the basic dynamics of group-think and the way ideas circulated within close social groups become amplified—there is nothing about this that is particular to young Muslim men. Nor is there anything that unusual about a tendency to glorify violence, and, among some, the tendency to behave in violent ways. Nor indeed about the tendency among some of those to want to justify, and ritualize even, great acts of violence: young men who carry out school shootings in the United States, for example, always have some kind of manifesto of grievance they wish to publicize as justification for their actions[63] and always seem to describe their acts as some kind of ritual with a deeper meaning.

But there is no denying that some young people respond to these common psychological and social phenomena by leaving their families behind and moving to Syria, where they often engage in grotesque acts of violence, while others join their local Green Party and grow vegetables together. Some celebrate the empowerment they find in radical ideologies by enjoying the spoils of war, such as money and sex slaves, while others do so by singing folksy songs around campfires at music festivals. Which is to say that the psychological and social drivers we have identified do not always push in the same direction. In fact, they can have radically different outcomes. Some produce profoundly pro-life, pro-social behavior, while others produce death cults. As Mohammad Sidique Khan, the leader of the London 7/7 bombings group, put it, "We Love Death As You Love Life." The obvious question

---

63 And in Norway, the mass murderer Thomas Brevik went to great lengths to try and justify his actions in political terms with a manifesto that quoted substantially from the arguments that are too easy to find on the European and North American far right about the threats of Islam, multiculturalism, and, of course, "cultural Marxism."

is, Why? What does, in the ultimate analysis, determine the different outcomes of these otherwise common phenomena?

Young Muslims in the West, and indeed in the Islamic world, face virtually the same problems as the majority of other young people around the world. Where they do find themselves in immigrant communities, they are not the only young people in immigrant communities. In Europe there are perfectly comparable immigrant groups from the West Indies, Eastern Europe, (Christian) Africa, and (Hindu) Asia. And some of these groups face exclusion and discrimination that is far worse, notably the Black African communities. In the United States the situation is similar, but here the largest immigrant communities are from Latin America. All these communities too feel aggrieved, are highly sensitive to social and political injustice, and are actively fighting against ongoing aggression from the powerful majority culture. Here too, as within the Muslim communities, there is an ongoing tension between the higher moral values for which they fight and petty criminality that is rampant, and often even necessary, for people to survive day to day.

Islamic radicalism has produced a mind-set that can be encapsulated in the expression "dead men walking"[64] to describe themselves. This matters, as even compared to other modern forms of terrorism there is no other group that is producing waves of suicide attacks against innocent civilians—no other group that even tries to do so in a concerted way. There are frequent attacks against mainstream society: random shootings, even bombings, riots and looting and so on, but almost always by deranged individuals, not by groups on behalf of groups. No other group sees itself as a group at war with the entire world and actively waging war on the entire world on multiple fronts, leading to the collapse of UN-recognized states and displacing millions of people.

The fact remains that even as we look at the process of radicalization that jihadi terrorists undergo and see what little role religion and

---

64 Of course just to prove that there is little that is totally new in this world, agents of the Soviet-controlled Comintern in the 1920s and 1930s often claimed to be "dead men on leave"—such was their certainty that their underground actions would inevitably lead to their arrest and execution.

ideology seem to play, the undeniable fact is that between this group and all other groups that could be expected to engage in similar kinds of violence and do not, there are no variables that differ except one: the Salafi-*takfiri* ideology that frames the jihadis' politics of grievance. That is the only factor that is materially different between them and the multitude of dispossessed, marginalized, and abused groups of the world. There are many, many groups of people who have grievance politics around the world, and have little means to express their grievance but through violence—but this is mostly aimed at their own state or other local groups. But it is only Salafi-Takfirism that has hundreds of thousands of mujahedeen to wage war on the entire world at once.

In light of the history of this ideology that has been developed from Wahhabism to today's jihadism, it is not surprising that such a mode of thinking can lead, in the right historical circumstances, to such generalized political violence. And here we must stress that both elements are necessary for these kinds of outcomes: both the conditions of exclusion, marginalization, and hopelessness, the feeling that Islam as a group is under attack from all quarters, and the ideology of Salafism, which at the same time sanctifies this exclusion and encourages active resistance against it.

THE PARTICULAR CHALLENGE OF SALAFISM

In all that we have said so far we have assumed it is self-evident that if you have an ideology in which the world is locked in a perpetual struggle between Us and Them, and They are of lesser moral concern before God, it becomes quite easy to seriously consider killing Them. Especially if They are *oppressing* Us, or attacking Us in "our lands." We have plenty of examples of what happens when this becomes the guiding belief system of both secular and religious movements. While we can draw on this history for understanding—and some possible solutions—the challenge is to deal with modern-day Salafism, not 1930s Stalinism or Fascism.

So how can we challenge Salafism? Given the underlying ideology, how do we explain the paradox of the peaceful Salafist? Why is it that so many individuals who subscribe to bigoted, xenophobic, and hate-filled ideologies, whether within Islam or within other religious frameworks, nonetheless manage to be, for the most part, peaceful? Why is it indeed that the majority of people who subscribe to such ideologies are in fact not vicious murderers at all? In part, it is that many are attracted to more austere creeds simply to give a structure to their own lives. They may accept the wider message of disdain for others, but this is not their own central motivation.[65] This matters, as it is clear that we need to break the current links between nonviolent Salafists and their violent close cousins fully committed to jihad.

Equally many movements are actually a combination of multiple prior strands of belief. So at one level, Marxism, via Lenin, came to inherit the French Revolutionary Jacobin emphasis on elite parties, terrorism, and state-sanctioned violence.[66] This led to the casting of those not deemed to be part of the class that was to inherit the earth (and with membership of this class carefully regulated by the state) as "others," who had no entitlement to the right to life.[67] On the other hand, Marx, and some of his followers, drew from the wider debates in European liberalism and socialism across the 19th and 20th centuries.[68] This strand, if not exactly tolerant (it still aimed at a particular form of society),[69] had few problems in coping with a diversity of beliefs and social movements.[70] By the 1970s, orthodox Marxism was in a degree of flux. Some had turned to terrorism in an attempt to force radical change, others clung to the verities provided by the USSR (or

---

65   Gurr, Why Men Rebel.

66   AS Cohan, Theories of Revolution: An Introduction (Exeter: Thomas Nelson, 1975).

67   Geoffrey Hosking, A History of the Soviet Union, 2nd ed. (London: Fontana, 1990).

68   Tom Rockmore, Marx after Marxism: The Philosophy of Karl Marx (Oxford: Blackwell, 2002).

69   Elzbieta Ettinger, Rosa Luxemburg: A Life (Guernsey: Guernsey Press, 1995).

70   Antonio Gramsci, Selections from Prison Notebooks, trans. Geoffrey Nowell Smith and Quintin Hoare (Southampton: Lawrence Wishart, 1971).

Mao's China), others started to engage in regaining Marxism's other set of roots—in the wider debates of the European enlightenment, such as pluralism and respect for human rights.[71]

Turning back to our focus, we can note that modern-day Salafism too is a hybrid. One parent is traditional Wahhabism, the second is the grafting, by the Saudis, of the view that Salafism is about personal rigor in belief. Clearly the second is an invention—but so are many powerful beliefs—and it has the capacity to help deal with the Salafist challenge. In effect the question is less why do some people find Salafism attractive and more why do some then go further into violent jihad?

I will return to this in a later chapter and closely examine exactly how the young men who have plotted or committed terror attacks, or the young (and not so young) men and women who travel to Syria, have gone from a closed and insular worldview to actually justifying or actively engaging in acts of grotesque, inhuman violence. We must look at the actual evidence on how these people walk along this ideological path. In doing so we will learn both about the psychological processes that are taking place inside the mind of a person as they radicalize, as well as the conditions necessary for radicalization to occur. For all the depressing frequency with which we humans kill one another, it is still not something that just happens. It is not something that we find easy.[72]

---

71 Joan Barth Urban, Moscow and the Italian Communist Party: From Togliatti to Berlinguer (Ithaca: Cornell University Press, 1986).

72 Some psychopaths potentially excluded. But even then, psychopathic individuals may be disproportionately more likely to commit violence, and violent crime, yet the majority of people who could be clinically diagnosed with psychopathic mental disorders do not engage in such actions. However, research into the membership of the Italian Red Brigades, after that organization collapsed in the 1980s, suggested that around 40 percent of the active killers in the group could be described as psychopaths. In effect engaging in terrorism was probably a simple means to enact their desires, the existence of an organized terrorist movement creating both opportunity and apparent justification for their actions. The rest had, one way or another, managed to convince themselves that murder was justified either by state violence (they commonly cited the violence of capitalism as their justification for opposing it with violence of their own) or the presumed advantages that would flow if they were to be successful (the idea of doing harsh things for the good of future generations being a common argument in many violent movements).

CONCLUSION

This chapter has sought to place violent Salafist jihad into the context of Islam as well as other extremist movements, both secular and religious, throughout history. One frame is where it shares much in common with other violent political movements, but while this is important, we need to be aware it is also different and has its own internal logic and rationale.

Looking at other terrorist groups and their logic is illuminating. In part, much of what we see and know from AQ, ISIS, and those they inspire is not so new. Allying reactionary goals to the use of modern technology was a feature of both anarchist and reactionary terrorist groups (such as the Russian Narodniks in the mid-19th century). Indeed radical anarchist groups developed and celebrated the "propaganda of the deed," whereby a particularly violent attack was seen as likely to strike fear into the state establishment and inspire their own followers.

Looking at previous studies it is useful to distinguish between the situations that seem to give rise to violent terrorist groups and the reasons why individuals might join them and take part. Conventionally, the argument is that such groups arise out of material deprivation or under conditions of political repression[73] (though rarely if the state can be accurately described as totalitarian). In reality these are common factors but are not sufficient to explain the rise of such groups or why some have a longer life than others.

Many European groups have developed within functioning democracies, which may well have their flaws but offer universal suffrage and a multiplicity of political parties. Thus groups as disparate as the left- and right-wing terrorism in Italy from 1969 to the 1980s; left-wing terrorism in Germany across the same period; the short-lived and ineffectual violent left in France at the same time; and separatist, nationalist violence of the type that plagued Northern Ireland and Spain from the early 1970s to 2000 all occurred in mature democracies. Equally, while the Muslim world produced some terrorist movements (most, at least loosely, connected with the Palestinian struggle but others sponsored

---

73   Abadie, "Poverty, Political Freedom, And The Roots Of Terrorism."

by various authoritarian regimes), it was not till the early 1980s that one could start to talk of Islamic terrorism as a separate entity. And here, in its first form, it was the Shi'a-led resistance to the Israeli occupation of southern Lebanon that was the original template.[74]

So we cannot trace the emergence (and continuation) of terrorist groups simply to the existence of social deprivation and state repression. Turning away from that, we then see that ideology offers some clues. Most of the leftist groups drew from a Marxist-Leninist concept of violent class struggle that needed to be led by a small, secretive, armed, vanguard movement. The far-right groups drew on the usual ideological mishmash of fascism with disdain for normal politics, a desire for an ethnically pure state, and a return to some mythical past regime. However, this again is not a sufficient explanation. If Italy saw sustained left-wing terrorism in the 1970s and 1980s, it was also home to Western Europe's largest Communist Party—committed to pluralism and peaceful political change. Equally not every right-wing nationalist movement has produced a terrorist wing (most have not). However, what is more informative is nuances of ideology.

Most orthodox Marxists would argue that class struggle is a central feature of modern society, but does this mean that anyone outside a narrowly defined working class has no rights? The mainstream socialist and social democratic traditions had long argued that working-class concerns were best pursued in the context of multi-class alliances.[75] The Italian Communist Party was committed to such alliances—to the extent that in its strongholds of Emilia-Bologna it created the basis for what became known as the "Third Italy," an industrial base built around small family-run firms. We may disagree substantively with such political parties, but they were not violent. Nonetheless they shared an ideology with those who used violence—as terrorists or as states.

So where lies the difference? The ideology used by groups such as the Red Brigades deliberately denied the basic humanity of those they

---

74 Fisk, Pity the Nation: Lebanon at War.

75 Donald Sassoon, One Hundred Years of Socialism: The West European Left in the Twentieth Century (London: Fontana, 1997).

targeted. Equally, in pursuit of a perfect future for humanity, harsh actions can be justified today. Regardless of the precise framing, we come back to the language of black and white, where anyone who does not meet some strict criteria is less of a human being. We also find ready justifications for violence against everyone else (most often the deepest hatred being reserved for those closest in ideological terms). Thus Salafism creates the intellectual basis within which violent jihadism can occur.

There is possibly another strand to explaining the emergence (and longevity) of violent political groups. They have their own traditions. The Red Brigades directly drew from those parts of the Italian resistance movement that had refused to lay down their arms in 1945[76] but also from the older tradition of anarchist violence that had been a major feature of pre–World War I Italy. In Northern Ireland, the IRA too was able to re-create itself by drawing on two centuries of violent republican campaigns against British rule in parts of Ireland. As we have seen, before 1980, violent Salafism did not really exist in its current form. However, it does have a tradition, and the intellectual underpinnings have been explored in this chapter.

Finally, if poverty and political repression are insufficient explanations for the emergence of terrorist groups, such groups still need an ongoing grievance to sustain themselves. This can be real, it can be simply a product of their own ideological framework, and it is often inconsistent.[77] Thus violent jihadist groups make much of various crimes by the "West" against Muslims to justify their own violence. As we will see later in this book, such narratives are often badly flawed but are often readily believed in circles with a lack of intellectual curiosity.

This shifts the focus to who joins such groups. The evidence is not clear—there is no simple "terrorist" type. Some groups seem to attract the well educated, others the less well educated. Some groups draw from the relatively well-off middle classes, others seem

---

76 This group was mainly based in Milan and Turin. By 1947 it had turned from any pretense of a political struggle to simple gangsterism. Some of its leaders fled to Czechoslovakia in 1949 and certainly had links to the leadership of the Red Brigades in the early 1970s.

77 Abrahms, "What Terrorists Really Want: Terrorist Motives and Counterterrorism Strategy."

to recruit from those who are socially excluded. Equally, while we might find using the label of "psychopath" convenient, the evidence is that most who join and carry out violent acts are not, in a clinical sense, psychopaths.[78]

What we are left with is two strong pieces of evidence. First, those who move into such groups tend to do so in stages and from other political or religious groups. As we have seen, the route is rarely from the orthodox parts of a belief system (the mosque or a communist party) and more often from informal groupings where zeal is prized above intellectual knowledge. Again, we can see in this how "mainstream" Salafism starts to form a bridge—it is often internally chaotic in its ideology, it does not prize conventional knowledge or learning, and it is based on a fundamental misreading of Islam. The second consistent finding is that once people join terrorist groups, they place the preservation of in-group ties above almost everything else—including the ideology they are notionally fighting for.[79] Again, this matters. As a matter of public policy, it is far easier to disrupt someone's journey from radicalism to terrorism than it is to convince someone to abandon terrorism—unless their movement is clearly losing.

In the following sections we will look closely at the role of Salafist ideology in creating the basis for violent jihadism. Equally we will explore how some, in what remains a mostly peaceful movement, make the shift from a fundamentalist interpretation of Islam to carrying out acts of violence and aiming to commit mass murder. For the moment, it is useful to discuss how Salafism differs as a violent terrorist movement from other historic examples.

At one level, the goals of these Salafists are apparently clear. Islam lost its way by the time of the Ummayad caliphate; this loss of the original purity saw a loss of God's divine guidance; and this in turn led to the decline of the early Islamic empires. Thus to recover the vigor of the early years, Islam must return to that original formulation of the faith. Key obstacles to this are Western (especially US) interventions in

---

78   Ferracuti and Bruno, "Psychiatric aspects of terrorism in Italy."

79   Abrahms, "What Terrorists Really Want: Terrorist Motives and Counterterrorism Strategy."

the Muslim world and the often corrupt local regimes that keep Muslims divided. Those who fail to challenge this lamentable state of affairs are, in turn, enemies. For the moment, let us set aside any question of the truth in this argument; even in its own terms it is highly contradictory. The wider Islamic world remained the intellectual center of the world for around four centuries after the Ummayad caliphate lost power. Even in its early years, it was evolving, taking one form where it was dominant (such as Arabia) and adapting in regions such as Syria or Iran, where the population was mixed and other religions were also important. In this section we have explored the issue of what Wahhabism really is and how it fits with conventional Islam, but for the moment let us note that this confusion as to what they are trying to establish has seen Salafism diverge among its adherents (we will look at the practical implications of this for the situation in Syria later in this book).

So do they really differ from their violent predecessors? Well no, not really. Some of their tactics, such as reliance on suicide bombing, are unusual, but their ideology is a typical form of the doctrines that had sustained other violent groups. They see the world as "us" and "them," "them" being a fundamental threat to establishing a world that is safe for "us." The relative few who embrace violence can use the language of an established ideology and swim in the sea provided by a large number of nonviolent fellow believers. Thus at one level, Salafist terrorism poses similar challenges to other forms and can be addressed using the same responses. Part of this response is one that fuses criminal justice with a military response—where appropriate. The other strand is to challenge the underlying belief systems.

We find that the recent research on radicalization[80] points to a myriad of causes as to how and why people do end up capable of killing

---

80   Crenshaw, M. 1981. The Causes of Terrorism. Comparative Politics, 13:4, 379-399, Cronin, A. K. 2002. Behind the Curve: Globalization and International Terrorism. International Security, 27:3, 30-58, Fearon, J. D. & Laitin, D. D. 2000. Violence and the Social Construction of Ethnic Identity. International Organization, 54:4, 845-877, Gurr, T. R. 1970. Why Men Rebel, Princeton, NJ, Princeton University Press, Tilly, C. 2003. The Politics of Collective Violence, Cambridge, Cambridge University Press, Tosini, D. 2007. Sociology of Terrorism and Counterterrorism: A Social Science Understanding of Terrorist Threat. Sociology Compass, 1:2, 664-681.

in the name of their religion, or their imagined community. Many factors do in fact need to be aligned, and no one factor is, by itself, sufficient. So ideologically mandated bigotry and hatred of the Other in the form of Salafism is not the sole sufficient cause for anyone to take up terrorism. But we will see that it nevertheless remains the case that the Salafi ideology makes the prospect of killing another human being altogether much easier for the psyche to process, in the right circumstances. The core of this ideology features a relentless drive to dehumanize the Other, the non-Salafi (or as Salafists would say, "non-Muslims"), and to impose as much an emotional distance between the *believer* and the *kuffar* as possible. In other words, it does a tremendous amount of the work required for the prospective terrorist to overcome the deeply ingrained impulse of empathy with other human beings, as well as all the pro-social conditioning they would have experienced growing up, which would otherwise overcome the intention to kill innocent strangers. And yes, while other similar ideologies or psychological pathologies can fulfill the same role, no other ideology is at this moment in time presenting such a clear and immediate threat to our societies and our understanding of civilized living.

PART FOUR
AN ISLAMIC CHALLENGE

We will return to the practical impact, and evolution, of both mainstream Salafism and Islamic terrorism in subsequent chapters. This short section looks at the response by mainstream Islamic scholars specifically in terms of condemning terrorism. As we saw earlier, ideologists for AQ and ISIS argue that terror is fully justified due to the need to protect Islam in a hostile world. A critical response by internationally renowned Islamic scholar Dr. Muhammad Tahir-ul-Qadri[1] argues not just that such acts are repellent but they cannot be justified on any reading of the Qur'an, and it is the extremists who should be seen as failing a key test of whether or not they are Muslims. In a key refutation of the arguments used by Salafists (and we will see later that this is common among those groups of individuals who radicalize themselves), only a "properly constituted state" can declare jihad—anything else is self-justified vigilantism. This argument matters profoundly, as it cuts across the common "do it yourself" simplicities that form the core of the Salafist ideology. His fatwa is especially clear on repudiating the tactic of suicide bombing.[2]

The fatwa sits in the same line of argument offered by other meetings of Islamic nations and scholars as to extent that AQ/ISIS step outside what is acceptable on the grounds of their violent methods. One of the earliest of these was the Amman Message,[3] originally delivered as a sermon and then elaborated by discussions of various Islamic scholars, which reiterated early Islamic repudiation of violent dissent and the use of violence against noncombatants. A later update was the London Declaration,[4] the result of an interfaith conference, which developed

---

1   Muhammad Tahir-ul-Qadri, "Fatwa on Terrorism and Suicide Bombings," (London: Minhaj-ul-Quran, 2010).

2   Jerome Taylor, "Sheikh issues fatwa against all terrorists," The Independent, 2010 http://www.independent.co.uk/news/uk/home-news/sheikh-issues-fatwa-against-all-terrorists-1915000.html.

3   Amman Message, "The Three Points of the Amman Message," (Amman2004).

4   The London Declaration, "The London Declaration," 2011 http://www.londondeclaration.com/.

similar themes and also stressed the similarities between the world's major religions. Both are explicit in describing any act of terrorism as un-Islamic and directly challenge the common Salafist argument of declaring this or that group of Muslims as apostates. This type of clear repudiation of violence on the grounds that its proponents can no longer claim to be Muslims has had some impact. Nine of the terrorists who killed 170 people in Mumbai in late 2008 were denied burial in any Muslim cemetery[5] on the grounds that such an act meant they were not Muslims. As he so often does, Friedman is guilty of simplifying to make the facts fit his opinions, but the basic argument is well based in Islamic jurisprudence. Those guilty of brigandage (*hirabel*) are not to be given a burial due to the terror their actions have imposed on wider society.

This short chapter explores these open repudiations of violent Islamist dogmas by the Islamic religious establishment and considers how their arguments can be used to challenge the ideology we explored in the previous chapter. However, it is worth noting that neither the Amman declaration nor Muhammad Tahir-ul-Qadri's fatwa are denunciations of Salafism as such. The Amman Message explicitly accepts the Hanbali school of jurisprudence as one of the main strands in Islamic thought, and it is this approach that Wahhabism claims sits at the heart of religious doctrines—though this is not necessarily the case. In turn Muhammad Tahir-ul-Qadri draws from openly Salafist preachers in building up the legal case for his condemnation of terrorism and especially suicide bombings.

THE AMMAN MESSAGE AND THE LONDON DECLARATION

It is useful to take these two declarations together, as they share much in common and do challenge some of the central elements of radical Salafist dogma. As we have seen, radical Salafism makes

---

5   Thomas L. Friedman, "No Way, No How, Not Here," New York Times, 2009 http://www.nytimes.com/2009/02/18/opinion/18friedman.html.

much of the view that they can determine which individuals or regimes are non-Muslim and thus can be attacked. To them, the Mardin Fatwa is important as it both justifies open revolt against any government not sufficiently Islamic and that this decision could be taken by individuals or groups outside any structured form of Islamic jurisprudence. This "do-it-yourself" approach to designating enemies has been used to justify attacks on notionally Socialist regimes (such as Nasser's Egypt), the Soviets after their invasion of Afghanistan, and, most recently, most regimes across the Middle East and any Muslims who do not share the extremist Salafist ideology. Equally once a group is designated as an enemy, to the Salafists there is then no restriction in terms of the level of violence that can be used against them.

The Amman Message directly challenges all these concepts, in particular around the definition of who is a Muslim, when can someone be declared an apostate, and who has the right to issue a fatwa.[6] The result was a clear statement that:

- Specifically recognized the validity of all eight Mathahib (legal schools) of Sunni, Shi'a, and Ibadhi Islam; of traditional Islamic theology (Ash'arism); of Islamic mysticism (Sufism), and of true Salafi thought, and came to a precise definition of who is a Muslim.

- Based upon this definition, they forbade *takfir* (declarations of apostasy) between Muslims.

- Based upon the Mathahib, they set forth the subjective and objective preconditions for the issuing of fatwas, thereby exposing ignorant and illegitimate edicts in the name of Islam.[7]

In effect, this restated the traditional view developed within the Islamic community that specifically legal debates about religion could

---

6   Amman Message, "The Three Points of the Amman Message."

7   Ibid. p. vi

only be conducted by those with suitable qualifications.[8] In particular, the Amman Message then goes on to restate the requirement that conversion to Islam should be voluntary and conducted with due respect—a far cry from the brutalities of Islamic State.

In terms of accepting approaches if a conflict does exist, the message restated the demand to protect noncombatants, and this led to the clear statement that:

> "we denounce the contemporary concept of terrorism that is associated with wrongful practices, whatever their source and form may be. Such acts are represented by aggression against human life in an oppressive form that transgresses the rulings of God, frightening those who are secure, violating peaceful civilians, finishing off the wounded, and killing prisoners; and they employ unethical means, such as destroying buildings and ransacking cities: Do not kill the soul that God has made sacrosanct, save for justice." (6:151)[9]

The London Declaration was less concerned with articulating a purely Islamic argument against extreme Salafism and was more of an interfaith declaration.[10] However, it restated a denunciation of terrorism essentially because it is usually aimed at the defenseless and noncombatants. In particular, it challenged the Salafist argument that those who live in states they decree as enemies of Islam become legitimate targets. Critically, the declaration stated, "Terrorism is never a legitimate and honorable act of war but is always a cowardly act of indiscriminate murder" and stressed the sanctity of the lives of the innocent.

Both these responses to the extremist Salafist ideology are valuable. In part the Amman Message particularly restates the importance

---

8   In this sense it is worth noting that the different legal schools acknowledged by the Amman Message all have differences on this point in particular about who can issue certain judgments. However, the key point is that each legal school does have such rules, and that fatwas and declarations that someone is apostate are not something that any individual can undertake.

9   Amman Message, "The Three Points of the Amman Message.", p.11

10   The London Declaration, "The London Declaration".

of proper jurisprudence in the development and application of Islamic law. While anybody can debate such points, the do-it-yourself approach so popular among extremists is fundamentally wrong. As we will see, this is important, as the creation of a personalized ideology built from some simplistic arguments is indeed the norm among extremists. The London Declaration reinforces the earlier message that even in a legitimate conflict there are laws and constraints and the deliberate targeting of innocent individuals is never acceptable. This direct challenge to the tactics of the extremists is the core element to Muhammad Tahir-ul-Qadri's fatwa, and we will examine how it challenges the approach so readily adopted by the extremists.

AN ISLAMIC REJECTION OF SALAFIST ARGUMENTS
THE RIGHT TO REBEL

One key aspect of the Mardin Fatwa for the Salafists is that it is the responsibility of each individual to make a judgment as to whether a given regime is in the abode of peace or of war and then act according to this distinction. There is a wider point here: defining when it is legal for a population to revolt against unjust rulers has been a point of debate from classical times up to the contemporary secular rules such as those enshrined in the UN charters. In effect, a body of argument has gradually been built up that variously sets out core rights and, to a varying extent, supports the right of citizens to resist, or rebel, if those rights are not granted.[11] Current non-Islamic law is not clear on when such a rebellion is legal (of course it is very unlikely to ever be seen as being legal by the current rulers of the affected state), but a general requirement is that it should be a revolt to acquire the rights embedded in the UN charter,[12] not in order to deny

---

11   Yulia Razmetaeva, "The Right to Resist and the Right of Rebellion," *Oxford Journal of Legal Studies* 21, no. 3 (2014).

12   Jack Donnelly, *Universal Human Rights in Theory and Practice*, 2nd ed. (New York: Cornell University, 2003).

human rights to others in that society. The UN charter thus proposes that a right to rebellion will arise if the rule of law is lacking and there is a need to protect key rights:

> "Whereas it is essential, if man is not to be compelled to have recourse, as a last resort, to rebellion against tyranny and oppression, that human rights should be protected by the rule of law."[13]

The problem, as ever, is in defining when the rule of law is sufficiently lacking so as to justify rebellion. As with our judgment about what constitutes terrorism (as opposed to resistance), there is a substantial danger that we accept revolts when we favor the goals and oppose them when we do not. It is clear that the denial of some rights does not mean there is an immediate right to rebel; instead, the legal case requires both denial of rights and lack of means of redress.[14] In turn, even in an instance of legitimate civil conflict, the body of international law about the conduct of war, treatment of civilians, and proportionality remains in force.[15] Again, to the ideologies of violent Islamism, the mere fact they have designated a state as not being part of Islam means that revolt is justified. And, as we have discussed, they then have no qualms or restraints in the actions they undertake.

This suggests that there are two strands to a response based on Islamic jurisprudence. When, if it all, is revolt justified, and if a revolt is justified, what actions are then acceptable? The following discussion of these points relies heavily on the fatwa of Dr. Muhammad Tahir-ul-Qadri.[16]

As discussed earlier, there are a number of accepted schools of jurisprudence within Islam, and each approaches this issue in a slightly

13 United Nations, "Universal Declaration of Human Rights," (New York: UN General Assembly, 1948).

14 Tony Honore, "The Right to Rebel," *Oxford Journal of Legal Studies* 8, no. 1 (1988).

15 Razmetaeva, "The Right to Resist and the Right of Rebellion."

16 Tahir-ul-Qadri, "Fatwa on Terrorism and Suicide Bombings."

different way. The Hanafi school distinguishes between those who use violence for personal gain (described as "brigands") and those who believe it is right to rebel against what they see as an illegitimate government but do so using illegal means.[17] The latter are often linked to the early ultra-sectarian Islamic sect of the Kharijites. In consequence, only those who rebel and do not use illegal methods are to be treated as "rebels"—even so, rebellion is not acceptable. If the ruler is wrong, or believed to be in error. The requirement is to give just counsel not to rebel. The Maliki school identifies rebels as those who act on their own interpretation and refuse lawful obedience. The Shafi'I school effectively denies the existence of a legitimate rebellion "even if the government is oppressive." The Hanbali school repeats the distinction between brigandage and rebellion and argues that if they use "self-styled and misleading interpretations" they should be treated as rebels. The Jafari school calls anyone a rebel "who revolts and fights against a Muslim state, and refuses to give it his rightful due." In effect, all these approaches are complex and based on readings of both past events and current motivations. However, in general Islamic law suggests that brigands should be treated more harshly than rebels—and the judgment between the two largely relies on the methods adopted.

This framework is at odds with contemporary international law in some ways, but a common theme is that rebels are those who "declare Muslims as disbelievers and justify extremism through their erroneous interpretation of the religion."[18] The classical interpretation of Islamic jurisprudence is that rebellion is illegal as it is not just a threat to wider society and the current state but "tantamount to waging war against God." Those who rebel are deemed to have ceased to be members of the wider Muslim community and, if they die, die outside the faith. This applies even if the government is "sinful and corrupt," so long as it is a Muslim government. Of course, the response of the jihadists is to use the Mardin Fatwa to redraw the boundaries of what a Muslim government is so as to escape the clear arguments of centuries of Islamic jurisprudence.

---

17   This is an important distinction, and we will return to the question of what actions are legitimate for a group of Muslims who are involved in armed conflict.

18   Tahir-ul-Qadri, "Fatwa on Terrorism and Suicide Bombings." p. 190

However, if revolt is impermissible against a Muslim government, are there any means to seek redress against a corrupt or overpowering regime? Muhammad Tahir-ul-Qadri suggests there are a number of tests. First is if the state itself explicitly rejects Islam; second, that there is "complete and absolute" consensus among jurists and scholars that the rulers have become disbelievers. Third is if the rulers stop believers from offering their prayers; the final test is if the rulers declare "lawful that which is forbidden." The second test is particularly important, as it can only be met if there is no scope for any alternative explanations.

If this leaves minimal options for an armed revolt, this is not the same as saying that a corrupt regime cannot be challenged. This leads to a form of jihad where the focus is on debate and argument and that, no matter how wrong the government is, there is no legitimacy for armed revolt against a regime as "long as they observe the prayer." This concept is repeated in various contexts: in effect, as long as a government allows Muslims to pray, then it has not lost all legitimacy and should only be opposed by peaceful means. This basic argument is endorsed by the official Saudi Salafist establishment, who frequently link the modern-day jihadists to the Kharijites of early Islamic history. In particular, if an individual (or state) indulges in sin, they are not a disbeliever (i.e., an apostate in the jihadist lexicon) unless they then also declare that such acts are lawful. So drinking alcohol may be subject to penalties, but someone remains a Muslim unless they declare that drinking alcohol is in fact legal under Islamic law (in other words declare that something is lawful when it is banned). From this, the ISIS/AQ acceptance of killing Muslims simply because they do not conform to this or that specific article of faith is a serious error against Islamic law.

It is worth noting that much of this argument about the illegality of open rebellion except in very specific circumstances was common in both pre-Christian pagan literature and the Christian writings on Just War.[19] Rebellion was almost always condemned, in part as a ruler was ordained by a higher power and in part as the damage caused by

---

19   David A. Ahrens, *Christianity's Contribution to Just War Tradition* (Carlisle: Strategic Studies Institute, Army War College, 1999).

civil conflict was deemed too dangerous. It may sound strange to our modern ears, not least given that many of us live in states that were formed by armed revolt against another state, usually with a period of civil war while such a conflict was waged. The reason for this change was the emergence of a new strand of political theory about human rights, and our entitlement to acquire and protect those rights, in the late 18th century. In different ways, this reformulation has influenced modern liberalism, socialism, and, as noted earlier, the UN's Universal Declaration of Human Rights.

This is not the place to debate which tradition on revolt is correct or to reflect that despite Islamic, Christian, and pagan strictures against rebellion, it is something that has happened across human history. What matters in this stage is that even given their over-interpretation of the Mardin Fatwa, modern-day Islamists stand outside the mainstream of Islamic jurisprudence in their focus on armed rebellion as the means to settle differences of opinion within the wider Muslim polity.

But even to gain the title of "rebels" carries implications. The Hanafi school of jurisprudence is clearest on this matter. Those who adopt the tactics of the early Kharijites—indiscriminate murder of their enemies, both Muslim and non-Muslim—are not even rebels; they are simply brigands and criminals. Thus to be seen to be a rebel (and in itself to exclude oneself at least temporarily from the wider community) means one still has to act in a particular way and observe certain rules. In effect, Islam not only offers its own Just War tradition, it has much to say about how war and conflict should be handled.

THE LAWS OF WAR

Cicero, famously and rather legalistically, claimed that "in war, laws fall silent." This was done in a trial where he was defending one of the many generals who rebelled against the Roman Senate in the last years of the Roman Republic. In effect, his argument has often been treated as suggesting that once a war commences, there is (or can be) no legal constraint on what happens subsequently. Historically, we have a depressingly long record of wars fought without mercy or restraint, including the Thirty Years' War, which devastated central Europe in the 17th century, and, far worse, the wars that blighted the 20th century. However, after the horrors of the Second World War, there was a conscious attempt to reintroduce laws to constrain actions in war drawing from both religious and secular traditions. The result now is the concept of war crimes; the International Criminal Court[20] was established to try those who step beyond the boundaries of what is acceptable, even in times of war. A case can be made that this has only been partially successful, but the intent is sincere and has been applied to crimes committed in various recent civil wars such as those in the Balkans and Africa.

In turn, Islam has a long tradition of law that sets out which acts are acceptable even in a war. We discussed some of this in the earlier sections when reviewing the first stages of Islamic history, but it has a particular relevance when applied to the tactics adopted by the violent jihadists, especially since 2001. There is a substantial body of Islamic legal opinion that insists that noncombatants, whether or not they themselves are Muslims, cannot be killed during a military struggle. A *hadith* is clear when it states, "Any Muslim who unjustly kills a non-Muslim with whom there is a peace treaty, God will make Paradise forbidden for him."[21] Other strictures include theft from non-Muslims, denial of their religious choices, and insulting them. Even if the precise boundaries of what is acceptable are unclear, from the start Islam has been clear that there are constraints, for example in this message from the Prophet to his military commanders:

Advance in the name of Allah, with Allah, on the pattern of the Messenger of Allah. That means do not to kill the elderly,

---

20 United Nations, "Rome Statute of the International Criminal Court," UN, 2002 http://legal.un.org/icc/statute/romefra.htm.

21 Tahir-ul-Qadri, "Fatwa on Terrorism and Suicide Bombings." p.98

infants or children and women. Do not exceed the proper bounds. Gather your spoils and make peace.[22]

The contrast to ISIS's actions in Iraq and Syria is stark.

One common argument among the jihadists is that random attacks in the West are justified, as these states are democracies so all citizens are responsible for the acts of their governments. Again this is a deliberate misreading of Islamic law, wherein waging war against those who are neutral (even if we disagree with them) is forbidden. As with the restraint on rebellion, the Islamic tradition is fully aware of how destructive war can be and, as such, seeks to minimize both its occurrence and its scope.

As we have seen in the last chapter, suicide bombing has become a tactic of choice for many groups affiliated with AQ or ISIS. However, we can be perfectly clear: Islam forbids suicide. The key argument is that human life is a gift from God, and this prevents the deliberate taking of one's own life—even in war. Running through Islamic jurisprudence is the argument that actions should be ascribed to those who perform them. This makes suicide in the form of carrying out a suicide bombing attack unacceptable, as the suicide bomber is using their own body as a weapon—thus it is not an act of courage that may cost their life but an act that must end (if successful) in taking their own life. Other interpretations suggest that those who order suicide attacks are equally guilty and that obedience of a Muslim can only be given to "that which is right."[23] Equally contrary to jihadists' claims of heavenly pleasures for those who carry out suicide bombings, Islamic scholarship is consistent in suggesting that the eternal penalty for suicide is hell.

This interpretation is endorsed by the Saudi Salafist establishment, which has argued, "To my knowledge so-called 'suicide missions' do not have any legal basis in Islam and do not constitute a form of Jihād.

---

22   Cited by: Shaykh Hisham Kabbani, "Jihad, Terrorism and Suicide Bombing: The Classical Islamic Perspective," The Islamic Supreme Council of America, 2017 http://www.islamicsupremecouncil.org/understanding-islam/legal-rulings/21-jihad-classical-islamic-perspective.html?start=15.

23   Tahir-ul-Qadri, "Fatwa on Terrorism and Suicide Bombings.", p.82

I fear that they are nothing but a form of suicide, and suicide is also prohibited in Islam."[24] As ever, context is important. Most military traditions acknowledge self-sacrifice on the battlefield and indeed often award their highest military honors for such acts. But the context is of bravery in the face of an armed enemy, not of deliberately killing oneself as a weapon designed to kill innocent civilians.

Again, there is a clear message underlying the consistent interpretation of Islam. Human life matters, and it should be preserved at almost any cost. Thus civil strife is almost impossible to justify by Islamic jurisprudence, and the clear intent is that dissent be handled by peaceful methods.[25] If war is justified, there are constraints, and one that is constantly repeated is the constraint against the killing of innocents. Equally, given the importance of preserving life, Islam is very clear in its condemnation of terrorism.

Of course, in practice, Islam, like any other tradition, has often failed to live up to these demands. Muslims have waged wars that are hard to justify, and civil strife has been a regular feature of Islamic history. Acknowledging this, placing such events into context, is as important as being clear that they represent failings to live according to the demands of the faith. If military conflict is to be justified, it must be acknowledged that "whether one likes it or not, the decision and discretion and right to declare war or jihad for Muslims lie solely with the various authorities as represented today by the respective Muslim states—and not with any individual, even if he is a scholar or a soldier."[26] Equally, as above, suicide is wrong.

Thus, the do-it-yourself ideology constructed by the extremists is at variance with both the consensus within Islam and the method by which Islamic law has been constructed and adapted. If you make arguments that declare this or that state as hostile to Islam, this or that group as apostates, and make use of any tactic that suits you, then you are deliberately ignoring the central tenets of the Muslim

---

24 Quoted in: Kabbani, "Jihad, Terrorism and Suicide Bombing: The Classical Islamic Perspective".

25 Tahir-ul-Qadri, "Fatwa on Terrorism and Suicide Bombings."

26 Mehdi Hasan, "Suicide attacks are un-Islamic," in *New Statesman* (2009).

community. Returning to very early Islamic history, it was this that led to the rejection of the Kharijites. Despite their ostentatious displays of piety, they were in fact rejecting the entire structure of the religion of which they claimed to be the purest adherents.[27]

CONCLUSIONS

This section has concentrated on what conventional Islamic jurisprudence has to say about when it is legitimate to revolt against a state and what actions are acceptable in case of armed conflict. As is clear, Islamic law is relatively straightforward on the subject of rebellion. This can only be sanctioned under very specific situations and where the great bulk of scholars, lawyers, and imams indicate their agreement that a given state has lost legitimacy. This test is stringent and heavily biased against there being any legitimacy to revolt. Readers who frame this question from the perspective of secular arguments that have been constructed since the late 18th century may find this restrictive and surprising. As such, this book does not argue that the interpretation in Islamic jurisprudence is more or less valid than contemporary secular arguments (as reflected in the UN charter on human rights) but, by definition, they are the rules that apply to Muslims.

This leads to a significant rejection of the do-it-yourself model of declaring states and individuals as un-Islamic, which is such a feature of the jihadist ideology. In the last section we explored the legal arguments they use, and we will see the practical implications of their approach in the rest of this book. However, here we can state, quite without any equivocation, they are wrong in terms of the religion and the legal tradition they claim to be the purest representatives of.

The second part of this section looked at what Islamic law has to say about the conduct of a war—or a revolt. As we saw, the Hanafi school

---

27   Tahir-ul-Qadri, "Fatwa on Terrorism and Suicide Bombings."

makes a distinction between brigands and rebels. Both are seen to be wrong, but there are levels of error involved. Brigands are those who use violence purely for personal gain (criminals in modern terms) or who rebel and use inappropriate tactics. It is only those who rebel and still accept the constraints of Islamic law concerning warfare who can be seen to be rebels rather than brigands. This matters, as by their tactics the modern-day jihadists are not even to be treated as rebels. They are, for all intents and purposes, brigands who are now outside the Islamic community. And that brings us back to the beginning of this chapter. The Muslim community in India refused to bury the Mumbai attackers in an Islamic cemetery precisely because, by their horrific actions, they were no longer part of the Islamic community.[28]

This equally returns us to an argument that runs across this book. Most Salafists are nonviolent and use that model of Islam to inform their own lives. As we have seen in this and earlier chapters, their interpretation is wrong, but that does not remove them from the community on the grounds of beliefs alone. Thus to most Sunni scholars, the sectarian Kharijites were still Muslims even if they held to an extreme deviation from the religion of the Prophet and were the most dangerous sectarian manifestation of the early Islamic faith, thereby deserving to be fought with impunity. It was not their beliefs that put them outside the Muslim community; it was their actions.

This is seen clearly in the numerous rigorously authenticated *hadiths* on the topic. However, there are a number of notable scholars, such as the Maliki polymath Qadi Abu Bakr, who argued that they were outside the fold of Islam, based on strong evidentiary proofs. One *hadith* describes them with the wording "they will pass through Islam," indicating their inconvertible exit from the Islamic faith. The Prophet also stated with regards to the Khawarij, ". . . and if I was to reach them, I would fight them even as (the tribe of) Aad were fought. . . ." Added to this are numerous descriptions of them in *hadiths*, such as "they are the worst of creation" and "the most hated of creation to God"—all of which, when taken together, indicate that they cannot be within the fold of Islam.

---

28   Friedman, "No Way, No How, Not Here".

RADICAL ORIGINS

In effect, there are limits to what can still be seen as part of Islam. The chief mufti of Saudi Arabi, the late Bin Baz, also ruled the Khawarij as being outside the fold of Islam.[29] Again, we are dealing with matters of degree. Quietest Salafists are wrong on many key issues but remain Muslims. But those that move even further from the central tenets of the faith—through their actions—may, like the early Khawarijites, cease to be Muslims.

I will return to these arguments later in this book. At the moment, such material is being taught and used, in particular in the context of Muslim-led responses to extreme Salafism. However, as with the lack of knowledge of our own history, the extremists are able to take advantage of a lack of understanding of Islamic jurisprudence. There is a need to move these counterarguments from the realm of scholarly debate and well-constructed specific programs. Such teaching, both of history and law, needs to be part of the routine of every mosque and every imam. Equally, we need to understand why those who find extreme Salafism so attractive are so often already outside the ambit of the local mosque. Finding the means to make the intellectual argument against jihadism commonplace is probably *the* main challenge now facing the wider Muslim community.

---

29   Mohammed, *Caliphate Reloaded: Past, present and future Muslim discourse on Power.*

PART FIVE
EXPORTING HATE

arlier, we saw how the alliance between the Royal House of Saud and the Wahhabi religious establishment gave birth to the ideologies and the political dynamics that would eventually give rise to Al-Qaeda. But the arrival on the scene of ISIS, and the way in which terror groups from Nigeria, Libya, Egypt, Pakistan, and even, recently, Russia all seem keen to join up under the banner of ISIS is rooted in far more than the internal politics of the Saudi kingdom.

The jihadist ideology is not global only in its outlook; it is global in its constituents. On all continents, in most, if not all, countries with significant Muslim populations, there will be Muslims who have already been seduced by this ideology of hate.[1] This cancer has reached stage 4: it has spread all over the world. And as the military (and ideological) successes of ISIS briefly grew in the deserts of the Levant, the cancer became increasingly active and malignant in other parts of the world as well. Even if ISIS's power in its original hub now seems to be waning, like Al-Qaeda before it, the fear is it will now go viral and spawn new offshoots. It has supporters and networks, it has drawn in militants from virtually every country, and it has already demonstrated its enthusiasm to wreak mayhem in Europe and America.

But the radicalization we are witnessing today is only the lifting of the veil. It is merely how we are finally becoming painfully aware that the cancer exists. This cancer, however, has been in our midst for decades—exported with great diligence and at great expense by both the state and the many religious charitable organizations of Saudi Arabia set up to promote its "Salafi" ideology globally. Saudi Arabia has invested upwards of $100 billion in just the last thirty years or so in this mission. This money has gone to building madrassas, reeducating preachers and imams to the more radical creed, educating foreign students in Saudi Arabia on scholarships, and printing and donating millions of copies of the Qur'an accompanied by textbooks

---

1   Kristof, "The Terrorists the Saudis Cultivate in Peaceful Countries".

that emphasize the Us vs. Them vision of the world and encourage intolerance towards all non-Salafis, Muslims or otherwise.

What we are seeing now is the coming home to roost of decades of investment in bigotry by the Saudi and Wahhabi establishment. The upper echelons of the Saudi state, the House of Saud itself, and the Ulema (the senior mainstream Salafi clerics) may not have anticipated that they would themselves become targets of the ideology they were promoting, but in the four decades since the jihadist attacks on Riyadh in the late 1970s, the money has not stopped flowing out of Saudi Arabia and into the hands of hate preachers across the world and jihadis in many regions of the world where we now have failed states and jihadist insurgencies.

But those were not the only jihadis who were receiving Saudi support. Though it is both impossible to prove and also quite unlikely that the House of Saud was directly involved, Senator Bob Graham, lead author of the Joint Inquiry into Intelligence Community Activities Before and After the Terrorist Attacks of September 11, 2001, has already indicated that Saudi Arabia has been found to be the principal financier of the hijackers—potentially even by individuals and institutions quite close to the Saudi government. Yet even now, the Saudis are either unwilling, or think themselves unable, to take on the ideology and the religious establishment, which has consolidated their hold on power, even when the Saudis remain one of the principle targets of that ideology.[2]

And equally, the United States, Britain, and the West are refusing to tackle this, the most fundamental cause of the global rise of Islamist terror, even as they face more and more acts of terrorism against their citizens. Instead, we keep happily buying the oil that eventually funds this ideology and its followers, and also happily selling tens of billions of dollars' worth of weapons and other military equipment to the Saudis: Saudi Arabia has military expenditure levels on par with Russia, France, and the UK, behind only the United States and China. Needless to say, some of these weapons do end up in the hands of jihadis. When the civil war in Syria broke out, the Saudis trained and armed

---

2   Ruthven, *A Fury for God: The Islamist Attack on America.*

anti-Assad groups to the tune of millions of dollars. Even though the initial Saudi efforts focused on groups not affiliated with Al-Qaeda and the Al-Nusra Front, it was inevitable that many of those fighters and their arms would eventually become ISIS assets. Not least in any civil war, weapons become a currency to be bartered, exchanged, or stolen in pursuit of other goals.

This link between billions of dollars, mostly *our* billions of dollars, and the ideology that is ripping apart the Middle East and killing our citizens on our streets here in the West must be broken. It can be broken either by forcing the House of Saud to change its approach to funding the propagation of Wahhabism internationally, or by removing the Saud-Wahhabi petrodollar-ideological complex from power. The latter prospect is not at all appealing. We have no idea of what might replace the Saudi government in the peninsula, and we may find that whoever emerges out of such a conflict may well be even worse than the current regime. This means we need to tackle the issue of Saudi sponsorship of Wahhabism. This will not be easy—but it must be done.

If our governments are reluctant to act on this, it is up to us, as citizens of democratic states to impose on them the need and the urgency for them to do so. Because until we do, until we tackle and suffocate the ideological underpinning of the wave of terror that is washing over the world, no amount of bombing or even troops on the ground in Iraq, Libya, or Syria will help. Until we tackle the ideology and its power base at source, we will be fighting a hydra. If we do defeat ISIS in the Levant, a replacement will rise in Nigeria. Or in Pakistan. Or again in Afghanistan. Or in any one of many other places where failed and failing states are struggling to come to grips with Islamist insurgencies or where a local Muslim population faces real repression and their cause can be easily exploited by ISIS.

The next three sections in this book explore these dynamics in detail and in particular the problems that occur once Saudi-sponsored Salafism starts to gain ground in any country. This chapter looks at the problems in Western Europe (and to some extent concentrates on the UK). This is of relevance to a US audience, as English has become the main language by which groups like ISIS seek to reach out to potential supporters. We will then turn to look at the early emergence of Salafism in Europe in the context of the various Balkan wars in the 1990s. The key lesson here is that Kosovo, postwar, accepted substantial Saudi and Gulf money to rebuild, and this has led to the emergence of a radical Islamist movement in that country. This discussion leads into developments in Iraq and Syria and the ways in which the Salafist movement is changing, and how Saudi sponsorship of its preferred form of Salafism is leading to its facing a growing threat from groups such as ISIS.

SPREADING PROPAGANDA

Let us first understand this one fact about the ISIS terror: we are currently losing the propaganda war. And one observation alone can bring home just how badly we are losing the propaganda war. ISIS releases propaganda videos on social media with some regularity. These videos depict some of the most barbaric, inhumane, and sadistic behavior towards humans that we have ever seen. They are, for lack of a better word, snuff movies. We allow these videos to be widely broadcast through social and traditional media and many of us watch them. In doing so, most of us react with revulsion. We despair at the depths of depravity to which human beings can sink. Not surprisingly the usual response is disgust and moral anger as people reject barbarism in favor of human decency. Most of us. But not all.

And those of us who are utterly scandalized by what we see perhaps then struggle to understand how another human could watch the very same videos and not be similarly moved to revulsion. When we watch these videos we cannot shake the feeling that we must somehow be a completely different species than the perpetrators of these abhorrent crimes. Which is why we often assume that they must be psychopaths or otherwise morally and emotionally lacking. And let no one doubt many of them are. But our lack of imagination here, our inability to understand how anyone could watch those videos and be moved by them to want to join ISIS, to want to move to Syria, is exactly the reason why we are losing the propaganda war.

The reason why well-educated young men and women, why mothers with their children, why whole families of three generations can look at these very same videos and react so differently is that what they see depicted in these videos is very different from what we see depicted. They do not see senseless, sadistic murder. They see righteous, ritualistic retribution. They see just retaliation against "oppressors," and *infidels*, lesser humans in the eyes of God. They see the unapologetic affirmation of an identity—that of a "Muslim"—which perhaps they hold strongly and which perhaps they have felt victimized for having. Regardless of the fact that if they were at all victimized, chances are it had very little to do with their faith, at least in the West. And regardless of the fact that the behavior of ISIS is completely at odds with the Qur'an and all the precedents established by the Prophet, as I have argued before. To them, these discussions are academic. As far as they can see it, ISIS affirms something that they themselves may have felt unable to affirm, and they see what ISIS is doing as liberating.

So how warped do your understanding of the world and your feelings and relations towards other human beings need to be to find the senseless slaughter of innocent civilians liberating and empowering for your own sense of identity? The answer, which we can draw from the previous chapters, is that such a warped perspective comes directly from the basic fundamental teachings of Salafism: the Us vs. Them, binary friend and foe, perpetual war view of the world, the siege mentality it entails, and the victim complex that often comes with it. In a very real sense, Salafis inhabit a very different planet from mainstream Muslims, and from everyone else who is sane, emotionally competent, and not beholden to an ideology of death. As it turns out, not much more than that is needed for an ideology to be able to trump the otherwise really very powerful influence of human empathy. Again, it is worth stressing that Salafism effectively shares characteristics of other totalitarian belief systems that were able to mobilize their followers to commit crimes against humanity just like the ones portrayed in these social media videos. Stalin's gulags and murderous secret police were run by people who believed that the "enemies of the people" deserved to die with no sympathy. The Nazi ideology required its believers to cease to see "others" as having any human status and thus be deserving of being murdered en masse.

And, in its Salafist form, all these things are being taught in Saudi-built mosques from Pakistan to Britain to the United States. Worldwide, an estimated fifty million people describe themselves as Salafis, with significant numbers in India, Bangladesh, Egypt, and the Sudan, and smaller communities all over the world. Not all of these are violent terrorists. We have already seen how diverse, complex, and idiosyncratic Salafi ideology can be. The large majority of followers will be peaceful, if somewhat xenophobic, living in introverted communities not too dissimilar to the ultraconservative Hasidic Jewish communities of north London, for example. But what does unite them is this way of looking at the world that is different from the way we would see the world. And in the context of that world, the propaganda videos of ISIS have a profoundly different significance than they do for us.

What is more worrying, however, is that Salafism is not just the best-funded strand of Islam, it is also the fastest growing, not least among young people—including on university campuses. And with an estimated $2 to $3 billion dollars spent by Saudi Arabia each year on the effort to globalize Salafism, it is not difficult to see why.[3] They are prepared to fund a mosque, train the preachers, provide funds for social relief. The end result, as is now clear in areas of Belgium, is that Salafism starts to permeate an entire community.[4] As far back as 2002 the Saudis were spending billions per annum and at that stage were supporting over fifteen hundred mosques, two hundred colleges, and two thousand schools. Chillingly in view of what has happened recently, a 2002 report notes: "In Europe, the Kingdom of Saudi Arabia has supported and contributed in the establishment of many mosques and Islamic centers among which the Cultural Center in Brussels,

3   Memri, "Saudi Government Paper: 'Billions Spent by Saudi Royal Family to Spread Islam to Every Corner of the Earth'," The Middle East Media Research Institute, 2002 http://www.memri.org/report/en/0/0/0/0/0/0/638.htm.

4   Clapper, "The Saudi Connection in the Belgium Attacks".

Belgium which has received total support of SR 19 million."[5] The result of this funding has been to lead young Muslims in Belgium away from the more relaxed traditions of their parents (many of whom came from Morocco or Tunisia) and to embrace Salafism.

At times the Belgian authorities asked the Saudis to remove particular preachers and imams, but overall Saudi funding has meant that religious education for Muslims in Belgium has long been provided by well-trained Salafists sent to Saudi-funded mosques by the Saudi state. The result is that young Muslims have become alienated from the Islam of their parents as well as from the traditions of the state they live in. As we will see in the next section, this dynamic of Saudi-funded mosques breeding a form of Islamic interpretation even the Saudis oppose has been repeated in Kosovo. However, this chapter concentrates on how their ideology is being reinterpreted by Western-based preachers and how these individuals have been able to disseminate their arguments to a wide audience.

HATE PREACHING IN BRITAIN

I f we are to deal with the Salafist challenge, it is essential to understand the complex links between authorized (i.e., Saudi-funded) and unauthorized Salafist teachers and their impact in spreading the belief in violent jihad. So far there have been relatively few home-grown Salafist hate preachers in the United States, but this has become a major issue in Britain. The discussion that follows concentrates on the UK, but the implications are global. Any person with an Internet connection can access their sermons and come to accept their arguments and worldview.

What is particularly regrettable is how long it took us to understand that indoctrinating generations of young people into bigotry

---

5   Memri, "Saudi Government Paper: 'Billions Spent by Saudi Royal Family to Spread Islam to Every Corner of the Earth'".

and hatred of humanity would pose a threat to our societies. In this sense Britain forms an interesting test case. It has more of a problem with self-radicalization than the United States, and so far there is only limited evidence that the various Islamist attacks within the country since 2005 have been directly organized and controlled externally by either Al-Qaeda or ISIS. Historically there has been a degree of tolerance of foreign radicals—as long as the individual is not actively and directly posing a threat to the British state, British citizens, and some key British interests, individuals used to be largely free to do or say as they pleased. And in keeping with this liberal attitude, Britain has over the decades provided a safe haven to a very diverse and eclectic mixture of political refugees from other countries: from Karl Marx[6] to Augusto Pinochet, to the Muslim Brotherhood[7] and many radical Islamist preachers.

One critical question is whether this history of relative tolerance can be sustained, given the new threat posed. After all, in the 19th century London provided refuge to a range of radicals, from those who tried to assassinate Louis Napoleon to Karl Marx (who was described as no threat to the British state when Prussia tried to have him deported).[8] The only real rule was that exiles should not engage in active politics that affected the United Kingdom. Underlying this was an assumption that their beliefs could not gain wider support among the population.

This underlying assumption may well have influenced British policy in the 1980s and the 1990s. It was not as if Britain was not aware of radical Islam. Throughout the '90s, radical Islamist "hate preachers," as they were called, made tabloid headlines with what were considered strident and deliberately eccentric claims. But while in the '90s many of their pronouncements were happily dismissed as the ravings

---

6   Eric Hobsbawm, "Dr Marx and the Victorian Critics," in *How to Change the World: Tales of Marx and Marxism*, ed. Eric Hobsbawm (London: Little Brown, 2011).

7   David Cameron, "Muslim Brotherhood review: statement by the Prime Minister," UK Government, Cabinet Office, 2015 https://www.gov.uk/government/speeches/muslim-brotherhood-review-statement-by-the-prime-minister.

8   Robert Justin Goldstein, *Political Repression in 19th Century Europe* (London: Routledge, 1983).

of lunatics, what was happening ran far deeper than just deliberately ostentatious media performances.[9]

As in many countries around the world, some British Muslim institutions had been readily accepting Saudi funding for decades, and subsequently facilitating the propagation of Salafi doctrines within the local Muslim populations. As this process developed, we have even witnessed a number of established Western academic publishing houses publishing historical accounts of Wahhabism that present it as a tolerant tradition. These effectively whitewash the dubious history that we have presented thus far, and facilitate Saudi Wahhabi efforts to convert Muslims who would never otherwise choose to associate themselves with violent, perverted readings of Islam from their own mainstream traditions.

As hinted above, these efforts were greatly enhanced by the crucial marketing coup of Salafism, which, unlike classical Wahhabism, can be peaceful. This pronouncement alone allowed the Saudis to happily go about promoting—in quite an explicit manner—intolerance, isolationism, and antisocial attitudes in general, as well as, what some critics specifically argue, hate for any "Other," with only a minimal amount of concern raised by the British state, and barely noticed by British public opinion. We never concerned ourselves very much with the impact that any of this might have on the minds of young people who grew up hearing about or reading all this stuff. We thought that any child or young person raised in Britain would instinctively see the value of inclusive, liberal multiculturalism as a matter of course. They might choose to personally live according to a more austere code derived from their religious beliefs, but this was seen as an essentially personal choice. This attitude sits well with a traditional laissez-faire approach to such matters, but the key issue is whether this can be sustained given the nature of the problem posed by Salafism.

And to be clear, the charge is not that the Saudi government has pursued a program to promote and coordinate terrorism in Britain, or elsewhere (at least as far as we are aware[10]). Indeed, at the surface

---

9   Pantucci, *"We Love Death As You Love Life": Britain's Suburban Terrorists.*

10   Kristof, "The Terrorists the Saudis Cultivate in Peaceful Countries".

level it has made a determined and sustained effort in combating it, especially since it itself is a frequent victim of the very same terrorism. Rather, in Britain, the global jihadist theology emerged from a renegade group of Salafi preachers who often entered into public polemics against the Saudi state and its policies, in much the same way that bin Laden did in the '90s. These preachers adhered to the jihadist strand of Salafism, and branched out of the Salafi mainstream in much the same way as we have seen in previous chapters. Their position had long been rebuked in the Arab world by mainstream Salafism and, at least since 1995, in Britain. However, one problem is that many of the leaders of these groups are from outside the UK (Omar Bakri, for example, is Lebanese), and their radicalized followers are rarely connected to the structures of traditional Islam such as the local mosques.

The development of Salafi Islam in Britain during the 1990s was quite complex. There was a contest for the hearts and minds of Muslims between the mainstream Salafism led by the Saudi clerics; Islamism spearheaded by essentially British-born groups such as Hizb ut-Tahrir (HT); and the more radical Islamism developed by people such as Abu Qatada, Abu Hamza, Abdullah al-Faisal, and then, later, by Omar Bakri Muhammad. This created a situation in which the dangerous Salafi dogmas were becoming more widely disseminated and were becoming, to some extent, normalized with no small amount of help from Saudi Arabia, by funding preachers and mosques. To a large extent the intense, energetic debate was between these radical elements, and this allowed them to marginalize the voices of mainstream Islam overall. As noted at the end of the previous section, the mainstream of Islamic teaching was either silent or unable to effectively intervene in this discussion.

And between them, and throughout the decade, these very visible hate preachers were able to lay the foundations for a "grievance theology" that infected the minds of many young Muslims, who would go on to carry out or plan terrorist attacks—and indeed of those who are now travelling to Syria to join ISIS. So even as we were keen to dismiss these hate preachers, while we perhaps ghoulishly enjoyed the tabloid spectacle they were offering, they arguably were the primary catalyst for the radicalization of many British Muslims.

How did these individuals contribute so much to the current landscape? A quick survey of their activities may yield lessons both on the process of radicalization and how to fight it, in Britain and abroad. Jihadists in Britain preached their theology of hate for up to two decades, unimpeded by the state. They specifically targeted young, disenfranchised Muslims, who were conscious of a number of conflicts involving Muslims overseas and who saw themselves as victims of an unjust political system. Whereas al-Faisal and Abu Qatada encouraged and incited young Muslims to commit terrorism and criminal offenses, Abu Hamza al-Masri and Omar Bakri Muhammad, in addition to this, used their organizations to assist them in carrying out acts of terrorism.

ABU QATADA

In 1993, a Jordanian national who had fought alongside the mujahedeen in Afghanistan arrived in Britain seeking asylum. Despite being convicted on terrorist charges in Jordan in 1998, Abu Qatada was allowed to remain in the United Kingdom. Highly regarded within radical Islamist circles for his knowledge of jihad, it is reported that he had met bin Laden in Pakistan in 1989. He attracted a host of radical Islamists from overseas, many who were later charged with and convicted of terror-related offenses. One of these, Richard Reid, who was later convicted of trying to blow up an airline, was said to have sought Abu Qatada for "religious advice."

An exponent of *takfir*, Abu Qatada was accused of turning "the whole of Europe into a recruiting ground for terror." A particular theme in his sermons was that it was legitimate to target both Muslims and non-Muslims. Videos of Abu Qatada's speeches were found in the flat of Muhammad Atta, the ringleader of the 9/11 attacks.

Abu Qatada was detained in 2002 in the UK under antiterrorism laws, and, after long and protracted battles over his status between various British and European courts, was finally extradited to Jordan in 2013, after Jordan met the requirements of the British and European courts over the concerns they had for the protection of his human rights in the expected trial. The Jordanian courts have since found him not guilty of plotting the terror attacks he was suspected of, but his contribution to feeding the ideology of hate in the Middle East and in Europe is beyond doubt.

ABDULLAH AL-FAISAL

A bdullah al-Faisal is a Jamaican convert to Islam who taught for two years at Brixton Mosque in south London from 1991 to 1993. He had studied in Saudi Arabia and subsequently toured Britain for a decade, giving lectures in which he openly "urged his audiences to kill Jews, Hindus, and Westerners by any means available," and even promoted the use of chemical weapons to "exterminate the unbelievers." He did have limits though—cautioning that a nuclear bomb could only be used on countries who had a population entirely made up of "unbelievers."

Al-Faisal said that jihad simply meant "to kill the *kaffirs*." He was known to have preached in Beeston, Leeds, where three of the four 7/7 bombers resided. Germaine Lindsay was said to have been "strongly influenced" by al-Faisal, and it was known that Mohammad Sidique Khan possessed a number of his recorded lectures. The British government accused him of preaching "his message of hate to [. . .] Richard Reid and [. . .] Zacarias Moussaoui," although al-Faisal denied this. He was jailed for seven years in 2003 for soliciting murder and then was deported to Jamaica in 2007. Subsequent attempts to spread his message to Africa saw him deported from Botswana in 2009 and Kenya in 2010. Whether simply deporting such individuals is a sensible approach for the British state is a different question. These people are not going to stop their preaching and may reach new audiences. In many ways this exemplifies the tensions between the rule of law, liberal traditions, and the threat from the violent Salafists. Like the pro-Soviet Communists before them, they are adept at using the freedoms they deride in order to function within Western society.[11]

ABU HAMZA AL-MASRI

A bu Hamza, an Egyptian national, arrived in Britain in 1979 to study engineering. Initially he worked as a nightclub bouncer; he found religion after he was said to have met 'Abdallah 'Azzam in 1987. After fighting in Afghanistan with the mujahedeen, he returned in the early 1990s with *takfiri*-jihadi hate-filled messages, urging Muslims to "hate even the shadow of [the unbeliever]." In a number of his lectures he urged Muslims to kill non-Muslims. He even stated that it was perfectly halal (lawful) to kill them, even if there was no reason to do so.

As the imam of the Finsbury Park Mosque (1997–2003), Abu Hamza quickly added to its existing reputation as a "hothouse for Islamic radicals," attracting both Richard Reid and Zacharias Moussaoui. The mosque itself acted as a central hub for recruiting young Muslims to his *takfiri* thought, raising funds for the mujahedeen in the Muslim world, and training young Muslims for jihad overseas. All four men convicted over the failed 21/7 attack in London had attended the mosque, and boasted to others about being bodyguards to Abu Hamza. He was arrested on May 27, 2004 and convicted in 2006 for soliciting murder, inciting racial hatred, and possessing a "terrorist encyclopaedia."

In October 2012 he was deported to the United States to face terrorism charges. In January 2015 he was found guilty of eleven charges (the charges also included those related to wider criminal activities), and was sentenced to life in prison without the possibility of parole.

---

11   Peter Hennessy, *The Secret State: Whitehall and the Cold War* (London: Penguin, 2002).

OMAR BAKRI MOHAMMED

Holding both Syrian and Lebanese nationalities, Bakri sought asylum in Britain in 1986 after he was expelled from Saudi Arabia. As head of Hizb ut-Tahrir (HT) in England in 1986, his mission was to persuade Muslims of the need to restore the caliphate in the Muslim world. He preached that participation in the democratic process was *haram*, as the concept was deemed *kufr*. Earlier on in his preaching, he argued that while voting could make you into a non-Muslim, since most people did so out of confusion or lack of knowledge, voting was an error. Once he formed the Islamic group Al-Muhajiroun, he shifted to arguing that voting was tantamount to apostasy and that those who did so had ceased to be proper Muslims.

During Gulf War II,[12] Bakri said that Prime Minister John Major was a legitimate target for assassination if he ever visited a Muslim country, something he was to repeat with regard to Tony Blair in 2001. Following 9/11, Bakri not only glorified "martyrdom operations" but also encouraged young Muslims to undertake them and travel to Afghanistan to fight against Western forces. He also warned that Muslims who condemned 9/11 and supported the coalition forces would be fought and even killed by "true Muslims."

In 2004, Bakri allegedly told Muslims as young as ten years old to "kill and be killed" by flying "planes into 10 Downing Street or into the White House." His organization, Al-Muhajiroun, insisted that "terrorism is obligatory in Islam." In 2005, Bakri had declared that Britain had become an abode of war, in which the "*kuffar*" had no protection from being attacked, and emphasized that "all non-believers were legitimate targets of jihad," wherever they may be, because of their governments' involvement in pursuing the war on terror. In addition, spokesmen for Al-Muhajiroun encouraged Muslims from *overseas* to attack Britain for its complicity in the invasion of Iraq.

Bakri had closed down Al-Muhajiroun in 2004, possibly sensing it would soon be proscribed by the government, which did ban it and

---

12   The conflict that followed Saddam Hussein's invasion of Kuwait, the First Gulf War being the long and bloody struggle between Iraq and Iran in the 1980s.

its successor groups, al-Ghurabaa and the Saved Sect, in 2006. Bakri himself left the United Kingdom for Lebanon in August 2005; he was banned from returning. In November 2010, he was sentenced by a military court in Lebanon to life in prison with hard labor for acts of terrorism.

Despite the closure of his organizations, Bakri sought to expand his propaganda influence and preached his message for more than twenty years as he toured cities, university campuses, and mosques until he was banned. Overall this had little impact, but along with his organization, Al-Muhajiroun (and its subsequent offshoots), Bakri was responsible for recruiting the largest number of radical Islamists, and even publicly acknowledged being the "spiritual advisor" to both Asif Muhammad Hanif and Omar Khan Sharif. Al-Muhajiroun claimed that Bilal Ahmed, Britain's first suicide bomber, was "one of their own," and many of the British Muslims fighting for the Taliban who have been killed in Afghanistan since 2001 had close associations with the group.

Bakri is referred to as the "godfather of British terrorism" because he inspired and was connected, directly or indirectly, to so many radicalized Muslims who either committed acts of terrorism or intended to engage in violent acts. Through his rhetoric, Bakri encouraged a climate of fear within mainstream British society, thereby contributing to a hostile environment for Muslims. This environment, in turn, provided fertile ground for his radical Islamist discourse, which indeed took root among a minority of Muslims who already felt the effects of Islamophobia and discrimination—two key factors made worse by Bakri's violent jihadi rhetoric.

IMPLICATIONS

What should stand out immediately is that none of these leaders of the jihadi movement in Britain were born or raised in Britain—unlike the young men who went on to carry out terror attacks. Their ideology of hate has largely been an import. And one that was not necessary or unpreventable. It is clear that, like the United States, the British state ignored the true nature of their allies in the war against the Soviet-backed regime in Afghanistan. Both states were later to make the same mistake in Bosnia and Kosovo[13] and may be repeating it in Syria. In effect there was a complacent assumption that radical Islamists had other enemies than the Western powers and, as such, offered no real threat. However, as argued in this book, the true nature of Salafist Islam was no secret even if the Saudis made efforts to overlay its brutal origins by presenting it as simply an austere interpretation of Sunni Islam. This blindness was willful and has had dangerous consequences.

The British state, as have many other states, already have in place the facilities by which their home secretaries, secretaries of state, or ministers of the interior can, at their discretion, ban selected individuals from entering their territory. In the current climate, it may well make sense to use these powers more often to prevent internationally prominent advocates of hate-filled, violent ideologies from entering and settling and then using this freedom to radicalize local populations. However, we still need to be pragmatic: banning someone from physically visiting a country is not the same as preventing their ideas being propagated via the Internet.

This suggestion seems obvious in hindsight, given the amount of evidence of their activity that we have subsequently collected, but even now to suggest that certain select individuals should be banned from entering the country is controversial—often we will lack clear evidence of their activities abroad. But the suggestion should no longer be as problematic as we might have thought of it in the '90s. We now know, sadly, just how poisonous these individuals can be to our society, and surely we understand that these people consider themselves at war with us—with all of us. It is therefore incredibly difficult to avoid the conclusion that we are indeed at war with this ideology of hate, and we must tackle it robustly, and by all reasonable and lawful means available to us.

---

13   Brendan Simms, *Unfinest Hour: Britain and the Destruction of Bosnia* (London: Penguin, 2001).

But I would argue that it is not only these kinds of individuals whom we must prevent from entering the country. Even more important is to stop the money that often comes in the country with the same purpose—to promote and disseminate hatred, social division, and sometimes even violence. If the argument to keep foreign jihadi preachers out of the country stands up, surely the argument to keep foreign Salafi money aimed at undermining the very fabric of our liberal, multicultural society—a society in which Muslims of all sects and creeds can practice freely, often more freely than they would be able to in so-called Muslim countries today—must also stand up.

To repeat myself, we will need to target the problem at source. We need to engage directly with the Saudis, and engage them about their relationship with their Wahhabi religious establishment. Some Saudi clerics have identified Wahhabist dogma as the core problem for the kingdom itself, but so far their voices have been muted. In consequence, the billions that the Saudis have poured into countries around the world to promote bigotry and intolerance have enabled hate preachers in many, many countries to replicate the feats of the hate preachers of Britain. And thus to feed the seemingly constant stream of eager, young jihadis eager to join ISIS, or Boko Haram, or the many other local and regional movements that are springing up in unstable regions of the world as we speak. Once you come to see the world as a game of Us vs. Them, locked into perpetual struggle, where you are the oppressed victim, you are little more than a charismatic hate preacher and two YouTube videos away from flying out to Syria. Against this, any protestation by the Saudis that they too are fighting against terrorism, however true at the surface level, ultimately rings hollow. They are part of the problem—by far the biggest part of the problem. And this is something that we need to understand, and something that they need to understand. Only then can we start moving towards actual solutions to a problem that at the moment seems otherwise insurmountable.

This leads us to the next conclusion. Individuals do not jump from being relatively well integrated with the society around them to going to Syria and taking part in ISIS's atrocities overnight (even though some can radicalize very quickly). As with societies that carry out acts of genocide,[14] there is a series of steps that pave this path. As we explored earlier, terrorist groups need wider networks, both an intellectual and social movement that provides some support and people prepared to actively help them organize their finances, weaponry, and safe houses. All this implies that one reason why the West faces the threat of Salafist-inspired terrorism is because the creed that the Saudis fund and promote provides such a supportive environment.

THE STAGES OF RADICALIZATION

Perhaps some of the best contemporary research on radicalization has been done by ARTIS Research,[15] a worldwide, multidisciplinary research institution bringing together some of the world's leading psychologists, social scientists, anthropologists, and policy specialists for the purpose of studying conflict and recommending evidence-based policy solutions to reduce it. Naturally, much of their recent work has been in the area of radical Islamism, and starting from the 2000s, they have produced some very innovative and insightful work on the dynamics underlying much of the conflicts in the Middle East, as well as the related spill-over conflicts in the West in the form of jihadist terrorism. This section broadly accepts their analysis, but in the end I feel they under-estimate the importance of Salafism as an ideology in influencing the forms of radicalization and violence that we currently face. As I have argued earlier in this book, Salafism really should be seen as a totalitarian ideology and presents the same dynamics as Fascism or Communism and others of that ilk.

Some of their conclusions may very well surprise the casual observer, but it is well worth exploring them here. Take, for example, their 2009 report, *Theoretical Frames on Pathways to Violent Radicalization:*

---

14   Adam Jones, "Genocide and Mass Killing," in *Security Studies: An Introduction*, ed. Paul D Williams (London: Routledge, 2008).

15   ARTIS, "General Information," 2016 http://artisresearch.com/general-information/.

Understanding the Evolution of Ideas and Behaviors, How They Interact and How They Describe Pathways to Violence in Marginalized Diaspora.[16] This is a collection of case studies and theoretical observations on radicalization based on some of the most infamous terror attacks in the 2000s—the Hofstad, Madrid, and Hebron terror attacks—with multiple authors, all leading authorities in the field: Harold Hawkins, Scott Atran, Richard Davis, Marc Sageman, Rogier Rijpkema, Dominick Wright and Jeremy Ginges.

They conclude that unlike the usual picture often peddled in the media, terror attacks in the West have had very little to do with the hierarchical organization or coordination across borders by any entity such as Al-Qaeda, or its affiliates or competitors. Or indeed with *direct* guidance and coordination from hate preachers embedded in such groups. Instead, the young people, usually men,[17] who go on to commit terror attacks live in an environment of slow-boil, simmering hatred and resentment, a world of Us vs. Them, where We, or Our People, are victims of oppression, injustice and indignity. Random events as they unfold either on the world stage (e.g., foreign interventions by Western governments in "Muslim lands") or in local communities (social and economic exclusion for immigrant Muslim groups) are interpreted in light of this view of the world, and these young people become increasingly incensed and morally outraged. They come together in groups of like-minded people, and group-think quickly sets in. In this echo chamber of ideas, their views harden, their resolve increases, and violent reaction against what they view as an assault on Muslims becomes more and more compelling.

This is not to say that there are not well-organized attacks. Recent events in Paris and Brussels should leave us in no doubt that ISIS seeks to do this and is well aware of the propaganda value of such actions. Other attacks seem to be a combination of the self-radicalized building their own networks and some external support from Al-Qaeda or ISIS. The recent attacks in Orlando, Florida, seem to confirm this

---

16 ———, "Theoretical Frames on Pathways to Violent Radicalization," (Arlington: Office of Naval Research, 2009).

17 Though women can sometimes also be marginally involved.

alternative pattern of self-identification with ISIS but with limited actual engagement.

Such attacks also involve very little planning, except in the very last stages of acquiring the arms and explosives necessary to carry them out. Instead, what we see are loose networks of young friends, people who grew up together, or met in prison or playing football,[18] who develop a worldview of Muslim exclusion (and persecution) together. In these loose networks, occasionally very intense bonds of friendship are developed around a common rejection of this rotten state of affairs, and these clusters become activists for what they see as the "Muslim Cause." And some of these clusters, in the right conditions, provided that they stumble on the right resources, may well find themselves in the position to act on their rhetoric and carry out attacks against "the West." Many such plans fail due to lack of preparation by the would be terrorists and due diligence by the authorities, but some are carried out successfully.

What most observers, especially in the media, often fail to account for is the prevalence of these dynamics. In effect, a great many young men in our society are radicalized and accepting of the Salafist dogma to some extent. Often they remain essentially ignorant of mainstream Islam, and their Salafist worldview (with its emphasis on avoiding contact with nonbelievers or those deemed to be insufficiently Muslim) actually further disconnects them from that wider tradition: not least, as with many sectarians, they often hate those most similar to them more than they hate their notional enemies.

At each stage of the radicalization pathway described below there are a number of people that fit the description. And well over 99 percent of people at each stage will never move onto the next stage. But a small number do. And from then onwards—it is simply a matter of probabilities that some will eventually reach the stage where they are willing and able to carry out attacks. And from those, a minority

---

18   Or in other similar social contexts. Really, the key point here is about communities of friends coming together to pursue common leisure activities. Sports are almost always a feature, and football is one of the most likely sports. But that must simply be a feature of the fact that football is so universally popular around the world—there does not seem to be any special significance about the fact that jihadis do in fact play football together very often.

again will be successful. Equally we need to be careful: terrorist groups need supporters who do not themselves engage in violence[19] to keep safe houses and provide a wider support network. Of equal importance, analysis of the Italian Marxist terrorist movements suggests that very few entered from the traditional parties of the Italian left (the Communist and Socialist Parties). [20] Most came from self-radicalization in small local groups or via fragmentary political movements. As we shall see, this is mirrored among Islamist extremists; few, if any, are being radicalized within the conventional structures of Islam, such as the mosque.

This suggests that working just with the existing structures of the Muslim communities is not sufficient, as that is unlikely to be the path by which individuals become radicalized. To understand this process, we must start from the bottom of the pyramid.

STAGE 1: THE BOTTOM OF THE PYRAMID: "WE ARE OPPRESSED"

In 2008, Gallup published a study of the views of the Muslim world towards the West and their own status in the global geopolitical order. A random sample of around fifty thousand Muslims from thirty-five majority-Muslim countries were taken to represent the views of the Muslim population in the Islamic world (i.e., excluding Muslims living in non-Muslim-majority countries). The findings made for some rather uncomfortable reading, especially for Muslim liberals who always claimed that their religion was being hijacked by a very small but vocal band of criminals.

Seven percent of the respondents felt that the 9/11 attacks on the United States were "completely justified." This 7 percent represents

---

19   Leonardo Sciascia, *The Moro Affair, trans. Sacha Rabinovitch*, 2nd ed. (London: Granta, 1987).

20   Donnatella della Porta, "Left-Wing Terrorism in Italy," in *Terrorism in Context*, ed. Martha Crenshaw (University Park, PA: Penn State Press, 2010).

some ninety million people in the Islamic world. Almost as many felt that the attacks were "largely justified." All in all, 37 percent felt that the attacks were at least "somewhat justified." Which is to say that fully one third, or well over 400 million, of the ordinary Muslims of the Islamic world felt that it was legitimate to attack the United States and kill its citizens in a terror attack.

But we need to be careful in this interpretation. There are not in fact 400 million Muslims who want to kill you. Rather, these people would not mourn your death if you were to die. They would see this as in some way a predictable response to previous US actions in the Muslim world, as in, they believe that we would not mourn them if they died. This background of distaste for, and distrust of, the West—our states and us as groups of citizens—is the core of the problem. Of these 400 million Muslims, few are actually willing to take up arms for a group like ISIS. The CIA has estimated that at the end of 2014, ISIS had only between twenty thousand and thirty-five thousand fighters.[21] Though nobody seems to know just how many jihadis there are around the world at the moment, there can't be more than about 500,000 between ISIS, Boko Haram, Chechen, Afghani, and Pakistani groups, plus disparate "wannabe" jihadis in other countries.[22] Probably many less if we just count those who are active fighters. And of course, the overwhelming majority of these fighters are concentrated in failed and failing states in and around the Islamic world, in Asia and central Africa, and have next to no practical interest in the West, except as a potential recruitment ground and for propaganda purposes.

Hostile attitudes towards the Other then would seem to have very little impact on the propensity of the individuals who hold such views to engage in violent action. The most stunning example of this is perhaps in the Palestinian occupied territories, as highlighted by the ARTIS report.

---

21   Daveed Gartenstein-Ross, "How Many Fighters Does the Islamic State Really Have?," War on the Rocks, 2015 http://warontherocks.com/2015/02/how-many-fighters-does-the-islamic-state-really-have/.

22   A Schmid, "Foreign (terrorist) fighter estimates: conceptual and data issues," (The Hague: International Center for Counter-Terrorism Policy, 2015).

This suggests that over 80 percent of the Palestinian population supported suicide bombings during the second Intifada.[23] That's an entire society that agrees it is a good idea to use some of the most extreme tactics of violence against its oppressor. And yet, very few individuals indeed went on to actually carry out such attacks. In the entire five years of the conflict, between 2000 and 2005, there were around 140 suicide attacks—a staggering amount if we think about it in terms of willingness to take the lives of other human beings in an appalling manner, but a vanishingly small proportion of the 4.5 million Palestinians who live in the occupied territories,[24] nearly four million of which, remember, say they support such acts of violence.

This matters, as the group of personally peaceful individuals who have embraced Salafist interpretations of Islam provides the most substantial challenge for policy makers. As we will see below, once an individual has moved to embrace violent jihad in a perverse way, they are easy to deal with (even if they have also become an immediate threat). Planning, never mind carrying out, such actions is clearly illegal, and as such, this individual become a matter primarily for the criminal justice system as well as of immediate attention to state security services. So how do we handle people who believe in something we may personally disagree with, and which, clearly, has some potential to develop into a personal commitment to violence? Especially since the ability to cope with this form of dissent has been a key characteristic of an open liberal society?

As briefly discussed in the introduction, perhaps the dominant feature of those who embrace Salafism is a deep suspicion of non-adherents (both other Muslims and the wider society), leading to a degree of self-imposed isolation as they seek to protect themselves against what they see as moral contagion. However, self-exclusion is variable, both between individuals and groups and over time, and

---

23   ARTIS, "Theoretical Frames on Pathways to Violent Radicalization."

24   Palestinian Central Bureau of Statistics, "Estimated Population in the Palestinian Territory," Palestinian Central Bureau of Statistics, 2016 http://www.pcbs.gov.ps/ Portals/_Rainbow/Documents/gover_e.htm.

this affects many strands within Islam. More specifically, Ineke Roex noted some of these contradictions in a study of Salafist identities:

> ... Salafists invest in a uniform group identity and express this by stressing brotherhood and sisterhood through their clothing, language and religious practices. For instance, Salafists can distinguish themselves by wearing certain clothing: women wear the khimar (a veil that hangs down to just above the waist, covering the hair, neck and shoulders, but leaving the face clear) and the niqab (a veil for the face that leaves the area around the eyes clear and is worn with an accompanying headscarf) and men wear baggy, short-legged trousers. They frequently use Islamic terms and expressions and follow ritual practices like the salat (daily prayer) with precision. These group symbols are used in many ways and sometimes only temporarily: they are subject to debate and thus to change. For instance, there is no agreement on the obligation and desirability of wearing the niqab in the Netherlands.[25] Only a few women choose this style of covering themselves and many of those who do, wear it only some of the time. The diversity in the use of group symbols makes the group boundaries unclear.[26]

Equally, the degree of nonengagement with those who do not share core beliefs is contradicted by a desire to ensure that all Muslims come to live the morally pure lives that Salafists believe they already follow.[27] This contradiction is managed by the concept of *hisba* (commanding good and forbidding bad [*al-amr bi-l-ma'ruf wa-l-nahy 'an al-munkar*]), which emphasizes living by the nonnegotiable rules of their own interpretation of the faith. However, a detailed study of the Dutch Salafist community[28] has indicated this in turn has led to fragmentation. As

---

25 To further complicate this we should note that there is a range of practice in terms of the type of headwear worn by women in Muslim communities, often dictated more by local cultural and class mores than any interpretation of the Qur'an.

26 Roex, "Should we be Scared of all Salafists in Europe? A Dutch Case Study."

27 Ibid.

28 Ibid.

with early Protestant movements,[29] seeking to reach past those who have interpreted the faith to the original "pure" source documents has in turn led to fragmentation, as there is no single authority that individuals can access; interpretations of the source material vary, and there is no acceptable central body that can adjudicate on such disputes. Even worse, if they believe they hold the only true interpretation, there is no place for the style of debate normal to democratic societies, where there is an acceptance of pluralism. Thus we have a community where adherence to narrow rules is seen as critical but which lacks the means to debate those rules either among itself or with the wider Muslim communities.

This in turn leads to the question of how to deal with both non-believers and those within the Salafist community who are judged to have erred from the true path. The evidence from the Netherlands is interesting in that:

> According to Sharia law, there are indeed punishments (corporal and otherwise) for committing sins, apostasy and failure to follow Islamic rules. This indicates that there are formal means of coercion in the Salafi movement. Nonetheless, Dutch quietist and political Salafists in the researched networks insist that these punishments should never be carried out in a Dutch context[30].

This contradiction perhaps sits at the heart of the wider dilemma. The Dutch Salafists in Roex's study fully embraced the concept of branding those who disagreed with them as *takfir* (heretics) but make a distinction between social or moral pressures to conform (i.e., personal beliefs) and actual punishment of those who do not conform, as this would contradict the wider social and legal norms of the state they live in—in this case, the Netherlands. In fact, those interviewed by Roex were at pains to stress that *"takfir* is a matter for scholars and

---

29   Cohn, *The Pursuit of the Millenium*; A.G. Dickens, *The Age of Humanism and Reformation: Europe in the Fourteenth, Fifteenth and Sixteenth Centuries* (London: Prentice Hall, 1977).

30   Roex, "Should we be Scared of all Salafists in Europe? A Dutch Case Study."

Islamic states to decide, and is not for 'average' Muslims to be carried out. A far-reaching consequence of denunciation is that a Muslim can be sentenced to death or violence against the apostate person can be justified. . . . The Salafists interviewed expressly stated that these punishments may only be imposed by Islamic judges in Islamic states, and not in the context of democratic states."[31]

In this framing the importance of self-discipline and self-perfection is stressed but, at least in theory, there should be no coercion—even if in practice the threat of exclusion from a community is a real threat. Equally it should be noted that the relative unwillingness to apply formal sanctions is contextual—they are not appropriate in the Netherlands, as the necessary jurisprudence and religious authority are missing. They may well be appropriate in an Islamic country that has fully embraced the Salafist ideology.

All this raises an important question of just what we are dealing with. If we ignore the Islamic aspect of Salafist beliefs, the practices of group identity, caution in dealings with others, and use of in-group sanctions against those who backslide are common. For example, many nonconformist Protestant groups retain the concept of male elders "holding their hands over" women and younger men in the community. In a small, remote farming or fishing community, such a threat was not idle—exclusion from the church also meant exclusion from the community. Equally, forming communities that are to some extent isolated from the rest of society has been a common feature of religious groups, and more recently of green or socialist group-ings who wish to live by their own precepts. Again, there has always been a degree of internal discipline in such groups—at its worst a malign direct imposition of power relations and at its best the ability to exclude those who break the chosen norms. In effect, before we decide on how to deal with the issue of Salafist communities creating and living by their own rules, we need to think about how we should respond to any group that seeks to do so.

Of course, at the moment, there is one critical difference. In the main, exclusive nonconformist Protestants or people who wish to

---

31   Ibid.

experiment with a more ecological lifestyle do not contain within themselves a small core of people who wish to impose those norms on everyone else in society and a smaller group again, that is prepared to use extreme violence in pursuit of this goal.

This has led a series of right-wing commentators and political groups to argue that any form of Salafism is a fundamental threat. The precise nature of this argument varies over time and by country, but one early formulation was by the British MP (and future Cabinet Minister) Michael Gove in his book *Celsius 7/7*.[32] A closely related book was by the British journalist Melanie Phillips: *Londonistan: How Britain is Creating a Terror State Within*,[33] which argues that any acceptance of any form of Salafist belief creates the basis of a fundamental terrorist threat. Both suggest that self-imposed concerns by the UK government (to, in their words, avoid giving offense or breaking "multicultural taboos") in the face of a struggle against what is described by both authors as a totalitarian ideology that presents a threat akin to that posed by the Soviet Union or Nazi Germany. From this has emerged an overblown but consistent narrative that all Salafists are a threat (because a few are), and this is often extended to regarding all Muslims as a threat (as some are Salafists and some Salafists are also terrorists[34]). Such views are now commonly presented as the West deliberately ignoring a mortal threat[35] that could plunge our societies into civil war.[36] The book by Phillips is typical in making the assumption that all Salafists accept violence and that our policies need to be constructed

---

32   Michael Gove, *Celsius 7/7* (London: Weidenfeld and Nicolson, 2006).

33   Melanie Phillips, *Londonistan: How Britain is Creating a Terror State Within* (London: Encounter Books, 2006).

34   Two contrasting and early presentations and rebuttal of this argument can be found at: Will Cummins, "Muslims are a threat to our way of life," The Telegraph, 2004 http://www.telegraph.co.uk/comment/personal-view/3608849/Muslims-are-a-threat-to-our-way-of-life.html; Bhikhu Parekh, "Is Islam a Threat to Europe's Multicultural Democracies?," *Religion in the New Europe* (2006).

35   CounterJihad, "Special Ops Command to Pentagon: Stop Ignoring Jihad," CounterJihad, 2016 https://counterjihadreport.com/tag/salafism/.

36   Chris Tomlinson, "Islamic Scholar: Europe may be heading toward Civil War," Breitbart, 2016 http://www.breitbart.com/london/2016/09/11/islam-scholar-europe-may-heading-toward-civil-war/.

with this firmly in mind. This mind-set is affecting mainstream policy makers as issues such as banning burqas and other forms of clothing have become common. Since Donald Trump's election as president, it probably now forms the dominant ideology underpinning the practical policies of the new administration.

However, as noted earlier, studies of Salafists in the Netherlands[37] suggest that they do accept the laws and norms of Dutch society. Nevertheless, banning items of clothing can be problematic. The study found that in Belgium (where clothing bans were in place in 2008) women in Salafist communities became more isolated. As they could not wear a form of clothing that was deemed appropriate to certain situations, they did not engage in those social situations. This fits with the evidence that women in such communities opt to use a range of clothing according to the situation and that very few opt to wear full face veils all the time. This leads to an alternative policy framework—one where we accept Salafism, acknowledge that many are sincere in rejecting violence, and allow them to present their views. This is not the same as saying we must agree with them or not maintain common laws and norms, but it is not effective to treat those who eschew violence in the same way as we treat those who do break the law.

How policy makers balance this debate is probably one of the most important issues in contemporary North America and Western Europe. The problem is if we give in to the theories peddled by the far right, we actually reinforce the core narrative of the most extreme in the Salafist community. By rejecting all Salafists (and let us be honest, most of these commentators really want to reject all Muslims), we build on the argument that Islam and the West are incompatible. On the other hand, the existence of a large group of quietest Salafists is the core reason why extremist ideas have gained such a hold. In particular, Saudi funding in the UK, Belgium, and Kosovo (to name but three instances) is closely linked to the subsequent emergence of violent jihadism.

So we cannot just tolerate Salafism, not least as at the moment it is too readily associated with violent Islamism. We need to challenge

---

37   Roex, "Should we be Scared of all Salafists in Europe? A Dutch Case Study."

the incorrect interpretation of Islam that sits at its core. While this does mean challenging the Saudis, it also offers a challenge to our own communities. But we must also challenge the newly emboldened voices of the European and North American right who want to attack all Muslims in the guise of challenging violent jihadism.

STAGE 2: "THEY ARE ATTACKING OUR PEOPLE"

E vidence found by ARTIS researchers in other studies suggests that the people who become actively involved in taking up the "Muslim cause," especially those under age thirty, are not primarily driven by oppression or humiliation targeted at themselves. Indeed, they found that Palestinians who were direct victims of oppression were relatively unlikely to engage in violence. Rather, it is primarily those who feel moral outrage at the oppression and humiliation of others who are the most likely to take violent action—or, at the very least, people who become radicalized tend to point not so much at hardships and humiliations that they themselves may have felt but rather to the hardships and humiliations of others.

As with the discussion about how to respond to nonviolent Salafists, this produces a serious public policy challenge. For good reasons, democratic states are cautious about prescribing what opinions are acceptable and which are not. This may argue for a laissez-faire approach where the most that is done is to challenge particularly egregious assumptions and errors. However, we have ample evidence that this is too limited. Stepping aside from the issue of the Salafist community, we are now becoming more and more aware of the role of "fake news" in creating a structured belief system with supporting "evidence." This is increasingly becoming the domain of the newly emboldened far right and of the current Russian state, where creating blocks of self-referencing information has led many to reject reality in favor of fantasy. Once this shift has been made, changing minds becomes increasingly difficult.

It is also at this stage that the group dynamics of the friendship groups of young Muslims kick in. They socialize together in their normal social groups, in their neighborhoods, in their schools, around (though very rarely *in*[38]) the local mosques, playing team sports together, and occasionally discussing politics. Kids in immigrant and descendant-of-immigrant communities will naturally have a global outlook to their politics, even if knowledge and understanding of all the issues involved is not always very well developed. And what they see is a global geopolitical system that reeks of injustice. There are huge disparities of wealth and power in the international arena. And given the long-standing and persistent failures of global governance on the world stage, it really does not take a conspiracy-theory mind-set to jump to the conclusion that those in a relative position of power globally, notably the United States and the West, have a lot to answer for with regards to the condition in which the rest of the world finds itself, for example in the global south. As indeed they do have a lot to answer for, regardless of whether the global system that has emerged in the postcolonial era was deliberately rigged by the wealthy north or not. The most obvious feature of what we would like to call—with no hint of irony—"the global village" is the failure of the international community to establish a fair and balanced world order for all the world's peoples. In this "global village," the Islamic world is not and has not been faring very well. The cultural zone from which these young people derive much of their identity, regardless of how religious they might otherwise be, is highly marginalized. As we have seen, this is unlike the way things used to be during the Islamic Golden Age, when the Islamic world was the cultural center of civilization, and it is something that still rankles. This region was for decades a battleground between the

---

38 The usual findings in the 2009 ARTIS report is that that even the most radical Saudi-funded cleric at a local mosque is likely to challenge the radical rhetoric and calls to action of activist young Muslims (even if for no other reason than because it represents a challenge to the religious authority of the local imam, who, whether he likes it or not, has to be accommodating to the sensibilities of other religious or non-religious communities in his area). Indeed, it is very common for such groups to find themselves excluded from their local mosque (whether by their own choice or otherwise).

United States and the USSR during the Cold War; it has been ravaged by conflicts between different sectarian and political ideologies; and in the postcolonial era it has almost always had one or more failed states within it. It is not hard for these young people to identify with the "plight" of the Islamic world, especially since they often find very little to identify with in host countries that reject, to a greater or lesser extent,[39] them and their heritage.

Inevitably, their politics become the politics of grievance. As well it should be. Young people across the Western world, indeed across the entire world, have much to be aggrieved about, Muslim or otherwise. And even if they did not, it would still be strange for the young not to chafe at the restrictions that older generations inevitably impose on them. But what is specific to many of these Muslim youngsters, especially the young men, is the shape that their grievance takes. According to the studies, this grievance is really not very much informed by religion or theology or well-developed social theories (like Marxism, for example). It is not inspired by the tomes produced by the Saudi Ulema. But it is always inspired by a simplistic Salafi-*takfiri* worldview, which actually borrows very lightly from Islamic beliefs.[40] The very same Us vs. Them, perpetual warfare, "they are oppressing our people" worldview that forms the core of Salafism, regardless of all the theological refinements, niceties, and halfhearted injunctions against violence that Salafi scholars and imams throw on top.

Where they feel in some way or other separate and excluded from mainstream society, they can find an ideology that says this outcome is desirable—that they *should* withdraw from the impure mainstream

---

39 Here we used to have routine comparisons between the models of integration pursued by different Western countries, notably the melting pot of the United States, France's monocultural *laïcité républicaine*, or Britain's multiculturalism (both in academia and in the media), though in recent months and years we have seen Muslims and Muslim communities become radicalized in most host countries. The fact of the matter is that it is almost inevitable that poorer sections of Muslim immigrant communities will feel that they are being marginalized specifically because of their religion and their identity, and from then on they will always come to identify with other oppressed Muslims around the world.

40 Lebovich, "How 'religious' are ISIS fighters? The relationship between religious literacy and religious motivation".

society and its corrupting influence! Where they feel that something must be done to make the world a better place, to right injustices and grant redress to themselves or to groups of people they identify strongly with (oppressed Muslims in the Middle East), they find an ideology that gives them carte blanche—do whatever you need to do, use whatever means necessary. A message that inevitably appeals to the temperament of some young men, especially those looking for a mission and a cause. In this respect it is worth stressing that many of those who go on to carry out terrorist attacks have a background as petty criminals, visiting nightclubs, taking drugs.[41] In effect, before they wrap themselves in Salafism, they are not especially observant but have already drifted to the margins of society.

This prior sense of alienation matters. All the evidence is that the bulk of Western-born fighters actively fighting for ISIS in Syria and Iraq are from French-speaking countries.[42] As we have seen, one reason is that the Saudis have funded a network of Salafist mosques in France and Belgium, creating a disconnect between younger Muslims and the more relaxed, somewhat eclectic Islam of their parents derived from the traditions of North Africa. However, in addition, both France and Belgium have long had major problems of concentrating poverty in particular districts, usually on the edge of major cities. For a long time such *banlieues* have been a breeding ground for social discontent. In post–World War II France they first became the bastions of the French Communist Party, then breeding grounds for violent criminals. Recently they have been the focus of violent street protests, and it is no surprise that such marginalized communities are now the main source of Salafist militants. In truth, there is plenty for them to protest against.[43] In effect, where at one stage militant Communism or violent

41   Timothy Peace, "Who becomes a terrorist, and why?," The Washington Post, 2016 https://www.washingtonpost.com/news/monkey-cage/wp/2016/05/10/who-becomes-a-terrorist-and-why/.

42   Chris Meserole, "The French Connection," Religion.org, 2016 https://religional.org/2016/04/05/the-french-connection-part-i-backstory/.

43   Angelique Chrisafis, "'Nothing's changed': 10 years after French riots, banlieues remain in crisis" The Guardian, 2015 https://www.theguardian.com/world/2015/oct/22/nothings-changed-10-years-after-french-riots-banlieues-remain-in-crisis.

crime was the common response, we now see such young people turn to Salafist dogmas.

However, young would-be jihadists "discover"—though sometimes "invent" would better describe the phenomenon—an ideology together, as a group of morally driven, upstanding young men, a band of brothers, in search of meaning in their lives and a better world around them. Which goes a long way towards explaining the disconnect in the ideological outlook between this generation of young people and their parents and grandparents,[44] who, in Western Europe, often come from North Africa or the Indian subcontinent (both areas where the traditional form of Islam is open and tolerant). They often grew up in something of a religious and theological vacuum. Their older generations have not been, on average, very religious at all. And perhaps in a bid to ensure that their children are better able to integrate in their new countries and their secular cultures, they have not insisted too much on passing down their own, mainstream understanding of Islam, like, for example, the famously relaxed Maliki school of thought, prevalent across Northern Africa, and from where most of the Muslims in Continental Europe trace their descent. Instead, identity and meaning are found in the communal discussion, interpretation, and understanding of world and local events, through the prism of the simplicities of the Salafi-*takfiri* worldview, which have been aggressively pushed.

This argues that the challenge to Salafist interpretations must come largely from within the Islamic community. It is here that the knowledge of how to interpret the core texts, as well as the lived experience of many disparate Muslim groups across the globe, resides. Alienation

---

44 As I mentioned in previous chapters, we are now witnessing something of a new phenomenon with multiple generations choosing to move to ISIS territories from the West, all together at the same time as a family. This may at first hand contradict the claim that radicalisation is a specifically youth-related and age-horizontal phenomenon. And indeed there will be exceptions to this picture. But so far, there is scant evidence of actual violence being committed as a family enterprise, rather than by "bands of brothers", and it still seems to be the case that even for older radicals, they would have been radicalised much earlier in their lives, one, two, even three decades ago. Many of the conditions we are discussing here were very much present at that time as well, even if perhaps not on the same scale.

is unfortunately a product of being rejected by the country one lives in, but the creation of false narratives has a larger consequence than just alienation.

This relates to the discussion at the end of stage 1. If Western policy becomes dominated by the anti-Muslim discourse of the far right, then alienated young Muslims will feel their mind-set is being reinforced. This has terrible consequences as every so often a group will resolve to do something about the morally outrageous state of the world.

STAGE 3: "THE BAND OF BROTHERS"

Once the resolve to resort to action to redress social injustices together sets in, the group congeals into more than just a bunch of friends. The core group members now become comrades for a cause greater than themselves. They become activists, organize meetings, proselytize, raise funds for group activities, and so on. At this stage, this network of friends goes from low-cost/low-risk involvement, to high-cost/high-risk. Many of these groups demand full-time devotion from their members, and their activities are likely to draw the attention of the authorities. Equally, family and other friends will often disapprove and try to dissuade the new activists from such high levels of involvement, not least because this will often mean that they will need to neglect many of their prior social duties. And the conflicts that may arise from this may further isolate the new activists from their wider social and family ties. In turn this will only reinforce the centrality of the cause and of the brotherhood to their lives, and cement their commitment to it.

Atran and Davis propose[45] that radicalization begins in earnest when priorities shift in the person's moral hierarchy such that taking action (violent or otherwise) in pursuit of the cause takes ever higher precedence over other everyday moral demands such as those of

---

45   In the ARTIS (2009) Executive Summary (p.11)

family, friends, and wider immediate community. As the identity of the new group of brothers gets stronger and individuals become more committed to it, the purported ideological foundation of the group's identity, that of the "Muslim cause," must become more and more important for the individual—these are the lessons that Atran and Davis draw from decades of psychological research in cognitive dissonance. In effect, individual members of the group, to the extent to which they identify with the group, must reconcile and absorb the group identity, real or presumed, to their own individual identity. This becomes especially salient when a given individual has to make a difficult choice between competing demands—*Do I go to preach Islam, or do I tend to my sickly father?* If the individual chooses the "higher calling" of preaching Islam, doing so will become very strongly entrenched as a priority above most other "mundane" moral demands: *If I am a true brother of the cause, I must do what everyone else in the brotherhood would do.* And as a series of decisions like this are made, all pointing in the same direction, the individual becomes more committed. It is thus that, little by little, they become "soldiers for Islam," or mujahedeen.

Worse, this need to correct for cognitive dissonance between the individual and the group identity ripples through the social network of the group. As individuals perceive that their friends are also becoming more radical—or, as they would see it, more true to the cause—they feel like they themselves risk deviating from the ideal normative identity of the group if they do not match this commitment. If they see their friends making difficult personal sacrifices and prioritizing the moral demands of the cause over that of the family—if, for instance, their friends choose to go preach Islam instead of tending to a sickly father—then they feel that they must make similar decisions when they are faced with similar personal dilemmas. And indeed, all members of the group will react very strongly in opposition to "hypocrisy"—say, if they see one of their friends advocating withdrawal and reducing their commitment to the group above other "mundane" demands. Even so they may still not make the leap to acts of violence themselves. As we discussed in the previous chapter, substantial amounts of evidence about members of terrorist groups suggest that group maintenance becomes their core goal—well above the notional cause for which they are fighting.

At this stage then, we see that the young activists are no longer just like-minded friends. They become a collective body that demands esprit de corps, much like elite units of regular armed forces would. When wannabe jihadis identify themselves as soldiers, as mujahedeen, it is not always fanciful or absurd. They do sometimes have a lot in common with soldiers at the psychological level. It is also at this stage that the problem of how to deal with Salafists becomes as much a security and criminal justice challenge as it is one for wider society.

STAGE 4: VIOLENT JIHAD

N ow comes the crucial step: that from rhetoric and activism to violence, either by joining and fighting for a militant group such as ISIS or by carrying out a martyrdom terror attack in their own country.

Except that even in stage 3, relatively few make the leap to actual violence. Talk, as they say, is cheap. And between young male bravado and genuine moral outrage that is quite common in all young people, including young Muslim people, to use jihadi or "tough talk" rhetoric online or between young male friends and go no further. So common, in fact, that Sageman in the ARTIS report[46] finds himself wondering why there are so relatively few attacks, or so relatively few young people going to join ISIS. However, from talking to law enforcement, he found that there is virtually no way one can tell from the rhetoric of young people who will commit an attack and who will not. For every individual who will genuinely attempt a terror attack, there will be hundreds who will match their rhetoric and the ideological commitments word for word but who will never come close to actually taking violent action. As Sageman puts it, "Terrorists swim in a sea of people

---

46   In his case study of the Hofstad attack, in ARTIS (2009, 15)

who share their ideas" (in 2009, 15). He goes on to conclude that there is a "mistaken belief that we are fighting violent extremism (a cognitive notion). No, we are fighting people who kill other people, a behavioral attribute of these killers. We are fighting extremist violence, and not violent extremism" (id.).

In a sense, this is correct in the extent to which, regarding the large group of individuals who share this ideology and espouse its rhetoric, we should be focusing as much as we can on those who will actually commit violent acts. When construed in this way, the problem of radical Islamist ideology becomes the fairly traditional problem of allocating resources to deal with actual criminality. And here, the most likely explanation of why some individuals do go on to kill, while others do not, is probably the simplest: only in a small number of individuals do the circumstances involved in the radicalization process end up overcoming the natural limits of empathy and the limits of sociality that were instilled in them growing up, and thus an ideology of death can overpower normal inclinations and behavior. At this point the difference may very well just be down to prior predispositions (e.g., psychopathy, or a predilection towards a zealot mind-set, or whatever else). Or whatever other explanation you favor for why criminality in general happens. But to say that the cognitive, which is to say the ideological, aspect is thus irrelevant would be a profound mistake. This is a conclusion that most of the ARTIS research seems to be drawn towards, and I find this to be a very strange reading of the evidence they present.

There is truth in their assumptions. We can see much the same pattern of thinking, alienation, and group identification but still a gap between "belonging" and violent actions in other circumstances. Members of street gangs show very similar dynamics—not all actively engage in violent crime even if they form part of the group and presumably share the collective beliefs of the group. More worrying, as we noted in the previous chapter, is that terrorist groups do not just need committed killers. They need those prepared to help, either actively, by money laundering, criminal actions, running safe houses, or passively, as supporters and propagandists. To be dangerous, terrorist groups do not need many active members. The Italian Red Brigades had around twenty to thirty active killers in their ranks,[47] the Provisional IRA in Northern Ireland around two to three hundred. But modern Salafist-inspired terrorism has its own logic too, and that cannot just be explained away by looking at related instances. Allen[48] suggests that they have taken much from their predecessors but have also added a very distinct Islamist aspect to modern jihadi terrorism.

This makes the Salafi-*takfiri* ideology the historically peculiar element. Exclusion, marginalization, and hopelessness among minority groups are not historically remarkable. They have always been a feature of any society, and unfortunately they are likely to remain so, at least for the foreseeable future. Which is not to say that we should not be serious about tackling any instance of social injustice and inequity. Of course we must. That ought to be our highest calling as social beings and citizens of democracies. But if we are looking for the causes behind why some individuals choose to attack the whole of society in protest against injustice in our world today, even when they usually end up hurting other members of society who are equally vulnerable and marginalized the most, we cannot avoid placing the majority of the responsibility at the door of the ideology that "loves death as [we] love life."

And it all starts at the very *bottom* of the radicalization pyramid. This is not primarily about "extremist violence" at the top, as Sageman wants to argue. Extremist violence, as individual acts of terror, is simply the statistically unavoidable outcome of the existence of a generalized state of "violent extremism" among millions upon millions of Muslims worldwide. All fed by a worldview framed by the fundamental principles of the deviant sect of Wahhabism: the Salafi-Takfirism of puritanical withdrawal from the world and active dehumanization of the Other. And all promoted around the world with billions upon billions of petro-dollars by the Kingdom of Saudi Arabia, as we have seen.

From this, Atran and Sageman beautifully capture the entire series of psychological and social phenomena in the social networks that

---

47   della Porta, "Left-Wing Terrorism in Italy."

48   Allen, *God's Terrorists: The Wahhabi Cult and the Hidden Roots of Modern Jihad.*

underpin radicalization and the undertaking of violent jihad: "The key difference between terrorists and most other people in the world lies not in individual pathologies, personality, education, income or in any other demographic factor, but in small group dynamics where the relevant trait [which organizes the group's behavior] just happens to be Jihad rather than, say, obesity[49]" At which point, the only question that remains to be asked is, from whence comes this jihad? And as we have seen, it is not a matter of if the jihad and the violence will come, but when.

SUMMARY

The research done within ARTIS, building on earlier research into the logic behind political violence, offers powerful insights into the dynamics of radicalization. I fully endorse their description of the process of radicalization but argue that they are ignoring the particularly Salafist element to the current wave of terrorism. In effect, they make a mistake when claiming that *theology* has very little to do with radicalization. However, we need to be careful with words here. Salafism has given rise to some very new dynamics in terrorism (not least the largely independent self-creating terrorist cells—or individuals—that we now often encounter), but it is probably better described as an ideology rather than, as it may appear, a theological current within Islam.

This chapter develops the material presented earlier about the ideology behind Salafism and the wider dynamics of terrorism in general and of Islamist-inspired terrorism in particular. It then looks at the impact of Salafist violence within Western Europe and North America and how Salafism has spread within the wider Muslim communities. This suggests three key themes.

First, we have to be clear that the root of modern Islamic terrorism is Wahhabism and its Salafist creation. The relatively close linkage

---

49   ARTIS, "Theoretical Frames on Pathways to Violent Radicalization."

between areas where the Saudis have funded mosques and districts that produce the most extremists is too close to ignore.[50] As we will see in the next chapter, the malign correlation between allowing the Saudis to fund religious education in a country and the growth of Salafism is also too close to ignore. Having said this, we should also acknowledge that the most militant forms of Salafism (as represented by ISIS and Al-Qaeda) are as much a threat to the Saudi regime as they are to the rest of us. Equally, Saudi-funded clerics do challenge the most extreme reinterpretations of their beliefs, but by the time individuals have adopted this mind-set, they are out of the reach of conventional Islamic religious structures.

Developing this, the problem is the belief system adopted by quietest Salafists is still fundamentally wrong. Their presentation of Islamic history is badly flawed (as discussed at the start of this book), and their reinterpretations of Islamic jurisprudence are equally incorrect. But this leads us to the second key issue. Most of the radicalization beyond the second stage (in other words to form a 'band of brothers') now happens outside the formal structures of the Islamic community. In effect small groups cherry-pick information that fits into their inchoate worldview (as do their opposite numbers in the anti-Muslim far right). Into this gap, with its unstructured search for knowledge, can step the hate preachers, such as the individuals already discussed. They provide a very simplistic set of axioms, all of which tend to increase the tendency of Salafists to exclude and fear "others." The hate preachers also provide a simple block of arguments that set (mostly) young people on the road to deeper involvement with extremism. This presents a major challenge to the Islamic communities in the West. How to challenge the ill-informed opinions, and how to ensure that those who are disaffected remain within the traditional structures of the community?

The final issue is how to frame public policy. As discussed, in a way the very few Salafists who make the final step into actively planning acts of violence are the easiest to deal with. Making bombs, buying guns, earning money via criminal means are all illegal. Equally, the

---

50   Clapper, "The Saudi Connection in the Belgium Attacks".

concept of the "lone wolf" attacker who has self-radicalized[51] has gained far too much traction; in reality most acts of mass murder (planned or attempted) end up having links back to either AQ or ISIS—even if the linkage is essentially viral. This presents law enforcement and intelligence agencies with a massive problem in tracking such links and such people, but there can be no space for tolerance of their attitudes or actions. Even so, we do need to think about how to give people in such groups an exit strategy and how to handle those who wish to now escape from terrorist networks.

However, at other stages in the pyramid we are faced with attitudes and beliefs we might find abhorrent, but we need to be more careful in our response. The Salafist dogma around *kaffirs* and *takfir* is repellent, and most people find it deeply unpleasant to be described in such terms. But let us be depressingly clear: are such demeaning terms really that different from phrases like *libtards* used so freely by the far right and popularized by websites such as Breitbart? Equally encountering individuals celebrating (or calling for) murder on social media is not something we should tolerate. But again, equally depressingly, it is not a form of discourse that is limited to the wilder extremes of the Salafist community. So yes, we need to challenge Salafism (at all its levels of adherence), but we need to be very careful how we do so.

The next two chapters move on to explore the emergence of Salafism in the Balkans and then the various ways it has changed during the wars in Iraq and Syria since 2003. Once we have a fuller understanding of how modern-day Salafism and its militant form is evolving, we can return to answering some of the questions posed above.

---

51   Peek, "The Roots of Lone Wolf Terrorism: Why the West's Homegrown Jihadists Are All Sunni".

PART SIX
A CASE STUDY:
SALAFISM IN THE BALKANS

B efore considering how the West should respond to the challenge of Salafism, it is useful to provide other instances of the shifting dynamics behind the emergence of Islamic terrorism. The sequence of conflicts in the Balkans from 1991 to 1999 is an instructive case study. It challenges the core Salafist argument that the (never quite fully specified) "West" has never stood up for Muslims, but it also provides a compelling study of how the Salafists were able to embed themselves within a campaign backed by NATO and the EU to further their own goals.

The state of Yugoslavia had been an artificial creation of the post–World War I peace processes. It was formed as a fusion of the existing Serbian kingdom with Croatia and Bosnia, with Herzegovina and Slovenia taken from the defeated Austro-Hungarian Empire. The region had long been a battleground between the Austrians and the Turks, and it had seen the rise and defeat of a mosaic of local kingdoms. By the 1880s, Ottoman power was waning, and they were finally expelled in the 1912–13 Balkan War. However, their long rule had contributed to the complex mix of ethnicities and religions across the region, in particular in the large Muslim populations in Albania and Bosnia-Herzegovina. The new kingdom of Yugoslavia was defeated by the Germans in mid-1941, and an independent state of Croatia was reestablished. While the rulers of this short-lived state enthusiastically backed the occupiers, many Croats fought either with the Communist partisan movement or the pro-Royalist groups (the Chetniks). By 1944, Tito's partisans had become a powerful fighting force, able to limit even Soviet intervention to assist with the liberation of Belgrade before the Red Army formations moved back into Hungary. By 1945 Tito had re-established the old Yugoslav state (and very nearly managed to add Trieste).

His rule was authoritarian, but he managed to keep out of the Soviet bloc and created the veneer of a single state from the previous patchwork of ethnicities and nationalities. After his death in 1980, it seemed as if the new state had managed to achieve a degree of stability, but increasingly the leaders of main national republics were seeking more power than the federal structures allowed them to amass. In 1991, Slovenia declared its independence and, mostly peacefully, broke away and established itself as an independent state. Next to leave the Yugoslav Republic was Croatia, and this set in motion an increasingly ethnically based struggle with Serbia that spread across Croatia, Bosnia, and Herzegovina from 1991 to 1996. The final act of this fragmentation of the previous state was the rebellion in Kosovo from 1998–99, which ended with the creation of a new state from that largely Muslim (and ethnically Albanian) province. By that stage the still existing Federal Republic of Yugoslavia essentially held the same territory that the Serbian kingdom had in 1914 and had become a purely Serb ethnic state.

The war in Bosnia was different from that in Croatia. Croatia's schism had an ethnic focus, but the battle was essentially fought between two states over a contested border region. In contrast, when Bosnia voted for independence in March 1992, the ethnic Serbs boycotted the referendum, and then, led by Radovan Karadzic, created their own breakaway state.[1] The conflict that followed was less a clash between regular armies and more one of vicious local ethnic cleansing as the Serbs sought to expel all the Muslim population from their self-proclaimed republic. The imbalance of power worsened, as the local Serbs could call on support from the well-trained Yugoslav National Army (JNA),[2] while the Bosnian forces labored under the constraint of an international arms embargo.[3]

The resulting war was complex. In the east it was mainly marked by easy victories for the Serbs followed by massacres and ethnic cleansing. However, some towns such as Srebenica held out under siege as the Serbs lacked the manpower to actively prosecute their war. The prewar capital, Sarajevo, came under siege and also became

---

1   Alec Russell, "Unforgiven, unforgotten, unresolved: Bosnia 20 years on," Financial Times, 2012 https://www.ft.com/content/8a698dbe-73af-11e1-aab3-00144feab49a.

2   Since Serbia did not accept the breakup of the Yugoslav federation, the army retained its old title in this period.

3   Misha Glenny, The Fall of Yugoslavia (London: Penguin, 1996).

the focus of international attention. In the northeast, Bosnian Muslim forces attacked and overran predominantly Croat villages.[4] Equally it was not a simple ethnic struggle. Many Serbs identified more with the multiethnic, multicultural Bosnian Republic than with the purely Serbian statelet being carved out in the east.[5]

Across this mosaic, the west, in particular the EU and NATO, intervened ineffectively.[6] Both multinational organizations and individual states, such as the UK, were too accommodating to Serb demands for territorial and political adjustments. Not least to many military observers, the Serbs looked like a proper army as opposed to the militias they fought against.[7] Equally the west imposed an arms embargo soon after the conflict started, which tilted the balance on the battlefields towards the Serbs, as they could draw on the well-equipped, prewar Yugoslav army for weapons and ammunition. Finally, and depressingly, Western diplomacy became dominated by a desire to appease the Serb leader Slobodan Milošević[8] rather than deal with the root causes of the war driven by Milošević's use of Serb nationalism to create a basis for his own regime.

However, by 1994, the dynamics of the war started to shift. Pakistan began to openly supply the Bosnian army with some weapons at the same time as the Bosnians and Croats settled their differences in order to fight the Serbs. Then, after a series of massacres by Serb forces such as Srebrenica and around Sarajevo,[9] NATO formally intervened in 1995. By this time, the Serbs were already losing ground to their opponents. The end result was the Dayton Accords,[10] which effectively partitioned

---

4   Alan Taylor, "20 Years Since The Bosnian War," The Atlantic, 2012 http://www. theatlantic.com/photo/2012/04/20-years-since-the-bosnian-war/100278/.

5   Glenny, The Fall of Yugoslavia.

6   Simms, Unfinest Hour: Britain and the Destruction of Bosnia.

7   Russell, "Unforgiven, unforgotten, unresolved: Bosnia 20 years on".

8   Glenny, The Fall of Yugoslavia.

9   Simms, Unfinest Hour: Britain and the Destruction of Bosnia.

10   Sabrina P. Ramet, "Bosnia-Herzegovina since Dayton," in Bosnia-Herzegovina since Dayton: Civic and uncivic values, ed. Ola Listhaug and Sabrina P. Ramet (Ravenna: Angelo Longo Editore, 2013).

prewar Bosnia along ethnic lines, with an ethnic Serb enclave being created in the east of the old unitary province. With the end of fighting in Bosnia, attention turned to the long-running dispute in the majority Albanian province of Kosovo. Here the Serbs were in the minority and felt (with some reason) that they were being attacked by the Muslim majority. The demands for either independence or unity with Albania had begun soon after Tito's death, predating the wider Yugoslav conflicts by ten years. In the aftermath of Bosnia, the conflict in the province escalated, and by 1995 the Kosovo Liberation Army (KLA) was engaged in an armed revolt against the Serb administration.[11] However, outside attention was still focused on the conflict in Bosnia, and the KLA was widely held to engage in its own form of ethnic cleansing as and had strong ties to organized criminal networks.[12] This mirrored the close cooperation with organized criminal groups that had become normal in post-Tito Yugoslavia as states sought to evade sanctions by smuggling or by acquiring weapons. But the KLA in particular was seen by many observers to effectively be a criminal gang rather than an independence movement.

By 1998, the Serb crackdown on Muslims and Albanians had become so brutal as to demand international attention. Unlike in 1992, the new administrations in the United States and the UK were not prepared to stand aside (especially as the Serbian army was now clearly weakened by its defeats in Croatia and Bosnia) and were prepared to intervene militarily.[13] The result was a short NATO bombing campaign against Serb targets in Kosovo, across Serbia, and also the notionally neutral state of Montenegro, followed by a land invasion. By 2000, Kosovo emerged as an independent state dominated by ethnic Albanians, and most of the prewar Serbian population fled to Serbia following a series of riots and ethnic clashes after the KLA took power.

To many Salafists, the Balkan conflicts are an important source of their narrative of how the "West" persecutes Muslims. Equally, as we

11   Simms, *Unfinest Hour: Britain and the Destruction of Bosnia*.

12   Misha Glenny, *McMafia: Crime Without Frontiers* (London: Bodley Head, 2008).

13   Simms, *Unfinest Hour: Britain and the Destruction of Bosnia*.

will see, both in Bosnia, and less so in Kosovo, Salafist groups were very active,[14] gaining military training and developing the tactics learned against the Soviets in Afghanistan. However, while there is much to criticize in the Western response to the various Yugoslav conflicts in the 1990s, the reality does not fit a simple rendering of the view that the "West" attacks Islam. Perhaps ineffectively, and too slowly, NATO troops did indeed fight to protect Muslims both in Bosnia and Albania, and Western governments invested substantial amount of time in trying to resolve the wars. Equally postwar, the EU has become the major funder of reconstruction in both Bosnia and Kosovo.

ISLAM IN YUGOSLAVIA

The expanding Ottoman Empire gained its first European foothold in the 1350s. Over the next century it completed the conquest of Greece and Bulgaria, and by 1470 it had gained tentative control over Albania, Serbia, Croatia, and Bosnia, as well as expanding into Hungary. Over the next century, a series of revolts saw the Ottomans lose and then regain control. By the earlier 17th century, Ottoman expansion was checked by the rising powers of Hapsburg Austria and Poland while Hungary regained its independence. By the 1880s, Serbia, Bulgaria, and Greece had gained their independence, and Bosnia was occupied by the Austrians. Turkey lost its final Balkan provinces in the 1912–13 Balkan War.

Across this period there was no large-scale resettlement of the Balkans from elsewhere in the Ottoman Empire. The little that happened was around major garrison towns as the Ottomans tried to consolidate their control by encouraging retired soldiers to live near the barracks and form the backbone of a local defense force. For the most part, conversion to Islam was voluntary, and, at least when not dealing with

---

14   Gall, "How Kosovo was Turned into Fertile Ground for ISIS".

a revolt, Ottoman rule was tolerant of both Shi'a and Sunni Islam and other religions. People converted either to avoid taxation (which fell heavily on the Christian population), to gain advancement (some jobs were reserved for Muslims, and Muslims had preferential treatment in the courts), or for personal reasons.[15] The result was that by the 20th century the Muslim population in the Balkans did not constitute a separate ethnic group. The main areas of Islam were Bosnia (where the Muslim population shared the same south Slav ethnicity as their Serbian neighbors) and in Kosovo (which remained ethnically Albanian). Thus in Bosnia, Kosovo, and Albania, Sunni Islam became the majority religion.

The Ottoman conquest of the region was driven not by a desire to spread Islam but by the need to deal with threats to their borders, and in turn to threaten eastern and central Europe. As such, Islam in the region developed as a tolerant and open faith, and as Ottoman power waned, for all practical purposes there was very little difference between Christian and Muslim populations.

In Kosovo, however, there was a relatively close relationship between ethnicity and religion. The bulk of the majority Albanian population were Muslims, and the bulk of the Serb minority were Orthodox Christians. In Bosnia, in effect the distinction was one of religious background rather than ethnicity or, particularly, how religion affected daily life, clothing, eating, or drinking habits. Oddly it was Tito's regime that chose to link having a Muslim religious identity (or heritage) with being a distinct ethnic group[16] that formed one of the constituent republics of the Yugoslav Federation. In effect, in order to treat Bosnia as a distinct political unit, the regime had to conflate religion with ethnicity in a province where there were often few indicators in terms of social norms.

---

15   There were exceptions, such as the forced conversion of the population of the northern part of Albania in the 1600s, mainly in an attempt to end a regular sequence of revolts. The conversions were successful, but they made little difference in terms of stopping revolts in a region that prized its independence.

16   Gabriel Partos, "Bosnia's Islamic heritage," BBC, 2003 http://news.bbc.co.uk/1/hi/talking_point/3104130.stm.

THE MUSLIM POPULATION AND THE BALKAN WARS

I n effect by 1991, there were two major centers of Muslims in Yugoslavia. One group was spread across the provinces of Bosnia-Herzegovina, living in mixed towns and cities with an Orthodox Serb population in the east of the region and a Catholic Croat population in the west and north. The other was the largely ethnically Albanian population that dominated the province of Kosovo.

Typical of the former was the town of Visegrad overlooking the Drina River in the east. The prewar population of twenty-one thousand was made up of 63 percent Muslims and 33 percent Serbs.[17] The town had developed in the Ottoman era from a small village. While the Yugoslav state masked some enduring religious tensions, the practical reality was of a mixed community sharing common resources: "We (Serbs and Muslims) went to the same school together. We played football and basketball together. Right until the war, we were all Yugoslavs . . ."[18] The town's most famous landmark is an Ottoman-era bridge over the Drina River.

By July 1992 some two thousand of this prewar Muslim population had been slaughtered, and the remaining eleven thousand fled for their lives to regions still held by the Bosnian government. Here, the "war" had lasted for four days until the Yugoslav National Army had conquered the region. What then followed was typical of much of eastern Bosnia in 1992. Many Muslims returned to their homes when the fighting ended, trusting promises of the new regime. Slowly people disappeared, never to return once arrested. Their property stolen or destroyed. It was a conflict between people who had once been neighbors. Some of those who were killed were thrown from the famous Ottoman bridge. When a local reservoir was drained in 2010, two hundred sets of human remains were found on the lake bed. Elsewhere in eastern Bosnia, either due to geography or ethnic dominance, isolated towns resisted both the Yugoslav army and local

---

17   Russell, "Unforgiven, unforgotten, unresolved: Bosnia 20 years on".

18   Ibid.

Serb militias. The destruction of one of these enclaves, at Srebrenica, was probably the catalyst to forcing Western governments to intervene decisively against the Serbs.

During the war a number of religiously motivated fighters arrived,[19] and some married into the local community. This new influence, combined with the separation of the various communities during the war, has seen the emergence of a degree of religious conservatism as headscarves become more common and radicals challenge the traditional relaxed interpretation of Islam. Since Bosnia remains multicultural and could not survive as a Muslim-only state, this has only made limited impact, but the situation in Kosovo is different, as will be discussed later in this chapter.

In Kosovo, as noted above, there was a closer connection between religion and ethnicity. Most Albanians were Muslims, and most Serbs were Orthodox. However, as elsewhere in the region, the form of Sunni Islam left by the Ottomans was tolerant, and religion, as such, was not the source of conflict between Albanians and Serbs. However, postwar, Kosovo has followed a different trajectory from Bosnia, in part as the great majority of the Serb population fled to Serbia, properly leaving behind an essentially ethnically and religiously pure state. More importantly, unlike in Bosnia, the Saudis have become the major funder of reconstruction—and where the Saudis put their money, they also install their own Salafist creed.

POSTWAR SALAFIST INVOLVEMENT AND NARRATIVES
BOSNIA

P ostwar Bosnia has tried to retain its multicultural identity as it recovers from its war. It is clear that the traditional tolerant form of Islam has come under pressure, but broadly the state still defines itself as secular and nonsectarian. While the heavy involvement

---

19   Partos, "Bosnia's Islamic heritage".

of the Malaysian government in funding the training the postwar political elite has led to some problems,[20] on the whole, Salafism has not gained a foothold in Bosnian society. For the most part, despite the war, Bosnia's Muslim population remains pro-Western and at ease with combining their faith with an acceptance of globalization and non-Muslim practices. In part as this fits their historical background and in part as, for all its flaws, there is a widespread acknowledgement that it was Western pressure that preserved Bosnia from being dismembered between Serbia and Croatia.[21]

Although the general consensus is that Bosnia has not been receptive to militant Islam, there are still worrying trends. A "Mujahideen Battalion" drawn from various Arab countries had arrived to support the Bosnians in 1992.[22] They came to some prominence not in the fighting with the Serbs but in the vicious war in the northeast with the Croats, where they were often involved in ethnic cleansing as the Croats started to lose control. The battalion also tried to impose their version of Islam on the local Muslim population. Equally, they briefly engaged with the British force sent to maintain a fragile cease-fire in the region. By 1995, the unit was around fifteen hundred strong, but they were under pressure not just from UN peacekeepers but also the Bosnian government, which was concerned about their brutality.[23] Equally many other Bosnian soldiers were repelled by their brutality and fanaticism, as one recalled:

I remember the Mujahideen were there but we all kept very far away [from them]. . . . It was unnatural, they prayed before an attack that they would die. . . . They wanted death for Allah.

---

20 Nazry Bahrawi, "Is Bosnian Islam going the way of Malaysia?," The Guardian, 2010 https://www.theguardian.com/commentisfree/belief/2010/oct/05/bosnian-islam-malaysia.

21 Ahmet Alibašić, "Globalisation and its impact on Bosnian Muslims practices" (paper presented at the Democracy and Global Islam, UC Berkeley, 2005).

22 Mark Urban, "Bosnia: The cradle of modern jihadism?," BBC, 2015 http://www.bbc.co.uk/news/world-europe-33345618.

23 The leader of the local Bosnian forces, Enver Hadzihasanovic, was later convicted at the Hague for crimes committed by the foreign fighters when they were under his notional command.

We were scared. None of us wanted death and none of us wanted anything to do with those fanatics.[24]

Most left Bosnia after the Dayton Accords, although a few remained, having married into the local communities. Those who left went to fight "jihad" in Chechnya, Pakistan, and Afghanistan, while two of the 9/11 hijackers had previously fought in Bosnia. Though they left a legacy of local Salafist adherents, who have subsequently gone to fight in Syria, in general their influence in contemporary Bosnia is limited. There have been regular reports of Islamist training camps in the country, and individuals associated with the extremists have carried out a number of attacks on the Serbs,[25] which is still worrying. However, to many Bosnians, Muslim or not, the extremists are alien and a major threat to the slow process of reconciliation and rebuilding.

More than the domestic impact of the mujahedeen, the importance of the Bosnian war lies in the realm of ideology and practice. Along with Afghanistan, Bosnia set the template for international jihad, the idea that devout Muslims should move to any region where Muslims are under attack and become mujahedeen. That the locals rarely appreciated their help, or that the UN, in the end, did more to protect the Muslim population than these fighters ever did, is readily forgotten in the Salafist narrative.

KOSOVO

If Bosnia has emerged from the war with its traditional form of Islam more or less intact, the same cannot be said for Kosovo. There are three reasons for this, and all point to the real problem of Saudi influence and what happens once Salafism is normalized:

---

24 Denis Dzidic, "Bosnia's Wartime Legacy Fuels Radical Islam," Balkan Transitional Justice, 2015 http://www.balkaninsight.com/en/article/bosnia-s-wartime-legacy-fuels-radical-islam.

25 Ibid.

1. First and foremost, postwar funding in Bosnia has come from a variety of sources, including Muslim countries, but in Kosovo, the Saudis have provided the bulk of the reconstruction funding;

2. In Kosovo, the war saw the flight of the Serb minority, leaving an ethnically and religiously pure state. Also, whereas many in Bosnia felt they were fighting for the Yugoslav ideal of a multi-confessional, multiethnic polity, in Kosovo it was mostly a struggle between Albanians and Serbs;

3. For all its weaknesses, the postwar Bosnian state could draw on a prewar infrastructure for security and rebuilding key social systems. In Kosovo, the expertise for this left when the Serb population fled, leaving a very weak state structure behind.

Of these three reasons, perhaps the critical issue is that it has been the Saudis, not Malaysians, who choose to use Bosnia as an example of its own willingness to help other Muslim states, having been the main external funder of reconstruction.[26] The consequences show up all the complexities of their involvement.[27] When the Saudis funded Wahhabist mosques in Kosovo, they undermined a traditionally tolerant religious region into one with a significant Salafist problem. However, in a twist of irony, the young Kosovars now fighting for ISIS either in Syria or at home are also a threat to the Saudis. The final chapter will explore this dilemma in more detail, but it is instructive to see how their investment in postwar Kosovo has been linked to the growth of Salafism. And this, in a country that in 2000 was so pro-American that it has a Bill Clinton Boulevard in its capital, Pristina.

The Saudi-funded mosques may teach their preferred "quietist" version of Salafism,[28] and, as we saw in the Belgian study, many who adopt

---

26   Gall, "How Kosovo was Turned into Fertile Ground for ISIS".

27   Scott Shane, "Saudis and Extremism: 'Both the Arsonists and the Firefighters'," *New York Times*, 2016 http://www.nytimes.com/2016/08/26/world/middleeast/saudi-arabia-islam.html?_r=0.

28   Ibid.

this are content to see it as a framework for their own lives. But it still excludes other forms of Islam and sees non-Muslims as a significant threat instead of simply people of a different faith. It is not a long step from that to involvement in more radical movements. And those who make this final step tend to be self-taught but are able to exist in the shadow of official Saudi mosques. In effect, Kosovo is now a case study for how Saudi funding leads to religious intolerance and then to the growth of militant Islamic terrorism. As in regions such as Indonesia, the arrival of Saudi funding leads to predictable consequences—a breakdown of traditions of tolerance and an increase in the numbers of people prepared to use violence to ensure there is no coexistence with those of different faiths or interpretations of Islam.

By comparing the continuation of the traditional, moderate Islam in Bosnia with the rise of Salafism in Kosovo, the role played by Saudi funding becomes clear. While Bosnia has seen around 90 individuals go to fight for ISIS, it is estimated that 314 from Kosovo have done so (including 44 women and 28 children).[29] This indicates that Kosovo has produced the highest number of recruits per capita from the whole of Europe. By 2016, the Kosovar authorities had become worried enough to start closing down suspected Salafist networks, especially those suspected of recruiting for ISIS. However, this response is hampered due to the expansion of Saudi influence. Some 240 mosques[30] have been built since 2000, all with Saudi money and, of course, all staffed with Saudi-trained imams well versed in the tenets of Wahhabism. As a result, younger Kosovars are turning against the Islam of their parents as they amend their behavior to fit with the exclusionary beliefs of Salafism. While most, as elsewhere, see this as a personal choice and a means to live their lives, for some there is a short step from seeing others as less worthy to being willing to use violence against those "others."

When Kosovo was still part of Communist Yugoslavia, Islam was tolerated as a signifier of ethnicity or parentage rather than as an active belief system. Education was coeducational, and, as elsewhere, in terms

---

29   Gall, "How Kosovo was Turned into Fertile Ground for ISIS".

30   In part replacing the two hundred or so burned down by the Serbs in the period 1996–1999.

of behavior there was relatively little to distinguish between Muslims and non-Muslims. The new state was determined to both rebuild what had been recently destroyed and to allow an expansion of Muslim identity to help forge a new society. Unfortunately the bulk of the help both to fund mosques and to provide teachers came from the Saudis. In Kosovo, the Saudis have not just built, they have also destroyed.[31]

Buildings and mosques associated with traditional Albanian Islam have been demolished. This onslaught has particularly targeted remnants of the Sufi and Dervish traditions, both seen as unacceptable from a Wahhabist perspective. In particular, shrines where people would go to pray have been destroyed as the new religious authorities try to break links to the past. Equally families that have accepted funding and welfare from the new mosques have had to adapt their lifestyles. Gender segregation and the veil have become common as Kosovo's former traditions have come under pressure. Violence has also been a feature, with attacks on imams who persist in teaching the traditional model of Islam.

The authorities in Kosovo were informed about the consequences, but the need for funding, as well as the desire to forge a new post-Yugoslav identity, required warnings, such as that by Richard Holbrooke in 2003[32] that they should not work with the Saudi Joint Relief Committee for Kosovo.[33] If this had the effect of partly reducing Saudi funding, the next wave of mosques was funded by Kuwait, Qatar, and the United Arab Emirates to the tune of €1 million a year to promote Wahhabism. There was no way local Kosovar imams could compete, financially or ideologically.

Adding to the problem in Kosovo is the fact that post–1999 it has become a single ethnic-state. Indeed while many in Bosnia fought to preserve some aspect of a "Yugoslav" identity, the KLA was open in seeking to drive the small Serb minority from the province. There is ample evidence that the KLA did not just engage in organized crime

---

31   Gall, "How Kosovo was Turned into Fertile Ground for ISIS".

32   Holbrooke had been the US special envoy to the Balkans and heavily involved in both the Dayton Accords and negotiating the end of the Kosovo war.

33   Gall, "How Kosovo was Turned into Fertile Ground for ISIS".

(including the drugs trade) to fund its revolt but was also involved in sustained human rights abuses—including organ trafficking[34]—aimed at the Serb population.

As the Serbs fled in 1999, they took with them most of the technical expertise needed to run the region. This followed the systemic removal of ethnic Albanians from public service jobs in the 1980s. Both left a vacuum of expertise and manpower. The pragmatic decision by the West to install the KLA as the new government might have been understandable, but it effectively handed over the province to a Mafia-like criminal gang.[35]

SIMILARITIES AND DIFFERENCES

I t is instructive to compare the dynamics of Bosnia and Kosovo, as there are some important lessons to be learned. In the end, Bosnia has managed to retain much of its multiethnic makeup and tradition of a tolerant brand of Islam. Kosovo, however, has become an Albanian state, and its traditional model of Islam is under sustained threat as Salafism becomes adopted by many of the young.

Both states faced a sustained, murderous attack by a Serbian leadership that aimed at ethnic cleansing. While this leadership also fought against Croats over territory, their main obsession in Bosnia and Kosovo was to destroy what they saw as the threat posed by Islam.

During the war, Bosnia received some help from Muslim states, especially Pakistan, while Malaysia has had an important role in educating the new postwar Bosnian elite. In addition, as we have seen, it was host to a small but violent cadre of international jihadists. During

34 Paul Lewis, "Kosovo PM is head of human organ and arms ring, Council of Europe reports" The Guardian, 2010 https://www.theguardian.com/world/2010/dec/14/kosovo-prime-minister-llike-mafia-boss.

35 Chuck Sudetic, "The bullies who run Kosovo," Politico, 2015 http://www.politico.eu/article/kosovo-hashim-thaci-un-special-court-tribunal-organ-trafficking-kla-serbia-milosevic-serbia-ramush/.

its struggle, Kosovo received relatively little outside help, in part due to its relative isolation. In the end, the Serbs lost because NATO, especially the United States and the UK, decided to back the KLA,[36] first by airpower and then by a land invasion. Postwar, NATO departed, and Kosovo has since been the recipient of much aid from Saudi Arabia and its Gulf State allies.

This was the turning point for Kosovo. Yes, Bosnia emerged with the remnants of a viable civil society and state structures, and yes, some of the new generation of Bosnian leaders have adopted a more radical form of Islam than their parents. But in the end, Bosnia has largely been rebuilt by EU and UN funding. Meanwhile, in Kosovo, Saudis rebuilt mosques and sent teachers and imams in droves, and the results are thus predictable. Salafism has gained a strong grip, and the Saudi funded mosques are quite deliberately trying to squeeze out the remnants of the older Islamic traditions. Bosnia has a problem with Salafism creating extremism—as do many countries—but it is not becoming dominant. In part this is a matter of political will; most Bosnian officials and politicians want to retain a multiethnic, multi-confessional state. It is also practical, as even now only 55 percent of Bosnians are Muslims—allowing the Salafists to gain influence would make not only other Muslims but also the large remaining Croat and Serb populations feel threatened. For a country dependent on EU funding, this is not a feasible social choice.

THE SALAFIST INTERPRETATION

In the Salafist worldview, however, Bosnia in particular offers a number of diametrically opposed lessons. First it indicates that Muslims are always under threat when they live as part of other communities. If the well-integrated Muslim community in Bosnia could find itself facing genocide, then surely the threat applies anywhere else. In

---

36   Simms, *Unfinest Hour: Britain and the Destruction of Bosnia.*

effect, being open as a community is, to the Salafists, no guarantee of safety even as you risk diluting the essentials of your faith. So the fate of the thousands of Bosnian Muslims between 1992 and 1995 stands as a stark warning of the risks of trusting your non-Muslim neighbors.

Second, Bosnia was the second opportunity to practice jihad in a foreign country. By 1992, the Soviets had long gone from Afghanistan, and their client state was on the verge of collapse. Chechnya offered an opportunity to fight for Islam but was hard to reach, and the Chechens were not particularly welcoming of outsiders. Bosnia needed weapons and manpower and was relatively easy to reach. The result was a generation of European and Arab jihadists who went to fight. If they did not leave the long-term mark they managed in Afghanistan, the Balkans provided a second opportunity to test out the process of both fighting in a different country and how to use the example of their militancy to change their host society.

In Bosnia, they largely failed, while, ironically, in Kosovo—where Salafism took stronger root—there were very few foreign fighters. However, both struggles are also often cited as examples of how the West attacks Muslims and fails to protect them. While it is easy to be critical of Western efforts to protect Bosnia, the reality is the Salafist narrative is simply untrue. In both regions, the "West"—whether defined as the UN, the EU, NATO, or the United States—committed substantial efforts to protect the Muslim population. In the end, the reason the Serbian genocide failed was Western support for the Bosnian government—belated, flawed, sometimes halfhearted, but there nonetheless. Equally in Kosovo, it was NATO's decision to intervene, first with airpower and then with a ground invasion that ended the Serbian attacks on the Albanian majority.

Instead, as I will argue in the final chapter, the real lesson is the risk that allowing Salafism to be unchecked *after* the initial war was over is exemplified in the problems of contemporary Kosovo. As we have noted, most Salafists simply wish to live by a set of tenets they believe reflect the original purity of Islam. That they are wrong in their interpretation of this purity is important, as these seemingly academic and theological errors create fractures in a society, which then open the door to far more radical actions.

PART SEVEN
IRAQ AND SYRIA

I n a way, the events in the former Yugoslavia can be seen as a staging post and testing ground for violent Salafists and their doctrine of violent jihad. To them, events in Bosnia and Kosovo provided evidence that Muslims can never be safe unless they live in a country they control. If the largely secular, well-integrated, Muslim communities of Bosnia could be massacred and driven from their homes in a few short months, then the threat must apply to all. For those who wished to wage violent jihad, Bosnia was also a useful staging post. While the numbers involved were always small, a generation of Salafists did go and fight, creating further evidence for the view that there was a duty to "protect Muslims" in any country where they were threatened.

However, in terms of practical impact, their intervention in the former Yugoslavia has been limited. As we have seen, in Bosnia they were left as a marginalized group with little popular appeal. In Kosovo, Salafism and Wahhabism has made more inroads—primarily due to the effects of Saudi funding post-conflict rather than the actions of those seeking to fight in the global jihad. By 2000, for Salafists, there were plenty of sources of discontent—the enduring treatment of the Palestinians, the poor standard of governance across the Arab world—and a ready ideology in the form of Al-Qaeda's interpretation of Wahhabism, but there was a lack of places to put it all into practice.

The US-led invasions of Afghanistan and Iraq after 9/11 changed this. To Salafists, both were examples again of the "West" attacking Muslims. This provided useful confirmation for their ideological model but left them the problem of how to react. In Afghanistan, for practical purposes, Al-Qaeda lost its safe base. Though it was able to re-create itself across the border in Pakistan, it also became isolated from its other "franchises," and thus the new war against the Americans and their allies was mostly fought by native Afghans rather than a recreation of the diaspora of international jihadists who had turned up to fight the Soviets.

Equally in Iraq, the initial violent response to the US occupation came from a disparate collection of local groups. The Shi'a communities took the fall of Saddam Hussein as an indication that they could now dominate the country. Backed by Iran, they commenced a campaign of violence from Baghdad to the south. The Sunni response was initially filtered through the old Ba'ath Party, particularly once the US administration disbanded the army and removed any party member from the civil administration. Over time, the Sunni response split into three main groups. Al-Qaeda established a formidable presence in the country and drew in numerous jihadists to fight. A number of tribal groupings found themselves at odds with the new Shi'a-dominated administration and with Al-Qaeda. Finally the old Ba'ath Party created its own resistance.

This led to a substantial US response between 2007–08 that effectively co-opted the tribal groups against Al-Qaeda and saw a significant defeat for the organization. Al-Qaeda's leadership tried to learn lessons from this: a key issue was that they felt their campaign, and the rule they imposed on controlled areas, had effectively alienated almost all potential allies. This led to a focus of working with any Salafist-inclined group in pursuit of a particular struggle—something that now marks their approach in Syria and elsewhere. However, Al-Qaeda's Iraqi (AQI) franchise already had a difficult relationship with the international leadership,[1] and this revision of tactics sat badly with AQI's own focus on a sectarian war aimed at Iraq's Shi'a majority and any Sunni groups that stood against them. Equally there is now little doubt that at this stage the old Ba'ath security apparatus in effect joined with the notionally religiously inspired militants.[2] If we see Al-Qaeda as an essentially religious organization, this alliance (which appears at times to be fractious and at others very close) with a secular political party may

1   Daniel L. Byman and Jennifer R. Williams, "ISIS vs. Al-Qaeda: Jihadism's global civil war," Brookings Institute, 2015 https://www.brookings.edu/articles/isis-vs-al-qaeda-jihadisms-global-civil-war/.

2   Isabel Coles and Ned Parker, "How Saddam's men help Islamic State rule," Reuters, 2015 http://www.reuters.com/investigates/special-report/mideast-crisis-iraq-islamicstate/.

seem odd. However, AQI always had seen Iraq's Shi'a as the enemy, a view readily shared with the hardened killers of the Ba'ath.

By 2011, AQI was increasingly ignoring Al-Qaeda's international leadership and by 2013 was in outright revolt as it branded itself the "Islamic State of Iraq and Syria."[3] The catalyst had been its initial move into Syria when there was already an Al-Qaeda franchise (Jabhat Al-Nusra) operating in that country. Its initial intervention ended in defeat, but by mid-2013 ISIS had seized Raqqa while Al-Nusra (the official Al-Qaeda franchise in Syria) and the Free Syrian Army were occupied in fighting forces loyal to the Assad regime. This not only cemented the break from Al-Qaeda, it also led to militant Salafism being split between three very different goals:

1. Al-Qaeda itself still argued that the United States (the "far enemy") was the primary enemy and was increasingly trying to build tactical alliances with other Islamist forces. It was also reducing its sectarian attacks on other Muslims as it absorbed what it saw as the main lesson of its defeat in Iraq in 2007–8;

2. The newly named ISIS sought regional domination with a primary focus on destroying the local regimes but with a fundamental goal of establishing its power over a defined block of territory. However, the lesson it drew from 2007–8 was one of betrayal by its notional allies. Thus it set out to purify regions it captured of both non-Muslims and any other organized force. While the difference to Al-Qaeda is important, it should be seen as a matter of initial focus, not of long-term differences. Al-Qaeda seeks to intervene in any conflict involving Sunni Islam, and ISIS has since built its own international franchise and managed to organize attacks in the United States and across Western Europe;

---

3   Ibrahim, "The Resurgence of Al-Qaeda in Syria and Iraq."

3. Finally, a disparate but important strand of Salafist militancy emerged that focused on national struggles aiming to change the governance of a particular state. In Syria these groups argue they wish to see a religiously led government where, as long as Islam rules, there can be space for a degree of democracy and other religious beliefs. In a way, they aim for something close to the Islamic Republic in Iran, which is ironic, given they are mostly fighting against Shi'a-dominated regimes.

What ties these three seemingly items together is a fourth point: Syria has reinforced the notion of international jihad. In the period 2011–2015 it was relatively easy to enter (and leave) the country through a complicit Turkey, and a large number of foreign jihadists went to fight for one or the other factions. This has left the militant wings of Salafism in some confusion as to who is the real enemy and the appropriate tactics to use (especially towards those whom Salafists regard as apostates), in addition to a split between two international "franchises"[4] while a large number of groups have really focused on their own local struggles. How these dynamics are evolving is the focus of this chapter. However, even as we explore how Wahhabist-inspired militancy is changing, it is useful to bear in mind that the underlying ideology is similar for each faction.

However, if first Iraq and then Syria have become the destination of choice for those looking to fight international jihad, we should bear in mind we are mostly looking at the actions of those Salafists who have decided to embrace violence—either to carry it out or fully support those who do. Some have also gone especially to Syria to live in what they believe is a pure state without the threat of contamination from outsiders. Thus in terms of the earlier discussions, we are looking at the actions of the few who have moved beyond seeing Salafism as the basis for their own lives to those who wish, violently, to impose it on all.

---

4   Byman and Williams, "ISIS vs. Al-Qaeda: Jihadism's global civil war".

SALAFISM IN IRAQ

U p to his defeat in the Second Gulf War[5] in 1991, Saddam Hussein's regime was notionally secular, socialist and pan-Arabist in line with Ba'ath ideology. In reality it carried all these labels lightly, being primarily a deeply authoritarian regime supporting his personal rule. It had split radically from its notionally sister regime in Syria and was not especially pro-Soviet (not least as it had suppressed the powerful Iraqi Communist Party after Saddam came to power in 1979–80), and its commitment to pan-Arabism was limited. His army used Western- as well as Soviet-supplied equipment (in fact he relied more on the West to fund his war with Iran than the Soviets). Equally Iraq did not fund any major faction in the Palestinian movement and was involved with small violent extremist groups but not to the extent that Syria or Libya sponsored such groups. Although the core of his power lay in his own tribal clan from Tikrit, his regime included Christians in prominent positions. Equally, during the long war with Iran, there was no substantial evidence of Iraqi Shi'a opposition to being expected to fight their Iranian coreligionists.

However, after his defeat following the invasion of Kuwait in 1990–1, Hussein started to stress his commitment to Sunni Islam. The period 1991–2001 saw a major program of mosque building, most notoriously the Mother of All Battles Mosque in Baghdad, built to underline Hussein's newfound religious devotion and to celebrate his resistance to the West in the period after his defeat in Kuwait.[6] Equally while his regime continued to have senior Christian members, the revolts in the south, and by the Kurds after his defeat in 1991, removed most support from the majority Shi'a population. In turn this helped cement his turn to some degree of Sunni Islam, as he wished to

---

5   For convenience I am treating the Iran-Iraq war between 1980 and 1988 as the First Gulf War.

6   Philip Smucker, "Iraq builds 'Mother of all Battles' mosque in praise of Saddam," The Telegraph, 2001 http://www.telegraph.co.uk/news/worldnews/middleeast/iraq/1335735/Iraq-builds-Mother-of-all-Battles-mosque-in-praise-of-Saddam.html.

consolidate regime support in at least one potentially loyal constituent part of Iraqi society.

In consequence, emphasizing his devotion to Sunni Islam was, to most observers, simply an attempt to shore up waning support for his regime. Certainly any clerics who failed to toe the Ba'ath-approved line were removed from post or murdered. As such the country was closed to Al-Qaeda even if by 2003 Osama bin Laden was calling on his supporters to support the regime, as "under these circumstances, there will be no harm if the interests of Muslims converge with the interests of the socialists in the fight against the crusaders, despite our belief in the infidelity of socialists."[7]

To the Salafist movement, the main role of Iraq at this period was to demonstrate the cruelties inflicted on Muslims by the West. US-sponsored sanctions slowed any recovery from the fighting, and food and medicines were under embargo under the guise of preventing Hussein from rebuilding his store of weapons. By 1995 it was estimated that 576,000 Iraqi children had died as a result of sanctions[8] as Iraq's previously effective health and social care systems collapsed. There was some relaxation of sanctions as a result, but it is feasible that over one million Iraqis died between 1991 and 2003 simply due to the West's desire to punish Hussein. All this was readily recycled by the Salafist groups as evidence for their worldview and their criticism that the "West" was a permanent threat to any Muslim.

The Anglo-American invasion in 2003, and the mismanaged postwar policies, made Iraq into the destination of choice for anybody who wanted to fight jihad.[9] From this perspective, by 2005, the country was almost perfect. The Sunni community was completely alienated, in part by being stripped of their jobs but also by the new dominance of the Shi'a majority. Practical governance had broken down, and there was no meaningful postwar reconstruction. Finally Iraq contained

---

7   BBC News, "Bin Laden tape: Text," BBC, 2003 http://news.bbc.co.uk/1/hi/world/middle_east/2751019.stm.

8   Barbara Crossette, "Iraq Sanctions Kill Children, U.N. Reports," *New York Times*, 1995 http://www.nytimes.com/1995/12/01/world/iraq-sanctions-kill-children-un-reports.html.

9   Ibrahim, "The Resurgence of Al-Qaeda in Syria and Iraq."

both a sectarian foe (the Shi'a community) and substantial numbers of American targets.

The emergence of Al-Qaeda in Iraq (AQI) can in many ways be seen as an exemplar, both as to the background of those who shift to violent jihad and the disputes present even among the most radical of Salafist movements.[10]

What was to become AQI, and then, from there, morph into ISIS, actually emerged in Jordan in the 1990s led by Abu Musab al-Zarqawi. By his mid-teens he had dropped out of school and was involved in drug dealing and petty violence. He was sent to prison for these crimes until 1988, when he was released. In jail he became involved with radical Islamists and after his release went to Afghanistan, returning to Jordan in 1992. As we have seen earlier, this is a typical route to violent jihad. In effect, a nonreligious young man who wishes to use violence against those he blames for his immediate problems found it easy to be absorbed into the world of violent Salafism. He was again arrested after organizing a failed suicide bombing. This time he spent his stay in prison issuing a series of messages and pamphlets calling for violent jihad, alienating other Salafists in the process,[11] especially those who saw themselves as having a religious education and orientation. Released again in 2001, Zarqawi returned to Afghanistan, where he met bin Laden. Reports suggest they disagreed about the focus of Salafist violence (Zarqawi wanted to focus on the Jordanian monarchy and a sectarian war against the Shi'a) and of the value of cooperation with other radical Islamist groups.

After the US invasion of Afghanistan, Zarqawi fled via Iran to Syria and then arrived in Iraq in 2002. Here he was able to create the nucleus of an Al-Qaeda network. The US-led invasion lifted the constraint on the group from Saddam's regime, and it quickly emerged as one of the most violent parts of the anti-US opposition. From the start its tactics differed from those preferred by Al-Qaeda's international leadership; their tactics also shaped AQI from its foundation to the current Islamic

---

10   MJ Kirdar, "Al-Qaeda in Iraq," (Washington: Center for Strategic and International Studies, 2011).

11   Ibid.

State. Very early on, the use of public beheadings, filmed and placed on the Internet,[12] was adopted along with that of suicide bombing.

As we have seen earlier, the latter came into the world of Islamist militancy via the tactics of the Shi'a Amal militia and then Hizbollah in Lebanon in the 1980s. However, here it was used against specific targets and as one of the options available to the group. The second Palestinian Intifada saw more widespread use, especially once Hamas became a major force in Palestinian politics.[13] To AQI, it became a tactic of choice. Infiltrating suicide bombers into large crowds was an easy way to kill large numbers of Zarqawi's real enemy—the Shi'a population—even if it was relatively ineffective against the US armed forces.

By 2006, AQI had diverged from Al-Qaeda both over tactics and targets. The international group still saw the Americans (the "far enemy") as the real foe and was increasingly prepared to work with any Salafist-inclined group. AQI, however, saw the local regimes, especially in Iraq and Jordan, as the true enemy (i.e., the "near enemy") and believed that other Sunni groups (whether Salafist or not) were foes and competitors; AQI attacked the Shi'a population and religious shrines with the goal of inciting civil war.[14] The result was to erode wider Sunni support for the organization—something that catalyzed around the large number of non-Iraqis who were fighting for AQI.

As we have seen, going to fight "jihad" has become one of the marks of Salafist militancy. However, unlike the situation in Syria since 2012, the great majority of those who went to Iraq in this period came from other Arab countries. Between April and October 2005, the United States reported they had captured 311 foreign fighters and all but six came from Arab countries (Egypt, Syria, and Saudi Arabia accounted for 60 percent).[15] However, this cadre of foreign fighters was resented

---

12   Douglas Jehl, "C.I.A. Says Berg's Killer Was Very Probably Zarqawi," *The New York Times*, 2004 http://www.nytimes.com/2004/05/14/world/struggle-for-iraq-beheader-cia-says-berg-s-killer-was-very-probably-zarqawi.html.

13   BBC News, "Analysis: Palestinian suicide attacks," BBC, 2007 http://news.bbc.co.uk/1/hi/world/middle_east/3256858.stm.

14   Kirdar, "Al-Qaeda in Iraq."

15   Alan B. Krueger, "The National Origins of Foreign Fighters in Iraq," (NBER, 2006).

by other Iraqi Sunni groups due to their violence, religious extremism, and lack of links within Iraqi society.

The backlash against AQI's extreme sectarian violence reached a height after the group bombed hotels in Jordan, killing sixty people attending wedding parties,[16] in late 2005. In response Zarqawi stood back from public leadership, and the group tried to emphasize its Iraqi base by rebranding itself as the Islamic State of Iraq.[17] Zarqawi himself was killed in a US airstrike in June 2006. His death did not change either the tactics or goals of the group, and this led to a growing revolt against AQI from the wider Sunni community. Between 2006 and 2011 the group lost momentum as it was marginalized and each generation of its leadership was killed by either the Iraqi state or US forces.

The US withdrawal in 2012 provided the space for it to recover. Its primary target remained the Shi'a population and Prime Minister Nouri al-Maliki's corrupt, Shi'a-dominated government[18] as it was able to take advantage of ongoing Sunni alienation. However, it was the descent of Syria into civil war from 2012[19] that created the circumstances for AQI to shift to ISIS and take on its current form.

In effect, Iraq offers a further step in the development of Salafist militancy. The background of Zarqawi is typical of many violent jihadists. There is little evidence that he was particularly religious before being jailed for petty crime. Equally, he never really developed a religious rationale for his violence and, conveniently for him, found that his version of Salafism identified two groups—the Shi'a and the Jordanian regime—as the real enemy, usefully fitting to his existing prejudices. Additionally, although AQI used the usual religious language of Salafism, it readily found a place in its ranks for ex-members of the Ba'ath Party looking to fight against the new Shi'a regime in Iraq.

---

16   Kirdar, "Al-Qaeda in Iraq."

17   All the evidence is that initially this was a false front for the group. However, it
      continued to diverge from Al-Qaeda's formal leadership, and by 2010 the group
      probably had become more Iraqi—not least due to the growing role of Saddam's old
      security police.

18   Ibrahim, "The Resurgence of Al-Qaeda in Syria and Iraq."

19   EU, "Syria crisis," (Brussels: European Union, 2016).

Again, we see the repetition of the idea of an international jihad, which had dominated the Salafist interpretation of their war in Afghanistan and had been a small feature of the wars in Bosnia. However, Iraq drew in Salafist militants from across the Arab world for the very first time.

The experience of AQI shows us some of the main divergent trends even among the most violent of Salafist groups. Within Iraq, it clashed with other Sunni militant groups that were focused essentially on the future governance of Iraq. Internationally it diverged from Al-Qaeda both in focus (it saw the real enemy as the Shi'a and local regimes, not really the United States) and tactics (AQI focused on sectarian attacks and other Sunni groups while Al-Qaeda was interested in making alliances where it could). If we now associate ISIS with a global set of Islamist attacks, this was not true before 2012—up to that stage the group only operated in Iraq and Jordan and had a very limited presence in nearby Lebanon.

SALAFISM IN SYRIA

B y mid-2012, Syria was suffering from what the Red Cross declared to be a civil war. This in turn created a new conflict where Salafism could take root. Historically Sunni militancy in Syria had been organized by the Muslim Brotherhood, which had led to the failed uprising in Homs in 1992.[20] However, while brutal and corrupt, the Assad regime was not particularly sectarian. Its core was dominated by the Shi'a Alawite community, but it contained many Sunnis and Christians in senior military and civil positions and staffing the military, police, and civil authorities. In a reverse of Iraq, in Syria the Sunni population was in the majority but partly marginalized by a Shi'a-led state. Aware of this, the Ba'ath regime took care to ensure that jobs were given to the Sunni community in order to bind them to the existing order.

---

20   Fisk, *Pity the Nation: Lebanon at War.*

Thus the initial revolt was also nonsectarian (even if it was Sunni dominated), and the initial armed resistance to Assad was mostly by deserters from the Syrian army. The latter were increasingly armed by Saudi Arabia and the Gulf States and, by August 2012, appeared to threaten the survival of the regime. This led to a shift in the nature of the war as first Iran stepped up its support for Assad (and Hizbollah sent fighters to Syria) and the opposition fragmented along regional and confessional lines (as well as in terms of their external sponsor). This led to four broad groups emerging, all opposed to Assad but equally looking to gain ground at the expense of the others. For the purpose of this book we can ignore the essentially ethnic Kurdish factions and the now mostly irrelevant Free Syrian Army (FSA). But even so, by 2013, Syrian had two major Salafist insurgent groups, and the differences between them are indicative of wider dynamics in the Salafist community.

SALAFIST GROUPS NOT ALIGNED TO AL-QAEDA

One element is a complex (and shifting) set of groups, mostly very local in their affiliation, which organized themselves collectively, first as the Islamic Alliance and later as the Islamic Front. In this guise they have been the main recipients of Saudi and Gulf State funding. Ideologically they offer a spread, from groups the United States has described as terrorists to groups that the United States, UK, and other Western powers are prepared to fund and support. Their relative power comes from the population they can control, as well as their ability to acquire weapons and control flows of funding and food. To some observers they carry a light baggage as far as ideology and religion, with a focus on control of territory and wealth (which, in a war zone, includes weaponry). This is probably too simplistic, but it does capture the range of groups that are notionally Salafist in orientation and their divergent goals.

The Islamic Front brought together a range of groups including Ahrar al-Shaam (with a typlical jihadi-Salafi inclination), Suqur al-Shaam and Liwa' al-Tawhid (both with roots in the older Muslim Brotherhood), Jaish al-Islam (Salafi and former Muslim Brotherhood members with substantial Saudi connections), and others. In turn, some of the groups in the alliance, such as Liwa al-Islam, are a coalition themselves—in this case, about fifty groups involved in the fighting around Damascus, and each with their own areas of geographical control. Equally these groups gain and lose strength according to the shifts on the battlefield or funding. The death of an important leader can trigger a collapse as fighters move to a group they believe to be more effective or as other groups seek to grab territory and wealth.[21] Equally each such death, and subsequent splits, sees a reorientation of groups in terms of their commitment to a hard-line or pragmatic interpretation of Salafist beliefs.

Even at the level of notional war aims, these groups have differing goals. Though most reject the original aim of the Syrian revolt to create a secular democratic republic, they differ in other important respects. For example, Liwa al-Islam has close Saudi links, and its leader has spoken of reviving the Omayyad Empire of the 7th and 8th centuries and creating an Islamic state ruled by scholars and jurists. For all practical purposes, their goals are the same as Al-Qaeda's, and the only differences are focus and immediate priorities. In particular, like most other domestic Syrian Salafist groups, they have expressed no interest in carrying out attacks outside Syria (and they probably have no capacity to as well). By contrast, the group Liwa al-Yarmouk is based in the south of Syria, notionally still part of the FSA structures, and has rejected calls for a clearly Islamist constitution for Syria despite sharing other aspects of the Salafist belief system.

By 2013, the Islamic Front had developed a broad set of proposals for the future organization of Syria.[22] This includes the replacement of the Assad regime with an Islamic state but one that will protect the rights of minorities. Their approach calls for a Sunni theocracy

---

21 Aron Lund, "Divided, they may fall," Carnegie Middle East Center, 2016 http://carnegie-mec.org/diwan/66413.

22 ———, "Syria's Salafi Insurgents: The Rise of the Syrian Islamic Front," (Stockholm: Swedish Institute of International Affairs, 2013).

where Sharia law is dominant. At this fundamental level, their vision for Syria is not a democracy, as Sharia is not subject to debate by men. However, they have indicated that:

> We separate between voting to select the best among candidates, and voting on the sovereignty [*hakimiya*] of Sharia; the first is acceptable to us, as long as it is regulated by the Sharia, but the second is of course not acceptable. However, as long as elections serve to choose between candidates who recognize the sovereignty of Sharia and its hegemony over the state, then we don't see a problem with that.[23]

In truth this is little but a common argument among Salafist groups as to their preferred form of governance. In many ways their ideal mimics the constitution of the Shi'a Islamic Republic of Iran, where certain roles are retained for those with the appropriate religious credentials and the scope of the conventional democratic system is curtailed. The Islamic Front has made its disdain for democracy and secularism very clear, which is heading for "the garbage heap of history." In reality it is feasible to divide the Syrian Salafist groups (and fighters) into two broad sections. One section has had experience of Salafist beliefs (and armed jihad) outside Syria and accepts the broad arguments of mainstream Salafism. In a way this is clearly reflected in the notional political program of the Islamic Front. The second is a cadre of young Syrians radicalized by the war who have adopted a form of Salafism as part of their desire to fight Assad. They are not particularly ideological and are likely to shift factions if they believe another is either more efficient or pays higher wages.

One issue that has split Syria's Salafist groups was the question of how to handle Al-Qaeda and its local franchise in the form of Al-Nusra. For both ideological and practical reasons many accepted the exclusion of Al-Nusra from the Islamic Front's formal structures. Primarily this can be seen as a pragmatic decision for foreign consumption, as they often cooperate on the battlefield. However, the exclusion of Al-Nusra

---

23   Quoted in: ibid., p. 19

has been essential to retain Saudi, Gulf State, Turkish, or US funding. Some factions, such as Liwa al-Islam, have argued for the inclusion of Al-Nusra, as this would force them to moderate their policies and ensure they did not form an alliance with ISIS. However, in general the Salafist groups in Syria have excluded Al-Nusra notionally over issues of ideology and tactics such as the killing of civilians (although the Druze and Alawite communities have been treated as combatants, as they overwhelmingly support Assad), branding other Muslims as infidels, and accepting the intellectual leadership provided by the official Salafist scholars promoted by the Saudis and the Gulf States.[24]

We will return to the issue of Al-Nusra below, but there are other groups openly supportive of Al-Qaeda. The Azzam brigades are mostly based in southern Syria and are also active in Lebanon. They have called on the Sunni population of both countries to attack Hizbollah and in late 2013 fired rockets at Israel across the Golan Heights.

AL-QAEDA'S OFFICIAL FACTION: AL-NUSRA

Al-Nusra became Al-Qaeda's official front in Syria by 2013. At a practical level it is hard to distinguish this group from the more radical of the "acceptable" Salafist groups in the Islamic Front. But it is important to note that, even from the start, Al-Nusra accepted foreign fighters (and most of its original cadre came from Syrians who had fought in Iraq after 2005), making it much more part of the international Salafi-jihadi community, whereas the Islamic Front only pulled fighters from Arab states. Also, in contrast to the other Salafi groups, Al-Nusra used suicide bombings as a tactic of choice with the predictable routine of issuing videos containing the final messages of those taking part.[25] Other groups have carried out some suicide attacks but mostly use conventional guerilla tactics in their fight with Assad's

---

24   Ibid.

25   Ibid.

forces. Of course, it is at the level of long-term goals where they differ most. As part of Al-Qaeda, Al-Nusra sees the United States as the real enemy and states such as Saudi Arabia as apostate regimes—victory in Syria is but a stepping stone, not an end in itself. The other groups see imposing a suitable form of government on Syria as their goal. Equally Al-Nusra has denounced those who take money from the Gulf States,[26] whereas other "acceptable" Salafist groups make no such distinction.

Al-Nusra also differs from the wider coalition of Salafist groups by being very selective in who it accepts, requiring new recruits to be vetted by its front-line commanders as to both their military and religious reliability. According to one of the group's leaders, Al-Amir Gazi al-Haj, this selective approach is what underpins their success:

> We have pure intentions. We fight only for Allah. We do not accept even small deviations [from God's law], like smoking. We walk a straight line, and you can see the results.
>
> Al Nusra Front's new recruits take an oath of allegiance or al-Bay'ah. The religious nature of this oath, swearing before God to follow the jihadist leadership, makes it a stronger, more personal contract than a simple civil oath would be. Breaking this oath carries significant danger, with jihadists in Algeria killed for refusing to follow the leaders to whom they had pledged allegiance. The religious basis of this oath means that recruits have no legal recourse should they wish to leave the group, as they have made a vow to submit to jihadist leaders entirely, unless their instructions go against the will of God.[27]

By 2014 the group had a substantial number of foreign fighters. Unlike AQI[28] (before its entry into Syria), these were drawn from Western Europe and the Caucasus (especially Chechnya) as much as from other Arab countries. Not all of these initially went to Syria

---

26   Ibrahim, "The Resurgence of Al-Qaeda in Syria and Iraq."

27   Ibid. pp 28-29

28   At this stage AQI still only held territory in Iraq, with most of its remaining foreign fighters drawn from other Arab countries.

to fight for Al-Nusra, but they gravitated to the group either as they personally became more militant or because it was better organized and paid higher salaries.

Even so, Al-Qaeda believes it had learned valuable lessons from the defeat of AQI in the period after 2007. One was that it needs to cooperate with other Salafist and Sunni groups, while the other is to moderate its interpretation of Sharia law in areas it controls. Given Syria's largely nonsectarian history, the group tries to appeal by playing down its dislike of other (and non-) Muslims so as to avoid triggering the rejection that occurred in Iraq. To stress its new orientation, the group claimed it no longer targets noncombatant civilians. Thus the group has claimed responsibility for a suicide attack in the usual terms but stressed that "no civilian perished in this martyrdom operation, to the best of our knowledge."[29]

Equally Al-Nusra was keen to be seen to provide effective governance in regions it controlled. It created a social welfare wing (Qism al-Ighatha) to distribute fuel, food, and clothing. Operationally this suggests that Al-Qaeda started to adopt aspects of the long-term approach of groups such as the Muslim Brotherhood (and, ironically given their hatred for the Shi'a militant group, Hizbollah)—gaining loyalty by charity rather than just out of fear.

AL-QAEDA'S OFFSPRING: ISIS

By the end of 2013, however, this was to change. AQI had completed its break from Al-Qaeda and sought to gain control of part of northeastern Syria to add to territory it had taken in northern and western Iraq. Initially they were driven out by a coalition of Al-Nusra and other Salafist groups, but by mid-2014, what was now called ISIS returned in force. In turn it provided a variant of radical Salafism that differed both from the Saudi-inspired "mainstream" and the approach

---

29   Lund, "Syria's Salafi Insurgents: The Rise of the Syrian Islamic Front.", p.22

now adopted by Al-Qaeda. The balance of this section forms a discussion of ISIS's changing approach.

This book is not the place to discuss the various dynamics and events in the Syrian war since ISIS captured large areas of the northeast. My focus primarily is on how ISIS's gains have influenced the debate within Salafism and what their approach tells us about the mind-set of the most militant. However, it is worth stressing one thing: ISIS's primary enemy has not been the Assad regime but other factions opposed to Assad. Nothing exemplifies this as much as their seizure of Raqqa, still the center of their self-proclaimed caliphate. The town had been taken from the Syrian army by a coalition of forces from the Free Syrian Army, the Islamic Front, and Al-Nusra. Most of the combat elements of this alliance were still engaged with the Assad regime to the west of the town when ISIS swept in and took control.

ISIS retained many of the characteristics of AQI. It saw other Muslims, especially the Shi'a but also Sunnis it deemed apostate (and that includes almost everyone not specifically aligned with their ideals), as the enemy as much as the United States or Western Europe. It has never shed either its brutality[30] or its interest in using the Internet to ensure its crimes are widely seen. If the "propaganda of the deed" has been part of the terrorist armory since the 1890s, ISIS has raised this to a new level. It is depressingly easy to find their well-made videos featuring extreme violence online. In part this is designed as a weapon of terror, to make the group's opponents fear for their lives, but primarily, as we have seen, to inspire their supporters.

ISIS also completed the break from Al-Qaeda both operationally and ideologically. Cole Bunzel of *jihadica.com* noted that ISIS persisted "in a state of outright disobedience to its supposed seniors in Al-Qaeda Central (AQC)"[31] even before the final split. The Brookings Institution's William McCants said, "In the twenty-five-year history of Al-Qaeda, no

---

30   United Nations, "The human rights situation in Iraq in the light of abuses committed by the so-called Islamic State in Iraq and the Levant and associated groups."

31   Cole Bunzel, "The Islamic State of Disobedience: al-Baghdadi Triumphant," Jihadica, 2013 http://www.jihadica.com/the-islamic-state-of-disobedience-al-baghdadis-defiance/.

affiliate has ever publicly disagreed with the boss so brazenly."[32] This led ISIS to not just develop its existing tactics and ideology but to aim to supplant Al-Qaeda as the force in international violent Salafism.

This can be traced through two main aspects:

1. The emphasis on holding physical territory as a "caliphate";

2. Creating its own international network.

Al-Qaeda had originally aimed to control territory, either an entire state or an area where it was the dominant power. Its longer term goal was to re-create its version of the early Muslim caliphates so as to bring all Muslims under a single governance—with this, of course, based on their own Salafist/Wahhabist ideology. In the short term, physical control of space was useful but not essential. The advantage, as with Afghanistan before 2001, was that it allowed the establishment of training camps and a place to plot. Having *de facto* control, as in Afghanistan, also meant they could isolate those they did not fully trust. Ironically this was the treatment meted out to Zarqawi's Jordanians when they arrived in Afghanistan in 1998,[33] as they feared the group included spies planted by the Jordanian secret services. It may be that his isolation at this time, and cool reception when he returned in 2001, all contributed to his antipathy towards the formal leadership of Al-Qaeda.

Equally Al-Qaeda often had to share its space with more or less willing hosts. The Taliban regime in Afghanistan saw Al-Qaeda as their guests, granted them much hospitality.[34] Some Taliban leaders were annoyed that their "guests" had brought down American wrath in the aftermath of 9/11, and this contributed to a split between factions in the Taliban and the international jihadists of Al-Qaeda. After being driven out of Afghanistan, Al-Qaeda developed a new operational

---

32   William McCants, "How Zawahiri Lost Al-Qaeda," (Washington: Brookings Foreign Affairs, 2013). P. 30

33   Kirdar, "Al-Qaeda in Iraq."

34   Ruthven, *A Fury for God: The Islamist Attack on America.*

model. In some places, notably northwest Pakistan and Somalia, it was able to carve out areas where it was dominant, in alliance with local supporters. Elsewhere it moved to a "franchise" model where regional or local groups swore fealty to the group. In return they received training, some funding, and the "status" of being a formal Al-Qaeda affiliate. But for all practical purposes they operated in their own region towards their own goals.

If Al-Qaeda did develop a theory of the importance of controlling space, it remained as it had been pre-2001. Such regions allowed for the establishment of training camps and networks and made it easier for senior leaders to avoid US attacks. However, the "caliphate" was something that would be established later, perhaps as jihadists took control of a number of Muslim states—starting with Saudi Arabia.

AQI seemed to start with the same model, but significant gains in the Sunni-dominated regions of Iraq leading into 2006 opened the prospect of actually ruling over territory it controlled on its own terms. As we have seen, even at this early stage, AQI was intolerant of even other conservative Sunni groups and was happy to attack other Salafists as well as the Shi'a communities. They had no intention of being "guests" in anybody else's country. The rebranding of AQI as the Islamic State of Iraq might have initially been cosmetic, but the choice of title was indicative as to the importance of the "caliphate" and ruling territory to the group's leadership. In both the period 2005–07 and after it regained its influence post-2012, practically the group controlled large areas of western and central Iraq, including cities such as Falluja. However, pragmatically this domination was little different from the ebb and flow of any guerilla warfare campaign.

However, by the time ISIS entered Syria in 2013, the control of territory, and of urban areas, had become central to its appeal and self-image. Indeed this insistence that it was a state, not a guerilla army with local concerns, caused significant problems with other Salafist factions in Syria.[35] These may have been prepared to deal with ISIS as they dealt with Al-Nusra (i.e., cooperate tactically, share control of districts, etc.), but they resented ISIS's claims that they were going to

---

35   Lund, "Syria's Salafi Insurgents: The Rise of the Syrian Islamic Front."

redefine what Syria really meant. By mid-2014, ISIS had established firm control not just over Raqqa in Syria but also Mosul in Iraq (as well as other towns and cities in both countries). With this, ISIS was able to argue that it had really created the first parts of the caliphate so central to Salafist beliefs.

This created a significant shift in who was arriving to fight for the group. Traditionally, jihad had been the function of men (and usually younger men) who went to a region to fight. This concept was central to the growth of Al-Qaeda in Afghanistan and was present, to a limited extent, in the Balkans. As noted earlier in this chapter, Iraq became a major destination after 2003, but again it was mostly young men going to fight (and mostly from other Arab countries). Equally Somalia, which attracted around five hundred fighters between 1993–2014,[36] saw most arrive either from the wider region or if they had some family ties to the region.

Experience in such wars was mixed for the foreign fighters. In Somalia they were not welcomed by local Islamist groups if they were seen as too closely aligned to Al-Qaeda (and later to ISIS). In Chechnya, very few foreigners appeared, and, for the most part, the Chechens went to fight elsewhere after the Russian victories in 2009. One reason given for AQI's defeat in 2005–06 was local resistance to foreign fighters, but since ISIS recovered after 2011, it has become the main recipient of external fighters. In 2013, it has been estimated that some fifteen thousand out of its thirty-one thousand fighters had arrived in the region from elsewhere.[37]

Three factors seemed to have played a role in making ISIS the main recipient of external jihadists. First, unlike Iraq in 2003–07, it was relatively easy to enter ISIS-controlled territory from the long (and poorly guarded) Turkish border. This opened the door to those from Western Europe and North America. Second, some came to Syria to fight for other factions and then defected. It has been claimed that

---

36   Isabelle Duyvesteyn and Bram Peeters, "Fickle Foreign Fighters? A Cross-Case Analysis of Seven Muslim Foreign Fighter Mobilisations (1980-2015)," (The Hague: International Centre for Counter-Terrorism, 2015).

37   Ibid.

the Saudis offered those facing death sentences full pardons (and substantial payment) to go to fight for their approved factions within the Islamic Front.[38] At the same time the Saudis made it punishable by death to fight for either Al-Nusra or ISIS, but in reality once the fighter was in Syria, the Saudis had little control over what happened next. Studies of foreign fighters suggest they tend to go to struggles that are both well known and seen to be successful,[39] and ISIS in mid-2014 met both criteria.

The third issue is where ISIS has diverged substantively from Al-Qaeda's past practice. As ruler of a state, it needs the veneer of normal life outside of fighting. So foreign fighters have been promised both slaves and willing brides. ISIS-controlled Iraq and Syria thus became a destination not just for those looking to fight but for those who wished to live in what they believed to be a pure Islamic state. For the first time, women (both married and unmarried) and their children started to arrive in support of jihad.[40] For reasons of basic ideology, groups in the Wahhabist/Salafist community have not made much use of women fighters unlike the older, secular factions like the PLO. The only substantive exception to this has been the Chechens,[41] where women have taken part in a number of attacks on Russian forces and civilians and acted as suicide bombers.

By 2015, it was estimated that around 550 unmarried women had travelled to ISIS-controlled Syria with the express aim of marrying one of their fighters and making a new life in the caliphate. Of those who were clearly identified, the largest group by far came from the UK, the youngest was aged fourteen and the eldest forty-five.[42] ISIS recruitment

38   G. Ingersoll, "REPORT: Saudi Arabia Sent 1,200 Death Row Inmates to Fight in Syria," Business Insider, 2013 http://www.businessinsider.com/saudi-arabia-sent-inmates-against-assad-2013-1?IR=T#ixzz35jkuX7QX.

39   Duyvesteyn and Peeters, "Fickle Foreign Fighters? A Cross-Case Analysis of Seven Muslim Foreign Fighter Mobilisations (1980-2015)."

40   Atika Shubert, "The women of ISIS: Who are they?," CNN, 2015 http://edition.cnn.com/2015/05/29/middleeast/who-are-the-women-of-isis/.

41   Paige Whaley Eager, From Freedom Fighters to Terrorists: Women and Political Violence (New York: Routledge, 2008).

42   Shubert, "The women of ISIS: Who are they?".

of women is quite deliberate, with a social media approach that mirrors the blood-sodden videos they produce for would-be jihadists. As we have seen in earlier chapters, many young Muslims, male or female, turn to Salafism in part out of alienation, in part out of a feeling of discrimination, and in part out of a belief that something is wrong in the wider world. ISIS plays on all this, and sought to present life in the caliphate as a brave new beginning.

Even in 2014–15 this "pure world" was quickly revealed to be false, as many women found themselves married off, sometimes repeatedly, as their husbands were killed. As ISIS has come under sustained attack, they now face the risk of being killed in airstrikes or when ISIS loses control of a town. Their passports were confiscated on entry into ISIS-controlled territory, and ISIS's restrictions on the movement of women makes it hard for them to escape. ISIS has been quite open as to the future of any women who travel.[43] In a report designed for women moving from Arab countries, ISIS has stated:

Women are encouraged to come to Syria and Iraq where they can live the "sedentary" lifestyle led by responsibilities in the home, which is their "divinely appointed right" in line with Shariah "and the methodology of life that was ordained by God."

Education should begin at the age of seven and continue no later than the age fifteen, according to the manifesto. Curriculum should focus largely on Islamic religious studies, Koranic Arabic and learning basic cooking, knitting and other skills, in order to prepare women for their role at the centre of the household.

It advises that there is no need for women to "flit here and there to get degrees and so on just so she can try to prove that her intelligence is greater than a man's.[44]

43   Heather Saul, "Life as a woman under Isis: Document reveals for the first time what group really expects from female recruits living in Syria and Iraq," *The Independent*, 2015 http://www.independent.co.uk/news/world/middle-east/life-as-a-woman-under-isis-document-reveals-for-the-first-time-what-group-really-expects-from-female-10025143.html.

44   Ibid.

However, going to ISIS-controlled Syria has not just attracted unmarried women. In some cases women have also taken their children. Some of these have gone to join family members who are already part of ISIS, but others have decided to escape the "decadent" West so their children can have an upbringing in line with Salafist beliefs. ISIS though is not just interested in controlling the education of children; it also uses them as fighters and to carry out a number of suicide bombings.[45]

GLOBAL REPERCUSSIONS

The split of radical Salafism into three main currents has had global implications. Policy makers in the West have to face up to the difficulty of responding to Salafist groups who aim solely to change the governance of their own country. At the same time, the strand in Salafism that does wish to destroy the West has splintered into two competing groups.

We may disagree fundamentally with what the Syrian domestic Salafist groups aim for, but they do not immediately offer a threat to the West or even to neighboring states. Indeed, it may be that the immediate appeal of such groups has more to do with the dynamics of civil war. Many who want to fight Assad are prepared to join Salafist groups simply as they are now the dominant force in the non-Kurdish part of the opposition. In this, as we noted earlier, there is an analogy to the short-lived appeal of orthodox Marxist-Leninist Communist Parties during and immediately after the Second World War. These parties had formed the backbone of the local resistance to both German fascism and Japanese imperialism. They had an organizational model well suited to the demands of underground violent resistance and,

---

45 Charlotte Alfred, "A Shocking Number Of Kids Are Fighting And Dying For ISIS," Huffington Post, 2016 http://www.huffingtonpost.com/entry/isis-child-soldiers_us_56c779b9e4b0ec6725e28d90.

through their links to the Soviet Union, were relatively well supplied with weapons. After the war, many quickly left, having decided that they did not actually believe in Marxism-Leninism and were no longer prepared to support the USSR. A similar dynamic is possible in Syria; as discussed earlier in this chapter, many of those fighting for such groups are not particularly well versed in Salafist ideology. Thus if the civil war ends, it is quite possible they will disengage from groups committed to extremist beliefs.

Even so, this leaves the West facing two strands of international Salafism, both violent, both seeking to carry out acts of violence but now in competition with each other. As discussed above, initially AQI/ISIS had no presence outside Iraq (apart from limited influence in Lebanon and Jordan). By 2015, it had become the dominant face of international jihadism.

Its approach to this has elements derived from Al-Qaeda and new innovations. Up until the emergence of ISIS, so-called lone-wolf or self-radicalized terrorists in North America and Western Europe were relatively rare.[46] Usually once the background of the terrorists was understood it became clear that they had received training and direct support from Al-Qaeda. Thus the group that bombed London's tube and bus networks in 2005[47] may have been inspired by British-based radical clerics but probably also had direct assistance from Al-Qaeda. Since 2014, self-radicalizing "lone-wolf" attacks have become more common—individuals pledge their allegiance to ISIS before undertaking an attack without ever having formally engaged with ISIS for training or without having travelled to ISIS-dominated regions. For various reasons, as discussed earlier in this book, ISIS is having the effect of providing a focus for the disaffected much more readily than Al-Qaeda did.

In addition, ISIS has also continued Al-Qaeda's approach of orga-nizing major terrorist attacks especially in Western Europe. In this

---

46 And as discussed earlier, may still be. While the early stages of radicalization can occur in relative isolation, acquiring weapons and explosives takes more organization than simply watching ISIS's propaganda videos.

47 Nic Robertson, Paul Cruickshank, and Tim Lister, "Documents give new details on al Qaeda's London bombings," CNN, 2014 http://edition.cnn.com/2012/04/30/world/al-qaeda-documents-london-bombings/?c=&page=0.

they are aided initially by individuals who came to Syria (or Iraq) to fight and then subsequently returned home. Also, especially as Syria has become increasingly isolated, ISIS is encouraging its supporters to carry out acts of jihad at home right away and not even attempt to come to Syria.

Finally, ISIS has been very successful at taking over existing AQ networks. In a way the expansion of ISIS into Libya is a clear example of how this happens and the consequence for jihadist actions when they do displace AQ. In Libya, AQ had originally sought to cooperate with the local Salafist opposition to Gadhafi (the Libyan Islamic Fighting Groups—LIFG). While many in the LIFG rejected AQ, some individuals worked with AQ in creating a local branch of AQ's wider network then being established across North Africa. However, the bulk of the LIFG opposed links with AQ, as their focus was on the governance of Libya, not global jihad.[48] While in prison, its leadership went further and came to the view that "the use of violence as a means of overthrowing governments in Muslim countries was illegal from an Islamic point of view."[49] This represented not just a tactical rejection of AQ (i.e., a local rather than international focus) but a split on a fundamental matter of ideology.

In consequence, prior to 2011, AQ only had a small network with this using the Ansar al-Sharia label. During and after the uprising against Gadhafi, this operated in a manner similar to Al-Nusra in Syria. It sought to cooperate with other Salafist groups who shared key elements of its ideology rather than insist on total acceptance of AQ's fundamental beliefs. By 2012, it was estimated that AQ had some three hundred members in Libya spread between the towns of Darnah, Sirt, and Kuffra, but with more influence among the other local militias than these raw numbers would imply.

Again, in a mirror of the dynamics in Syria, ISIS started to establish themselves in Libya from early 2013. As in Syria, they have largely rejected the option of cooperating with other Salafist groups and have

---

48   Library of Congress, "Al-Qaeda in Libya: A Profile," (Washington: Federal Research Division, 2012).

49   Ibid. p. 9

instead tried to impose their own agenda and organization. The Quilliam Foundation has translated an ISIS document that sets out their initial strategy in Libya.[50] In particular, in order to create a substantial cadre of militants, ISIS tried to build up their presence in part by stopping the flow of Libyan fighters to Syria and in part by fusing with some local militia groups who were sympathetic to their goals. Key goals included:

- Treating Libya as a new "province" of the caliphate;

- Extending ISIS into Libya to lessen pressure on Syria/Iraq, not least as they could reach both into Saharan Africa and across the Mediterranean;

- Using Libya as an easy place to gain access to military supplies, which could be used to fuel other conflicts (such as in Mali).

However, while the ISIS document identified Libya as an important option, it also suggested that the group faced a limited time frame in which it could consolidate its control. ISIS first based itself in Dernah, after absorbing the local AQ network, in January 2013.[51] The murder of western tourists in Tripoli and the beheading of twenty-one Egyptian Coptic Christians briefly led to discussion of joint action between Egypt and Italy. However, other EU nations and the United States insisted on diplomatic actions and even maintained the existing arms embargo on the Libyan government, leading to the rapid collapse of the Italian-Egyptian initiative. The EU and United States at this stage were unwilling to intervene despite ISIS's provocations, as they feared that ISIS would be able to exploit the presence of Western troops to generate additional support for their cause.[52] In turn, ISIS established a

---

50   Charlie Winter, "Libya: The Strategic Gateway for the Islamic State," (London: Quilliam Foundation, 2015).

51   Mattia Toaldo, "Europe's options on Libya: no easy way out," Aspenia, 2015 https://www.aspeninstitute.it/aspenia-online/article/europe%E2%80%99s-options-libya-no-easy-way-out.

52   Ibid.

presence in a number of coastal towns—in effect the same towns that AQ had earlier infiltrated—and in particular established its main base in Sirt. Here, it effectively took over the existing AQ network (again, as in Syria, some AQ militants swapped allegiance). However, its brutality and sectarian approach provoked a local backlash, and it briefly lost power in late 2015 before regaining control of the city in early 2016. At the point of this book's publication, it is estimated it still has some fifteen hundred fighters in the city. This is a substantial increase over the AQ numbers in 2011, which the Guardian suggested to be just one thousand fighters, in August 2016 at the start of US air attacks.[53]

SUMMARY

T he last two chapters have traced the shifts in global jihadism since it first took its modern form in Afghanistan. As we have seen, some aspects of what could be called the "Afghan model" have been consistently applied, but equally both tactics and ideological goals have shifted. Underpinning the entire period from the early 1980s to date has been much the same ideology. All the Salafist groups draw on the same interpretation of Islam that we have explored earlier. The same thinkers reappear, and the same justifications are used for violence, for the need to return to what they see as the purity of early Islam along with the same sectarian disdain for any who do not share their worldview. At a practical level, the concept of going to fight jihad where there is a struggle has been a common thread throughout modern history.

However, against this shared background we can see emerging differences and a steady evolution in approach, culminating in ISIS, what is happening in Syria, and an increase in lone-wolf attacks around the world. One important change is the emergence of Salafist movements

---

53   Spencer Ackerman, Chris Stephen, and Ewen MacAskill, "US launches airstrikes against Isis in Libya" The Guardian, 2016 https://www.theguardian.com/world/2016/aug/01/us-airstrikes-against-isis-libya-pentagon.

that see their focus as the governance of their own country. As we have seen in Syria, and briefly discussed in the context of Libya, this has led to such groups either completely rejecting cooperation with AQ or ISIS or wishing to limit such cooperation to purely tactical issues. Thus in Syria, elements of the Islamic Front have cooperated with Al-Nusra on the battlefield but have tried to keep a clear distinction at a political and organizational level—even if purely for the pragmatic reason of wanting to retain access to Saudi and Gulf State funding.

In turn this adds to the problem of how Western policy makers should respond to the challenge posed by Salafism. As we have seen, most adherents are "quietists," rejecting violence and seeing Salfism as a template for their own lives. We are now seeing the emergence of violent groups (mostly in the context of repressive regimes or situations of civil war) that aim for their own state being ruled on Salafist principles. We may not like this outcome, but is it a serious threat to the West? These debates inform the discussion in the final portion of this book.

Within what can be called international Salafism, we now face two main players with similar long-term goals (reestablish the caliphate) and increasingly divergent strategies. AQ has not gone away, even if it has been sidelined by ISIS,[54] and its approach is still marked by three main aspects:

- The United States (the "far enemy") remains the primary foe;

- AQ will make local alliances with other Salafist groups and, in some cases, with non-Salafist groups. Linked to this, AQ franchises are toning down their interpretation of Sharia law to avoid alienating the population in areas where they take control;

- Flowing from this, AQ is prepared to share space with other groups. In consequence, it regards ownership of

---

54   Byman and Williams, "ISIS vs. Al-Qaeda: Jihadism's global civil war".

territory as a tactical issue (safe spaces, training camps, etc.) rather than as a core part of its identity.

ISIS has diverged on each of these points. In particular:

- Since 2014 it has become more "international" in its goals and its ability to inspire or organize acts of terror. However, it still seems focused on toppling the regimes in particular countries (or removing parts of countries from state control);

- It has avoided alliances and takes a very sectarian approach even towards other Salafist groups;

- Fundamentally it seems to value control of space where it can in turn act as a state. It is this that drives its rejection of other strands within Salafism and has also changed the nature of those who go to fight jihad. Once the sole preserve of those who wanted to fight, ISIS now seeks to attract people who want to live their lives under its rule.

In turn both groups have retained the "franchise" model that AQ created from the early 1990s. Here local groups swear allegiance to the notional leader of each "international" group. The consequences vary. As we saw in Iraq, this can lead to a battle to gain or retain the allegiance of a group that first emerged to offer allegiance to AQ. On the other hand, as say in Nigeria, a local indigenous group such as Boko Haram will simply shift allegiance, but this will make very little difference in practice. The group remains isolated from global jihadism and focused very much on its own local struggle.

Finally, events in Bosnia, Kosovo, Iraq, and Syria have created opportunities and new problems for the Saudis. As we have seen, they had relatively little influence in Bosnia or Kosovo during the actual fighting in those countries. Postwar, Bosnia received substantial funding from the EU, making it less reliant on Saudi funding. In turn it has largely escaped the problems that arise once Wahhabism takes root in a country. Kosovo has not been so lucky. The Saudis (and their

Gulf State allies) took a substantial role in funding its reconstruction and, in particular, imported their religious structures as they created a network of mosques and schools. The result has been the spread of intolerant Salafist beliefs and a substantial number of Kosovars going to fight for ISIS.

Saudi involvement in Iraq was initially relatively limited. Their long-standing enmity towards the Ba'athist regime was reinforced by the events during the 1990–1 Gulf War, but they took no formal part in the US-led invasion in 2003. Even once AQI started its violent war against its enemies, Saudi Arabia played a relatively limited role. Its citizens certainly turned up to fight for AQI but seem to have been outnumbered by those from Egypt.[55] Iraq has become important to the Saudis less as a place to spread Wahhabism and more as a major arena for its struggle against Iran and against the revival of Shi'a influence.

It is Syria that points to all the problems and difficulties that the Saudis face in trying to promote their agenda around regional power and spreading official Wahhabism while at the same time curtailing AQ and ISIS. First, Syria is yet another place where the Saudis are trying to limit the growing influence of Iran and the wider Shi'a community.[56] Second, they have sought to create a client Salafist movement that will accept their money, religious approach, and arms while steering clear of AQ. As we have seen, they have sent convicted prisoners to Syria to fight for their approved groups while declaring that fighting for AQ/ISIS is punishable by death. The messy realities of a civil war makes such distinctions very opaque. Many fighters in Syria serve a group they believe is effective, or reflects local goals, and the line between groups is porous. Even ISIS has fighters in its ranks who probably would be mainstream Salafists if ISIS were less powerful.

Here we must be clear. AQ or ISIS would not exist if the intellectual framework of Wahhabism did not exist, in the same way that European terrorist groups such as the Red Brigades relied on the existence of

---

55 Duyvesteyn and Peeters, "Fickle Foreign Fighters? A Cross-Case Analysis of Seven Muslim Foreign Fighter Mobilisations (1980-2015)."

56 It should also be noted that Saudi hatred of the Syrian Ba'ath regime stretches back to the 1960s, while they have long had a hostile relationship with the region reaching back to the early emergence of Wahhabism in the 18th century.

orthodox Marxism-Leninism. This is not to say that something else would not have arisen instead, but the form of these groups relies on their wider ideologies. Specifically there is no reason to disbelieve the Saudis when they say they are opposed to AQ/ISIS—after all, their own regime is an explicit target of both organizations. But at every turn, by spreading Wahhabism, the Saudis feed the initial foundation necessary to create and sustain AQ and ISIS. The final part of the book looks at the policy implications of the resulting problem both for the Saudis and the West.

PART EIGHT
THE ANTIDOTE

W e are at war with ISIS and Al-Qaeda. But that is not *the war*. The fundamental conflict is against bigotry, in this case in the form of violent, radical Islamism as derived from the bigoted ideology of Wahhabism. This bears repeating again and again until our representatives in Congress and our mainstream media journalists and commentators get it into their heads and start changing the way they talk about this issue. In a conventional war against a state or against a militant group, the solution to the problem is essentially one of military force: throw bombs and bullets until the problem goes away. And if this war were that kind of war, we would have won it long ago. The United States remains the undisputed military power in the world, and we retain the capability of completely destroying any state's military apparatus within weeks. That is what we did when we went in and overthrew the Taliban in Afghanistan and Saddam's regime in Iraq. We went in and destroyed their states and armies with ease. But did we win those wars or simply a single phase of a much longer struggle?

Dealing with Saddam Hussein's organized state is not the same as dealing with ISIS. This is not that kind of war. This is a war against an *ideology*. Ideologies survive the destruction of their armies, and give birth to new conflicts. And conflicts between ideologies never end if they are fought solely with military means. We destroyed Al-Qaeda, and ISIS rose in its stead. If we actually go in on the ground in Syria, we would destroy ISIS in a matter of weeks. But we would solve nothing. A new organization with a new label and the same aims and ideology would rise again somewhere else. And we would be left with the costs of trying to administer a broken country—as we found out in Afghanistan and Iraq. It should have been obvious all along that fighting a war of ideology with the tactics of a conventional war is futile. But just for good measure we now also have ample, painful, and very expensive evidence from the last fifteen years of trying to do just that.

So what tactics do we use to fight a war on an ideology? I will not deny that the military aspect of this remains important. The propaganda value for ISIS from its earlier military success in the Levant cannot be understated. And military setbacks matter, not least as these will cost them people they have already recruited and make it harder for new fighters to go to Syria. But new potential recruits? They will still be out there, radicalizing every day. They may be dissuaded from joining ISIS if the group no longer appears successful, but they will look for other ways to fight their jihad, either by joining other groups or just committing lone-wolf terror attacks in the West—the likes of which we have started seeing more of on our streets in the United States in the last year even as we've been managing to contain ISIS in Syria and Iraq.

The fundamental question, however, is how to contain the spread of their poisonous doctrine and reduce its appeal to Muslims here in the United States and everywhere around the world. I propose that we need to approach this as a public health crisis. The spread of this ideology resembles the spread of an infectious disease. We need to stop it at its origins. We need to do our best to first inoculate as many people as possible from the jihadis' Radical Virus, and to cure as many of those who have already caught the bug as possible. And in the same way that we understand that all of us must be able to recognize and take precautions against infections in ourselves and those around us when we have a pandemic outbreak, so too we must understand that we all have responsibilities in tackling this kind of radicalization in our societies.

We must also understand that it is absolutely crucial that our response to this crisis is not driven by hysterical shock jocks on radio and on television, by knee-jerk reactions, or by "simple truths" of those who surround President Trump. Our response should be driven by the prescriptions of those who have carried out careful, thoughtful research and analysis of the problem and have identified the best ways for each of us to respond to issues as we see them rise around us. We would not trust Glenn Beck to be able to tell us the best way to protect ourselves from a flu pandemic. We ask doctors and epidemiologists. We must not trust people who have prejudice, bigotry, and fear to sell to tell us how to best inoculate against prejudice and bigotry. We must trust the people who have successfully implemented de-radicalization programs, and those who have done the psychological and sociological research.

The recommendations contained in this final section are aimed at all members of society, both Muslim and non-Muslim. They are designed to deal with Saudi Arabia's "special export," the virulent brand of Wahhabi Salafism washing over the shores of other countries in the Middle East and in the West, like an oil spill, since the 1970s. This is an ideology bulging with doctrine, piety, and ritual—for its adherents a spiritual lodestar in a globalized world full of sin and moral chaos.[1] This ideology has been on the road for some time now, and has travelled far from its home country. It has consoled, motivated, and soothed the mujahedeen of the Afghan war. It inspired insurgents to occupy the Grand Mosque in Mecca in 1979, in the belief that the Mahdi, the Islamic redeemer at the End of Days, had arrived on earth. The Arabic text has been drummed into generations of children in the madrassas of Pakistan, who then become mere cannon fodder for ongoing disputes in that country, disputes that continue to pose an existential threat to the state and continue to destabilize Afghanistan. Another "Mahdi," Abu Bakr al-Baghdadi, the so-called caliph of ISIS in Syria and Iraq, is the product of the very same ideology. The terror attacks of 9/11 and the localized shootings we have started seeing in the past year stem from the same wellspring too.

Throughout this book I have tried to explain the nature of this ideological virus and its origins: fundamentally, the virulent element of this radical ideology that is Wahhabi Salafism. Its violent offshoot, global jihadism, is merely the symptom of this virus, which we are most likely to recognize in attacks against us on our own streets. By way of final clarification, global jihadism is a hybridized evolution of Wahhabi Salafism, infused with the Islamist thinking of Sayyid Qutb

---

1   In that sense, it has very much in common with the rise of the Moral Majority type of political Christianity we have seen in the United States in particular. Out of the chaos of the 1970s we have seen a resurgence of fundamentalist religion as people in the Middle East, as in the West, hanker for the "lost" moral certainties of an idealized past. The major difference, of course, was that thankfully the Christian fundamentalist resurgence did not result in the same level of generalized violence— abortion clinic bombings aside.

of the Muslim Brotherhood, taught by Abdullah Yusuf Azzam, a founder of Al-Qaeda, first brought to reality by Ayman al-Zawahiri, and globalized by Osama bin Laden and Al-Qaeda. Finally, the current leaders of this ideology are Abu Bakr al-Baghdadi and Abu Omar al-Shishani,[2] respectively the leader and the senior commander of the Islamic State of Iraq and the Levant, who sit atop a pyramid of global jihadism spreading its tentacles to almost all countries where there are sizeable Muslim communities that are susceptible to radicalization—while what has made them susceptible to radicalization in the first place is the initial spread of so-called peaceful Salafism with the aid of Saudi money.

It should be understood that this hybrid of Wahhabi Salafism and jihadi ideology makes jihadism into a revolutionary millenarian movement that intends to destabilize the world. Their goal is a major transformation of the current political ordering of the world that will allow its adherents to reenact an idealized past—their semi-mythical version of the Rashidun caliphate. At the heart of global jihadism is a belief that the Muslim *Ummah* are being attacked and humiliated, and that the community should stand together as one against the ravages of the United States, the West, and the Jews. As they plot their course to the ultimate victory promised by their millenarian creed, the global jihadis have a number of practical goals they believe they need to achieve along the way.

First, evict the United States of America from Iraq and the Arabian Peninsula; second, destroy the state of Israel; third, topple the corrupt apostate governments within the Muslim world; and finally, reestablish the caliphate in its full glory.[3] These objectives are at the same time simple and far-reaching, and many jihadis are convinced that they are well on the way to achieving all of these. The global jihadis see themselves as part of an epic life-and-death struggle, which they cannot lose as they have God on their side. They are locked in an End of Days

---

2   David Aaronovitch, "What is IS ?," BBC, 2015 http://www.bbc.co.uk/programmes/b06sdlmb.

3   Richard H. Shultz, "Global Insurgency Strategy and the Salafi Jihad Movement," (INSS Occasional Paper 66, 2008).

battle between themselves, representing the forces of good, against the evil forces that are the infidels and apostates—basically anybody who is not part of their ideology, including most Muslims. It would be tempting to dismiss these things as the lunacy that they clearly are. But I argue that we should absolutely take their threats seriously, as they have written them down, in the same way we should have taken seriously the threats written down by Adolf Hitler in his book *Mein Kampf* prior to the Second World War and the Holocaust.

In 2004 a book was published on the Internet entitled *The Management of Savagery*, by Abu Bakr Naji.[4] This is a text aimed at Al-Qaeda and other global jihadis on how to establish the Islamic caliphate. This is the modern-day equivalent of *Mein Kampf*. Their blueprint for global domination is not a hypothetical concept—it already exists. We cannot say that we haven't been warned. Our challenge is to respond to the rise of global jihadism and ensure that the values that underpin our civilization—the values of liberty, tolerance, peace, and cooperation between peoples irrespective of race and religion—come out on top.

However, this response has to reflect the complexities of the task. The last three chapters have looked at the ways in which Salafism has emerged and evolved in Western Europe and North America, the Balkans, and Iraq and Syria. As we saw in those chapters, the Wahhabist ideology that is exported by the Saudis both forms the core of the jihadist problem and, in consequence, becomes a very direct threat to the Saudi regime itself. There is a challenge to the Muslim communities. Salafism is still a minority strand in Islam, but it needs to be addressed directly. It does not simply offer a choice between a more or less austere lifestyle;[5] it is based on a fundamentally incorrect reading of Islam both as a religion and as a historical record.

---

4   Abu Bakr Naji, *The Management of Savagery: The Most Critical Stage Through Which the Umma Will Pass*, trans. William McCants (John M. Olin Institute for Strategic Studies, Harvard University, 2006).

5   In the way that individuals in Jewish communities opt for more or less Orthodox or liberal forms of worship.

Finally, there is a real challenge to Western policy makers. We cannot indulge in the simplicities of Breitbart or nativist parties like UKIP in the UK and decide that since a very small number of Salafists go on to commit acts of violence, all Muslims are responsible. Equally, while we may find Salafist beliefs unpleasant, and a challenge to our ideals of a shared polity, we need to find a well-calibrated response. Making the holding of particular ideas a criminal act, or subject to penalties, is a dangerous step for any society that prides itself on being free. As I have argued, dealing with the odd violent jihadist is the easy step—depending on circumstances, this is a challenge for the criminal justice system, intelligence agencies, or the military. Dealing with the bulk of quietest Salafists and the foundation Salafism lays for these aforementioned violent jihadists is not so simple.

The balance of this discussion works through these three challenges. As we will see, they interact, and dealing effectively with one part of the problem will make it easier to respond to another. However, since the Saudis are the core force behind the spread of Salafist ideas, we really need to start by considering how to deal with Saudi Arabia.

THE ROLE OF SAUDI ARABIA

S audi Arabia is absolutely critical to any discussion about how to handle the challenge presented by Salafism. But before going any further, there is one thing that I need to deal with. I need to clarify my position on the House of Saud. Throughout this book I have been very critical of the Saudis and of the Saudi state. I do not believe that this criticism is undue or in any way out of proportion. But I feel I must stress that the criticism is not malicious. I do not have any particular, private axe to grind, just as Senator Bob Graham, chair of the Joint Inquiry into Intelligence Community Activities Before and After the Terrorist Attacks of September 11, 2001, did not have any axe to grind against the Saudis when his inquiry explored the links between the

Saudi government and the Saudi citizens involved in the 9/11 attacks. And just to emphasize, the US courts have cleared the state of Saudi Arabia of involvement in the attacks.[6]

Nor am I calling for the Saudi monarchy to stand down, or be removed from power in the kingdom. Saudi Arabia has indeed played a significant part in the birth of global jihadism by promoting Wahhabi Salafism around the Muslim world since the late 1970s. Nonetheless it is too simplistic to lay the blame entirely at their door for the terrorist activities of jihadis. Global jihadi Salafism is the ideological eye of a storm in a multilayered and exceptionally complex fight for resources, influence, and power between nation states such as Iran, Russia, China, Pakistan, the United States, Turkey, Saudi Arabia, and the United Kingdom. The battles are being fought in failed or failing states such as Iraq, Syria, and, once again, Afghanistan, while on a smaller scale other deadly skirmishes take place on the streets of European cities, where disaffected second- and third-generation Muslim immigrants draw on the potent appeal of global jihadism to justify barbaric acts against ordinary citizens. The crazy millenial aspects of global jihad may hold their own perverse fascination, but we should never forget that the rise of the ideology was aided by the continuing support it received in terms of funding and political backing from the Saudis, the British, the United States, and various others, since its early days as Wahhabism.

This should not be shocking. In the history of the dangerous dance we call geopolitics, this sort of thing is par for the course. What should be shocking is that we are continuing to support the very same structures, the same system of alliances, the same funding channels, the same power bargains with the Saudi state, with their religious establishment, and, ultimately, with the nongovernmental religious foundations that bear the largest responsibility for the spread of the Wahhabi ethos around the world.[7] This funding has led to the ultimate rise of

---

6   BBC, "US judge clears Saudi Arabia in 9/11 lawsuit," BBC, 2015 http://www.bbc.co.uk/news/world-us-canada-34405451.

7   Max Fisher, "How Saudi Arabia captured Washington," vox.com, 2016 http://www.vox.com/2016/3/21/11275354/saudi-arabia-gulf-washington.

first Al-Qaeda and now ISIS. What this book has sought to do so far is to untangle the complex web that constitutes these structures. What I propose now is how we should start unraveling this web. This, you may be surprised to find, does not mean that we should remove the Saudis from power. Indeed, in the volatile internal politics of Arabia, that may yet be the worst possible thing we could do. It is not far-fetched to suppose that the Saudi royal family is the only thing that is standing between the status quo and a second ISIS-style "caliphate" in the region. In their own way, they are making efforts to reform their own state and economy.[8]

The Saudis formed their alliance with the Wahhabi establishment initially for political expediency. During the first and second Saudi emirates, they pursued this alliance with a rather earnest commitment. But from the founder of the current kingdom through to today, the House of Saud has been committed to organizing a viable, modern state. Their relationship with Wahhabism has been one of uncomfortable give-and-take. When the secular authority has been on the rise, they have sought to modernize the kingdom and have introduced numerous reforms that have sparked the ire of the Wahhabis. When there was a sufficiently strong pushback from the Wahhabis and the ultraconservative constituency in the kingdom, they made concessions—concessions which we may find regrettable, but which they regarded as necessary for the survival of their unstable state.

It is for this reason, effectively reflecting internal Saudi power politics, that they initially adopted the policy to encourage and fund the proselytizing of Wahhabi Salafism around the Muslim world. One initial reason was to challenge the spread of socialist, secular doctrines in the Arab world. Thus Salafism, in their eyes, had the potential to act as an ideological buffer against Soviet-backed secular Socialist regimes in the region and, in the wake of the 1979 Iranian Revolution, against the resurgent, militant Shi'a Islamism promoted throughout the region by the Iranian mullahs. Both provided templates for revolutionary movements that could ultimately topple the Saudi kingdom, and the Saudis calculated that their home-grown style of ultraorthodox,

---

8   Kemp, "Saudi Arabia's dwindling oil revenues and the challenge of reform".

conservative Islam would be the best counter to these rival ideologies. And we in the West, and in the United States in particular, have been more than happy to support this approach, and to add our own input into the funding and training of the mujahedeen who went to war in Afghanistan against the Soviets, for example.

But now, with the benefit of hindsight, we can see that this has been a grave error. Let us at least try to not commit any further such errors by adopting shortsighted quick fixes. A realistic worldview in 2017 means that we must first acknowledge that the Saudis are at least as high on the terrorists' target lists as we are and that they are doing invaluable intelligence gathering in our joint counterterrorism work. We must then continue to support them in their fight against our common enemies. But we certainly need to start doing things a lot more intelligently. Not least, in our dealings with the Saudis we should always remember they are an independent state committed to what they see as their interests—and those goals and ours may not always coincide.[9]

The Saudis recognize the threat that global jihadi Salafism poses to their rule and the very survival of the Saudi monarchy. In addition, the Saudis would now be exceptionally foolish to fund the very terrorist organizations that would see them overthrown. Saudi Arabia now has some of the most stringent measures in place to prevent terrorism and recently has imprisoned more terrorists with links to Islamic State than any other country in the world. The Saudis are also working hard to prevent financial assistance from seeping out of the kingdom via unofficial channels, though Western governments, and our own government in particular, must continue to monitor the financial activities of the Saudis. There is no time like the present to start reconfiguring the structures that have nourished the rise of the jihadist ideologies.

However, even as we push the Saudi state to shift its attitudes towards the jihadist ideology they have spawned, it is important to remember that the bulk of funding to groups such as ISIS now comes from private individuals in Saudi Arabia and the other Gulf states.[10]

---

9   Fisher, "How Saudi Arabia captured Washington".

10   Peek, "The Roots of Lone Wolf Terrorism: Why the West's Homegrown Jihadists Are All Sunni".

This has created a uniquely unstable position: there is state backing for the ideology behind the Salafist movements, and in Syria, the Saudis (and other Gulf states) are backing some Salafist factions, while the bulk of the funding to groups like ISIS in 2016 came either from ISIS's own resources (oil sales, etc.) or private funding. Again this returns us to one of my key points. This may well be a war with an ideology, but it is not a war with a conventional state. We need to challenge both the ideology and the multitude of ways in which it is funded.

Here are concrete first steps that we can take now. Policy makers must stem Saudi Arabia's financial and political support for the propagation of the Wahhabi doctrine that is so often the parent to violent radicalism.

They can do so, first, by altering the power dynamics between us and the Saudis. At the moment the Saudis know that they are in an unassailable position. We need their oil. It is as simple as that. As long as that remains the case, we can preach at them about the dangers of promoting Wahhabism abroad all day long, but they will have no reason to listen to us. To them, the threat posed by the ultra-conservative elements of their country and the potential conflicts they might have with the religious establishment will be much more immediate, as long as they can implicitly assume that their position with us is safe. In addition, Saudi policy makers are focused on their fears about the goals of the local Shi'a population, backed by Iran, in the region. In effect, we are not the only external voice trying to catch their attention.

Thus we need to reduce our dependence on Saudi oil here in the West, and we need to do so urgently if we are to gain the necessary leverage. We can do so by exploiting our own shale reserves, but that would give us only a temporary reprieve, and we would need to go back to begging for oil again within a decade. We could secure supplies from Iran, which has a potential production capacity that is similar to that of the Saudis if properly exploited. But the Iranian regime is hardly more reliable or less dangerous. Making ourselves as dependent on them as we are on the Saudis would solve none of our problems, would help fund Iran's sponsorship of their own terror groups in the region, and would remove whatever leverage we do have over the Saudis. Alternatively, we could develop renewable energy technologies locally and ensure that we will never again be dependent on foreign countries for our energy security—even if that may come at a moderate up-front cost. At this moment in time, there is nothing we could do to alter the geopolitical map of the world more than winning our energy independence now and in perpetuity. Renewable energy technologies are the only way that can guarantee this.

Our leaders can, secondly, form alliances with key figures within the regime to persuade Saudi Arabia to stop exporting Wahhabism. Prince Muhammad bin Salman al Saud, the young, dynamic new "power behind the throne" who has been serving as defense minister, seems very much intent on modernizing the country, updating its infrastructure, and reshaping the economy away from oil exploitation and towards a viable, productive, Western-style market economy. He seems friendly towards the West and is more likely to be receptive than any Saudi leader in the past. Saudi Arabia is currently suffering economically and fiscally as a consequence of low global oil prices. Surely now more than ever would be an obvious time to encourage them to save the $2–3 billion per annum expenditure they commit to Wahhabi propaganda abroad.

Our leaders must also encourage Saudi Arabia to manage and create platforms for theological dissent, while appreciating the sensitivities of the Saudi monarchy, as history shows that when Wahhabism interacts with more moderate forms of Islam, it itself becomes more moderate. The current approach the Saudis are taking of executing people left, right, and center for atheism, heresy, treason, even peaceful protest[11] is very much the wrong approach to take. Whenever people are prohibited from expressing their grievances in public in peaceful ways, they will eventually start expressing them in violent ways. It has been argued that such repression is a major driver of radicalization, not a deterrent, and according to Amnesty International, the Saudis are some

---

11 Last year Saudi Arabia had more executions that at any time in the last two decades (Associated Press, "Saudi Arabia: beheadings reach highest level in two decades," The Guardian, 2016 http://www.theguardian.com/world/2016/jan/02/saudi-arabia-beheadings-reach-highest-level-in-two-decades.)

of the worst offenders in this regard.[12] In this context, Saudi Arabia is basically breeding terrorists—an ideological and political pressure cooker. It is no coincidence that so many of the global terrorists come from the kingdom, including so many of the ones in the 9/11 group.

In the same vein, more cultural exchanges between Saudi leading clerics and their European/Western counterparts should be encouraged, to expose them to new ideas and ways of responding to radicalization. But these exchanges should happen on vastly different terms than they do now. Now they tend to happen sponsored by Saudi money, where the Wahhabis are in control of the discussions and the agenda. That way, they often radicalize those they meet. This should be done the other way around, so that the Wahhabi clerics are exposed to proper Islamic critique of their fundamentalist zealotry and have to respond to the ways in which their own fundamentalism is heterodox and at odds with the Qur'an and the *hadiths*, as well as the historical precedent established by the Prophet's Constitution of Medina. The Salafi Ulema of Saudi Arabia have for too long been sheltered in its billion-petrodollar echo chamber, where the oil wealth of the country has insulated them from the need to respond to serious Islamic critique of what they teach in Arabia and what they preach around the world.

THE ROLE OF RELIGIOUS LEADERS

Religious leaders can have a tremendous amount of influence over the trajectory their congregations take. They will perhaps be the most important people in developing and maintaining cross-community relationships at the local level. This will be especially true of imams, though this also applies to Christian and Jewish religious leaders. But the imams in particular must understand the crucial

---

12 Amnesty International, "Saudi Arabia 2015/2016," (London: Amnesty International, 2016).

role they have to play and the fact that their duties stretch far beyond teaching Arabic and the Qur'an to their own flock.

The imams must be the first to engage in conversation with the other communities. They must be the first to explain what the Muslim community is about, why it wants to integrate in Western society, and how it is going about it. They must also be transparent and candid in acknowledging the challenges posed by the Wahhabi Salafist ideology to their flock, and must be creative in responding to those challenges. One of the biggest challenges faced by the Muslim communities in the West is that they are perceived as *foreign* and, behind the "closed walls" of the mosque, secretive. Of course, we as Muslims know that the doors to our mosques are open to anyone. But this is not something that Westerners often know is the case. This enables an atmosphere of mistrust and mutual suspicion to set in. It makes our integration in Western societies more difficult, it makes Westerners wary of us, and it perhaps even fuels latent prejudice and racism. Ultimately, as this alienates our young people, it makes them more susceptible to the divisive message of the Wahhabis and the jihadis. Cross-community communication is perhaps the most fundamental thing we can do, and our religious leaders are the people who can do the most to enable and promote it.

A very heartening example of this happened in 2013 in England.[13] A group who called themselves the English Defense League (basically the English version of the German PEGIDA) marched on a mosque in the English town of York to protest against the Islamization of the West. There was a lot of noise, flags, half a dozen arrests for disrupting the peace. In all, the usual kind of thing for a far-right rally.

But one thing was different this time. The imam of the mosque did not do what most of us would do when there is a mob outside asking that we be removed from our societies—try to ignore a hostile crowd. Instead, he and a handful of members of the community went outside and set up a tea stand. They invited the protesters to a "cup

---

13 Mohamed El-Gomati, "How to tackle the EDL," The Guardian, 2013 http://www.theguardian.com/commentisfree/2013/may/31/edl-english-defence-league-york-mosque.

and a conversation." They spent much of the afternoon talking to each other, about their lives, their fears, about what drives their communities, what affects them and how to best approach the many challenges they found they shared. In the end, they had a friendly football game between the representatives of the two communities, and discovered just how much they had in common. Not too long after that, after a number of such encounters with imams, the leader of the English Defense League stepped down from the group, and the rest quickly disbanded.[14]

This is the power that religious leaders can have, and this is their responsibility. This is what imams, rabbis, priests, and pastors should do, more than anything else, every week. And these religious leaders will be the best placed to know the specific requirements and circumstances of their communities, and how to best approach these situations. There really isn't anything more that I can usefully say on this. But if they take these duties seriously, that alone will save more lives on our street than any domestic anti-terror legislation any Congress will ever pass. Dialogue and transparency, candor and empathy between communities is what is required. Not to say that achieving these things is simple. But it is also very possible to achieve them.

Looked at from this angle, as I have noted in this book, radicalization is not a phenomenon that is specific to Muslim communities, but it does take on a particular form within that community, and it does affect them much more. Quintan Wiktorowicz has done some excellent work, and he identifies a trio of factors that will encourage a person towards radicalism. He first identifies economic factors, such as joblessness and blocked mobility; second are cultural factors such as racism; and third, political repression or torture.[15] If we examine Wiktorowicz's points one by one, however, we can see some difference between Islamist and non-Islamist radicalization. The first set of factors—the lack of economic opportunities and

---

14   Though of course many others have since stepped into the vacuum.

15   Quintan Wiktorowicz, *Radical Islam rising: Muslim extremism in the West* (London: Rowman & Littlefield Publishers, 2005)., especially pp.17-20

the collapse of the old Western social contract, which assumed that each generation would have a better life than their parents—is something that is common to both the West and to the Islamic world. And in Europe and the United States, it is common to both Muslims from immigrant communities and those born in-country, especially those from poorer communities who feel they have been left behind by globalization and who are the wellspring of support for resurgent, isolationist nationalism.

But for Muslim radicalization specifically, the situation is exacerbated by the other factors. Both European and American societies are still, unfortunately, rife with racism and prejudice. This creates unequal economic opportunities, but also helps feed the jihadist "grievance theology," which is why Muslims in these countries can be radicalized to the next level of intensity. Lastly, there is the issue of political repression and torture. This is not a generalized issue in the West, though Guantanamo Bay and the memory of Abu Ghraib should still weigh heavily on our collective conscience and still serve as potent symbols that support narratives of radicalization. However, this is a rampant issue in the Middle East, especially in the chaos since the Arab Spring, and this continues to fuel the instability in the region as more and more people are drawn into this generalized state of conflict and are increasingly radicalized by it. For all the Westerners who do go to Syria and other places to join the jihad, most of the fighters are still from those countries in the region with the worst human rights records. That is what underpins Wiktorowicz's analysis.

When dealing with those already radicalized, the challenges deal with criminal justice and enabling people to break free of such groups. Around the world, various governments are cracking down effectively by arresting, charging, trying, and imprisoning those engaged in terrorist activities, while other measures are being implemented to prevent funding from reaching terrorist organizations. I firmly recommend the measures taken as part of the UK government's Prevent strategy[16] and wholeheartedly agree with and endorse the

---

16   Prevent Strategy (London: HMSO, 2011)

further apolitical measures being taken to prevent, protect, pursue, and respond, which comprise the European Union counter-terrorism strategy.[17] In addition, there are a number of initiatives currently being deployed by the Organization for Security and Co-operation in Europe (OSCE), described in their guidebook *Preventing Terrorism and Countering Violent Extremism and Radicalization that Lead to Terrorism.*[18] These policies are based around the more formal aspects of community engagement and law enforcement. They all play a significant part in the eradication of violent extremism.

There is much to say also in favor of the measures included in the United Kingdom's Counter-Terrorism and Security Act 2015, as well as the EU-US Terrorist Finance Tracking Programme of August 2010, which has led to around three thousand reports to counterterrorism enforcement agencies around the world and which provides vital intelligence surrounding the financial support networks of some of the world's most deadly terrorist groups, including Al-Qaeda, Al-Qaeda in the Lands of the Islamic Maghreb, Al-Qaeda in the Arabian Peninsula, Al Shabaab, and Islamic Jihad Union.[19]

Former British prime minister Tony Blair made a good point when he argued over eight years ago that Islamic religious leaders should be welcomed in and encouraged to attend British universities. We should do this across the West. This way we would ensure that the next generation of community leaders in the West and even back in the Middle East gains an understanding of the West that transcends the caricature you get in Saudi Wahhabi religious textbooks. It would also develop a religious education that is up to

17   European Union, "The European Union Counter-Terrorism Strategy," (Brussels: Council of the European Union, 2005).

18   OSCE, "Preventing Terrorism and Countering Violent Extremism and Radicalization that Lead to Terrorism," (Vienna: Organization for Security and Co-operation in Europe, 2014).

19   European Commission, "Joint Report from the Commission and the U.S. Treasury Department regarding the value of TFTP Provided Data pursuant to Article 6 (6) of the Agreement between theEuropean Union and the United States of America on the processing and transfer of Financial Messaging Data from the European Union to the United States for the purposes of the Terrorist Finance Tracking Program," (Brussels: European Commission, 2013).

date on the challenges of the modern world and can deal with current realities—so that they do not fall into the trap of concluding that the only way to be a Muslim is to live in a society that looks like 7th-century Arabia.[20] We need imams and preachers who have a good enough education to know how to make Islam work for the 21st century, not against it.

Beyond universities, we must keep a close eye on what happens in religious schools. In the United Kingdom the government is monitoring faith schools that are teaching a fundamentalist view of Islam—especially those that focus on Wahhabi Salafism. Recent United Kingdom Office for Standards in Education (October 2014) inspections found that the Ebrahim Academy,[21] an independent secondary school catering to boys of mainly Bangladeshi and Somali heritage, was judged to be inadequate, teaching a very limited curriculum while not actively promoting British values. The London East Academy was also found to be teaching a very restricted view of Britain, and most of the school's library books were in Arabic. The Al Mizan Primary School was only teaching religious education in terms of Islam, and the East London Islamic School was teaching children to recite religious texts by way of memory and repetition. The Islamic Marahirul Uloom School[22] situated above the Marahirul Uloom Mosque was found to have a curriculum that focused almost exclusively on Islamic themes, and students were unable to tell the government inspectors whether they should follow Sharia or British law.[23] In 2007 the King Fahd Academy, a London faith school owned, funded, and run by the Saudi Arabian government, was caught in a furor as it was found to be using textbooks written in Arabic supplied by the Saudi Ministry of Education that called Jews "apes" and

20   Graeme Paton, "Universities 'to reform Islamic teaching'," *The Telegraph*, 5 June 2007.

21   Office for Standards in Education, "Ebrahim Academy," (London: The Office for Standards in Education, Children's Services and Skills, 2015).

22   Hannah Richardson, "'Radicalisation risk' at six Muslim private schools, says Ofsted," BBC, 2014 http://www.bbc.co.uk/news/education-30129645; ibid.

23   Office for Standards in Education, "Marahirul Uloom School," (London: The Office for Standards in Education, Children's Services and Skills, 2014).

Christians "pigs."[24] But the British authorities have reacted vigorously, and over the last few years, thanks to the UK government's oversight, the King Fahd Academy has improved significantly.

The lessons learned by the UK should certainly be applied here in the United States. We do respect the freedom of certain types of schools, or even of homeschooling tutors, to teach those things that they think will serve as the best education for their pupils. But we must demand that that freedom is exercised responsibly. The fundamental tenets of liberalism, which we need to agree on for diversity to be able to flourish peacefully—the key concepts of tolerance, mutual understanding, and respect for diversity—must be at the top of the agenda for all government agencies involved with education; including all parents and all teachers. We must maintain the utmost vigilance to ensure that the Wahhabi Salafism or any other ideology of intolerance and bigotry is challenged and countered wherever it is found.

We have noted in earlier chapters that many of the young Muslims who fall into Salafist extremism do so outside the mosques and the conventional structures of the Muslim communities. This presents a particular challenge to all Muslims: Why is this happening? Why do some young people turn to the simple verities of Salafist dogma as opposed to the rich and nuanced arguments of orthodox Islam? They have become alienated not just from Western societies but also their own religious traditions.

Some reasons are connected with the disconnect often found in second- (and later) generation immigrants who tend to identify less with their parents' backgrounds (and are sometimes less accepting of the compromises their parents made to attempt to integrate). However, Salafism presents a clear challenge to the wider Muslim communities, and one significant issue is to understand just why the traditional structures of Islam fail to hold the loyalty of the small proportion of younger Muslims who find it easy to accept Salafism's message instead.

---

24   Evening Standard, "We do use books that call Jews 'apes' admits head of Islamic School," The Evening Standard, 2007 http://www.standard.co.uk/news/we-do-use-books-that-call-jews-apes-admits-head-of-islamic-school-7189965.html.

RECOMMENDATIONS FOR WESTERN POLICY MAKERS

While this section is addressed to policy makers, it is essential to note that dealing with the threat posed by Salafism involves almost all of what we would call civil society. As I have argued in this book, Salafism is underpinned by a fundamental misreading of Islam, which has unfortunately spawned an equally flawed response by the far right in Western Europe and North America that is also based on a flawed understanding of Islam.[25] These two erroneous worldviews oddly find a sympathetic relationship with each other—both are quite content to argue that there can be no compromise, no coexistence, and one side must win for it to be safe. This is at odds with every basis for a democratic society, so it becomes important that all the pillars of a democratic society contribute positively to the debate about the problems posed by Salafism, as opposed to reinforcing the arguments of right-wing Islamophobes. With this in mind, I start this section with a discussion about the challenge to wider civil society, before looking more narrowly at the policy perspective.

FOR TEACHERS

Teachers, in their own way, have duties that are similar to those of religious leaders. In their classrooms they need to balance the issues of culture, race, religion, and community every day. They too must exercise the utmost responsibility and sensitivity in how they deal with these issues, and how they teach their pupils to negotiate the often difficult social consequences of these concerns.

But there is also a handful of more concrete and obvious things that they can do. One area that is explicitly their responsibility is the

---

25   See for example: Gove, *Celsius 7/7*; Phillips, *Londonistan: How Britain is Creating a Terror State Within.*

teaching of history. Our curriculum on international history must expand to include the history of the Middle East and of Islam. This is complex, even as sketched out in this book, but there is a need to bring the realities to wider attention. There should be no illusion that teaching it will be much easier. But in many ways, teaching children the difficulties and the complexities of that history—the history of the exchanges between Judaism, Christianity, and Islam, and the effects those exchanges have had on the rest of world history and, ultimately, on our own culture today—is exactly the point. This matters, as it is the ability to handle contested narratives and information in a manner that leads to greater understanding that is at the core of advancing human knowledge.

What jihadis, and indeed what fundamentalist Christians, teach in the way of history is full of easy facts and clear moral certainties. But that is a history that is merely constructed as a vehicle for moral parables, not a description of any reality. And if that is how you raise a child, you should not be surprised if they struggle to accept the difficulties, complexities, and moral shades of gray of our modern world. But as any real historian or anthropologist will tell you, our societies have never been underpinned by black-and-white facts. They have never been in clear, moral harmony. Our founding fathers established a nation of free men with self-evident, inalienable rights for all—and they have done so on the back of black slaves. That really should be the perfect metaphor to guard against any idealization of the past, and especially those rewritings of history that are used to sow division among us today.

Teaching history properly is teaching children all these complexities. And a key aspect is in drawing comparisons between the complexities of the past and the complexities of the present. We cannot dumb down this knowledge. We cannot afford to condescend to our children that they would not understand such complexities. They can, and sooner or later they will have to if they are going to be able to build successful societies together. We achieve nothing by teaching history as moral parable. We should leave moral parables to the pastors and the imams.

But teaching history properly is also teaching its proper lessons, such as how the Islamic caliphate was most prosperous and successful at the time when it was most open and willing to embrace the new and the different. It was then that Islam built the most advanced civilization on earth. The Golden Age of Islam came into existence not despite of, but precisely because of, this openness and willingness to explore new ideas. The scientific and cultural achievements of the Abbasids did not stem from the culture of camel-riding Arab clansmen. It stemmed from the energy with which these camel riders pursued, over the course of several centuries, the knowledge of the Greeks, Romans, Egyptians, Mesopotamians, Persians, and Indians, and the dedication with which they improved on that knowledge.

The success of the United States in the last century can easily be attributed to the very same approach. We have taken in wave after wave of the best ideas, best scientists, and best entrepreneurs from around the world, and we have given the world its current dominant civilization. But here we must not forget the lessons of the Islamic world. When they thought they were done, when they thought that the rest of the world no longer had anything to teach them, the Islamic world stagnated. And ultimately declined. We must not close in on ourselves in such a way. Arrogance, indifference, but most of all fear of what is different and foreign . . . if we let these dominate who we are, what our country does, the way our political leaders speak, we will suffer the same fate. That is unacceptable. And it is, ultimately, un-American.

But there are also more practical aspects of pedagogy that need to be addressed. It is not just the teaching of history that can inoculate against prejudiced and ultimately self-defeating narratives. We must also teach our children a robust, positive vision of our own values of freedom, tolerance, and citizenship. And we must impress on our children that these are their inheritance, fully and properly, regardless of ethnicity, race, or religion. It is thus extremely important that we impress on our students the value of their citizenship. That these freedoms and opportunities are their birthright, but also their responsibility to retain and build on. And it is their responsibility to earn these rights by protecting those same rights for all members of our societies. We must all assume responsibility not only for our own rights and liberties but also for the rights and liberties of everyone around us—especially those whose rights are threatened from any quarter, be it the government, religion, ideology, or anything else.

In this, teachers will have an extra duty of care. They will need to be trained to recognize when some of their pupils might become seduced by intolerant and bigoted ideologies, when they might become radicalized so that they would fail to heed the rights and liberties of others, and especially when this might spill over into violent action. I have mentioned multiple examples of this already being examined in various countries in Europe. We must learn from those initiatives. And we will, sooner rather than later, need to take measures to introduce such training in the normal course of accreditation and continuous professional development for teachers. And we can expect such an initiative to have a positive impact beyond just the threats of Islamist radicalization. Other kinds of radicalization, such as the kinds that ultimately lead to the all-too-common school shootings, may also be mitigated to some extent. After all, our target in this initiative is not Islam—it is bigotry, intolerance, and hatred in all its guises.

FOR JOURNALISTS

Next, in terms of those who shape our culture and our society the most, we need to discuss the role of journalists, and of journalism in general. At this moment in time, journalists, news anchors, and TV pundits in the United States are probably the most unhelpful people we have in terms of fighting the poisonous ideology of Wahhabism and its jihadist offspring. And the main reason is this: the fundamental premise is that the world is caught up in a war of Us vs. Them, Muslims vs. the West. And what does our media do? It wholeheartedly endorses the sentiment! You can almost hear them: "Oh yeah?! Well we're at war back at you, buddy! Bomb the shit out of them!"

The jihadis talk absurd nonsense about an End of Days final confrontation between good and evil, and we're giving them one! The media has done more to validate the jihadist recruitment pitch to disaffected Muslim youth in the West and indeed in the Islamic world than five hundred inarticulate fatawa by ISIS Internet "imams." Now it's not difficult to see why. American culture itself is very much given to the romantic and dramatic appeal of a big fight of good vs. evil. Most of our Hollywood films are some kind of variation on the theme. And our culture is also quite militaristic by international standards—even if we set to one side the extent to which our armed forces are lavishly funded by the federal government. We talk about peace but we're always itching for a fight. News outlets are simply giving their audiences what they want: combativeness, a narrative of war, and a story of good against evil.

But that is insanely irresponsible. It's not just "giving the people what they want." We know that most mainstream media outlets have followed Fox News down this hole, and have long since abandoned the notion that their job is to report the facts. But with the recent spate of jihadism-related shootings in our country, this nonsense is now costing American lives on American streets. Is this *really* what the people want? Does the media think it has no moral responsibilities or duty of care towards the citizens of this country beyond providing them with entertainment?

Journalists, reporters, and TV pundits are fully responsible for the way in which they choose to frame and present the issues they present to their audience, and that polarized Us vs. Them reporting of issues involving minorities such as Muslims in the West is incredibly counterproductive. It goes beyond saying that the media has a responsibility to report that radicals do not represent Muslims as a whole. Insofar as parts of the media are spewing out nonsense that is basically the jihadist recruitment pitch from the opposite direction, the supposed clash of civilizations, about the intransigence and belligerence of the West, about a lack of common ground between Islam and the West, I would say that some of the blood spilled on our streets today is on the hands of those in our media who are basically inadvertently running a massive ISIS recruitment campaign.

Our media and opinion leaders need to start taking responsibility for the consequences of their actions. They cannot just pander to the ignorance and xenophobia of specific target audiences chasing click-throughs and viewing figures. Thought leaders have a duty to inform themselves about the issues they discuss and the consequences of the choices they make in the way they discuss these issues. Ultimately they have a duty to inform and educate their audiences, not reinforce them into ignorance.

This is not something that we can, or should, legislate. The First Amendment is, and should remain, sacred. This is not a matter for regulation either, even if that could help. This is a matter of conscience. If you are a true American, you do not endanger the lives of other Americans on our streets for cheap laughs and hollow applause on television or radio. Rather, you do the right thing. "Not because it is easy. But because it is hard."

FOR POLICY MAKERS

All of the above present a real challenge to policy makers. Salafism is a problem not because of the extreme violence of AQ and ISIS but because it has attracted a significant degree of support from the wider Sunni Muslim population. In turn, its emergence has fed into the poisonous arguments of the European and American far right that the problem is not jihadist terrorism but all Muslims. To address this means we need to address why young people are turning first to Salafism and then, for a few, to violent jihad.

My initial recommendations are at the macro-political level and are aimed at our leaders and policy makers in the West, who must make much better progress towards resolving the crucial ongoing geopolitical disputes that have served as the fertile ground in which the ISIS fungus has grown. They must find a solution to the seemingly intractable problem of Palestine; the United States must finally close Guantanamo Bay and ensure that they never allow another Abu Ghraib. These are issues that are a source of so much rage in the Muslim world, and feed into the jihadis' narratives every day. It almost goes without saying that our leaders cannot stand by and watch any longer the continued rise of ISIS while the wider conflict in Syria fuels the ongoing refugee crisis in the region and the European Union, a mass movement of people that is destabilizing politically all the countries affected. Solving the crisis in Syria will also stop the migration of European jihadi recruits in the opposite direction, towards Syria. The stabilization of Iraq and once again Afghanistan, where ISIS-affiliated groups are making a worrying amount of progress at this moment in time, are all matters to which our leaders and peacemakers must give their closest attention.

But first and foremost, we must begin to challenge the ideology itself, directly. It is exceptionally hard to kill an idea, but it can be done. The secular ideology of communism, for example, is now bankrupt. Yes, there are still adherents, but as far as mainstream culture is concerned, they are discredited and have no real purchase on the public's imagination or on their political aspirations. Fascism has proved harder to defeat. There were periods when it waned, but unfortunately at the moment it is making a comeback in the guise of narrow nationalist movements that make a hatred of Islam their core philosophy.

Despite the relative defeat of these two 20th-century creeds, secular liberal democracy has not exactly triumphed, after all, as we prematurely celebrated in the '90s.[26] A new ideological challenger has now emerged—global jihadism. But to this has now been added a reactionary, nationalist conservatism, both abroad—the most notable example is Putin's Russia—and at home, where the Donald Trump phenomenon is in many ways an American doppelganger of Putin.

Both of these forces, both global jihadism and reactionary nationalism, are responses to the issues raised by the globalization championed by the United States and the West since the Second World War. Globalization has been an incessant challenge to deeply rooted nationalism and has destabilized many local identities, in countries all around the world. European governments in particular are struggling with how to respond to a large number of mostly young, second- and third-generation Muslims who do not identify as being British, French,

---

26   Francis Fukuyama, *The End of History and the Last Man* (New York: Free Press, 1992).

German etc. and who are attracted to the internationalist radical ideology of Wahhabi Salafism. And they are similarly struggling with ultranationalist reactions from similarly young and disenfranchised groups of white (often but not always) young people, who vote for the Front National[27] in France, PEGIDA (translated as Patriotic Europeans Against the Islamisation of the Occident) in Germany, various neo-Nazi parties in countries ranging from Sweden to Poland, Hungary, and Greece, and so on. Just as the political situation has felt increasingly precarious in the United States after the rise of the Tea Party—with polarization of the political discourse between Republicans and Democrats, to whom scoring party-political points has become more important than actually governing the country; with increasingly hostile, xenophobic discourse about Latin American immigrants; with culmination of the reactionary politics of fear encapsulated in Donald Trump's presidential campaign—so Europe is being pulled apart by the same forces. The same factors are at play in the Middle East. Much of what happened since the Arab Spring can be understood as the manifestation of the same forces. But unfortunately, the fabric that held together many of these countries has proven much weaker than the fabric that is keeping together our own societies, and so we have seen many states shattered by these events: notably Syria and Libya, though it is worth noting that even Egypt, literally the oldest nation on earth, has also been teetering on the brink at times.

So we in the West must look long and hard at our own political discourse. Yes, this involves the media, as discussed earlier, but it also involves the pronouncements of official politicians—some of whom are leaders of important Western nations.

Second, we must raise awareness of the Saudi promotion of Wahhabism in the national debate, so that *local* politicians and administrators at home learn to respond to it, and learn how to prevent it or mitigate its potentially negative effects. We have plentiful evidence

---

27   Whose founder, Jean-Marie Le Pen—who is also the father of the party's current leader, Marine Le Pen—was found guilty of Holocaust denial (Henry Samuel, "Le Pen found guilty of Holocaust denial," The Telegraph, 2008 http://www.telegraph.co.uk/news/worldnews/1578053/Le-Pen-found-guilty-of-Holocaust-denial.html.).

now that taking Saudi money for mosques leads to the displacement of other Islamic traditions. This will require a great deal of political acumen and intercultural sensitivity to achieve successfully, but as some local communities will learn to do this effectively, they can share their experiences with other communities and establish a pattern of cooperation that ensures long-term success. See for example how our different local police forces cooperate with each other, and share their experiences and innovations with each other. It is very important to take those short-term measures of robust law enforcement and counterterrorist activities that have a proven record of being effective in combating global jihadism.

We must also be especially vigilant in our schools and universities to ensure that the narrow Wahhabi Salafist worldview is not the only interpretation of Islam that gets advertised, and it is essential that we take to the airwaves and the Internet. We Muslims need to speak out in our mosques and community centers to say that there is no worldwide conspiracy to humiliate Muslims, or assault their lands or people, and that we as a community must adopt the more progressive teachings of Islam. It is thus absolutely crucial that we find our own cadre of charismatic, Arabic-speaking moderates who are able to take on the Wahhabi Salafists wherever they are engaging with our communities. We can, for example, adopt the stance that scholar Rachid Ghannoushi calls "realistic fundamentalism," a position that aims to achieve Islam in all areas of life but is also tempered with the social, political, and economic realities of the day.[28]

The point of education, however, really ought to be made much more broadly. It is not just at home that it is important to get education right. We must, now more than ever, understand that the education that each and every child receives anywhere around the world is of consequence to the entire world—all of us will ultimately be affected. What we do now is what will decide whether the next generation finally cures cancer, or whether they will be fighting the same absurd and stupid wars that their parents are

---

28 Kumar Ramakrishna, "Delegitimizing Global Jihadi Ideology in Southeast Asia," *Contemporary Southeast Asia* 27, no. 3 (2005). (p. 360)

fighting. It is thus desperately necessary to improve the education of children in the poorer parts of the Muslim world. If children have a broad education based on mathematics, humanities, and science, they will have a better chance of getting a job and are less likely to fall into the hands of radical Islamic extremists. If they learn critical thinking skills, they will be better able to see through the gaping flaws in logic of uneducated, but charismatic, radical preachers and self-styled "imams."

There are excellent initiatives out there, such as One Laptop Per Child,[29] which has donated five hundred robust, energy-efficient, Internet-ready laptops to children in Pakistan and five thousand laptops to children in Afghanistan. It is a promising start. But needless to say, it is very far from what is required to counter the billions invested by the Saudis in madrassas in those countries and many other similar ones.

If we could build on this and donate thousands more laptops (which cost $199) to children in the region, this would allow them to connect to educational courses, such as those on offer at Future Learn,[30] an online learning initiative developed by the British Council where students of all ages, all abilities, and from all around the world are using the Internet to study a variety of subjects. Then there is also the exceptional Khan Academy,[31] which offers free online courses in mathematics, science, the arts and humanities; all that children and teachers need to access the academy is access to the Internet and an email address. Our entrepreneurs have done a great job of putting the educational resources of the West up on the Internet so that they can benefit everyone, wherever they might be on the planet. But now we must make sure that those kids who would otherwise end up in Wahhabi Salafist madrassas have access to these educational resources and know how to make the most of them, rather than simply tuning in to the same Wahhabi Salafist channels on the web that already surround them at home.

---

29   One laptop, "One laptop per child," One laptop per child, 2016 http://one.laptop.org/.

30   Future Learn, "What would you like to learn," 2016 http://www.futurelearn.com.

31   Khan Academy, "You can learn anything," 2016 https://www.khanacademy.org./

An example of an initiative that does just that is the brilliant Dell Youth Learning[32] project. Dell sponsors a local champion, who works hard to ensure that obstacles to learning, such as scarcity of food and security, are addressed while accessing Dell-provided grants and technology to provide educational opportunities. This project has been rolled out in fourteen countries, including Jordan and Indonesia, but due to high security issues has not yet been implemented in countries such as Palestine, Lebanon, Pakistan, Afghanistan, and Iraq, arguably some of the countries that could benefit from it the most. It is vital that we extend educational opportunities to children in countries where they are at risk of being exposed to extremism, although until we can solve the problem of security in these places, this recommendation may be some years away from fruition. We must demand these policies and initiatives from our political leaders, and this is what we need to hold them to account against each and every election cycle. We must show that bombastic statements about who would "bomb the shit out of *them*" best, as we sometimes hear on television, is not the solution, or a way for such elected official to continue to hold on to their office.

This leads to a third key recommendation. Money. Investing in global development, poverty reduction,[33] and education is a vital step to reducing the appeal of Salafist militancy. In the same way that the post–World War II Marshall Plan went a long way to reducing the appeal of pro-Soviet Communist Parties in Western Europe, a commitment to international development will go a long way to undermining the arguments of Islamic extremism. When the West pulled out of Kosovo, it left a financial void. When Saudi money stepped in to fill it, Wahabbi Salafism followed, pushing traditional Islamic traditions out and paving the way for extremists in training.

Finally, we need to understand the nature of terrorism and terrorist groups. While the modern form of jihadism is new and presents its own challenges, it still shares much with its (unacknowledged)

---

32   Dell, "Youth Learning," 2016 http://www.dell.com/learn/us/en/uscorp1/power-possible-learning.

33   P. Nel and M. Righarts, "Natural Disasters and the Risk of Violent Civil Conflict," *International Studies Quarterly* 52, no. 1 (2008); J. Podesta and P. Ogden, "The Security Implications of Climate Change," *The Washington Quarterly* 31, no. 1 (2007).

predecessors, such as violent anarchism in the late 19th century and left-wing and right-wing terrorism in later years of the 20th century. Almost regardless of notional ideology, we find very similar dynamics. From the earlier chapters, three key issues stand out:

1. The route into such extremist groups is rarely through the standard structures of a wider belief system. Young people making the journey to Salafist extremism do not do so via the mosque, in the same way that young Italians attracted to the Red Brigades did not do so via the large and powerful Italian Communist Party. As I noted earlier, this presents a challenge to the wider Muslim communities, but it also has a policy dimension;

2. As individuals become more radicalized and more committed, their allegiance actually shifts from their notional ideology to in-group maintenance of their new social setting. This means that counter-radicalization policies need to work at many levels, presenting alternative social structures, as well as arguments to stem growing commitment to extremism. The more young Muslims are isolated from wider opportunities, the more vulnerable they are to extremism. Equally, the more we present Islamic terrorism as some inexplicable belief system as opposed to seeing it as profoundly wrong, the less we will be able to deal with it;[34]

3. Even at the level of dealing with those fully committed to murder and mayhem we should not overmilitarize our response. In some places and some instances, the application of military power is the only response, but more often than not, terrorists can (and should) be treated as a challenge of the criminal justice and intelligence communities.

---

34   Nicholas Searle, "To defeat terrorists we have to get inside their minds," The Guardian, 2017 https://www.theguardian.com/commentisfree/2017/mar/17/defeat-terrorists-terrorism.

This basic approach defused the long period of left-wing terrorism in Europe (which was effectively ended by the early 1980s) and of nationalist terrorism in Northern Ireland and Spain (by the early 1990s).

So the policy challenge is complex. We need to work with the Saudis to ease their transition towards a more conventional state and away from their domestic reliance on the Wahhabist clergy. We need to stop accepting Saudi funding for religious institutions in the West and step up our own appropriate funding of programs and institutions that support education and preserve traditional Islamic practices where relevant. We need an approach to Salafism that understands exactly why it is a flawed dogma but in turn understands why it is appealing to too many young Muslims. Finally, we need to avoid the sort of rhetoric that simply reinforces the Salafist narratives about the hostility of the "West" towards Islam.

FOR ALL OF US

Finally, it is all very well to point fingers and demand that somebody else fix everything. It is reasonable to expect that our leaders—political, religious, and cultural—do what is necessary to combat the rising tide of intolerance and bigotry, as well as tackle the specific symptoms of violence in radical Islamism and jihadism. But that is not enough. We must all do our part as well. No politician can fix everything on his own from a big white building somewhere far away. We must take responsibility for the success, or otherwise, of our own communities.

It is an unfortunate fact of life that the Wahhabi Salafist ideology, which can be the gateway ideology to violent global jihadism, is here to stay. And it will always affect some parts of our societies. So what remains is to offer better ideas. We must also try to ensure that Salafism becomes simply an austere form of Islam chosen by its adherents as a model for their own lives, but not something that inspires a turn towards violence and bloodshed. Within Muslim communities, we shall have to explore and embrace more pluralist readings of Islam to counter the extremist narrative. And within broader society in general, we must assert with confidence our commitment to a peaceful, shared life together. We must not allow those who would sow division between us to do so, whether they are some radical Islamic preacher or some bombastic radio host.

The innovative and groundbreaking work of Abdullah-X[35] in Britain is a good example of an alternative approach to how we do society together. This project is the brainchild of a young British-based Muslim and former radical who once followed the teachings of the so-called and self-appointed Islamic scholars Abu Hamza and Omar Bakri before turning his back on extremism. He has since worked with the European Union to produce and promote the Abdullah-X cartoon series on YouTube. Using the catchphrase "Mind of a Scholar, Heart of a Warrior," Abdullah-X's videos are designed to encourage critical thinking and act as a counterargument to the slick propaganda videos of the "Call of Duty" wannabe warriors who swell the ranks of ISIS as foreign recruits. As Abdullah-X says, he aims to win "young Muslim viewers over one YouTube click at a time."[36]

This is an excellent example of how, ultimately, ordinary people like us are the best at talking to the ordinary people who might be susceptible to radicalization, and how young people are the best at talking to young people who are passionate about injustice and feel a burning need to engage with it and do something about it. We are the people who will best understand the daily lives of these people, and sharing our experiences with each other is the best way we can make sense of our shared societies. The best way to ensure that we tackle the problems facing society is by working together, not by demonizing and fighting each other.

---

35   Jason Farrell, "Abdullah-X Cartoon Aims To Deter Jihadists," Sky News, 2014 http://news.sky.com/story/1300364/abdullah-x-cartoon-aims-to-deter-jihadists.

36   Atika Scubert and Florence Davey-Attlee, "Abdullah X:' Former extremist's cartoon aims to stop young Muslims joining ISIS," CNN, 2014 http://edition.cnn.com/2014/10/07/world/abdullah-x-cartoon/.

Abdullah-X is showing us one way in which we can be savvy with our public engagement. We must support those voices who rise up from the Muslim community to make their impassioned pleas for a society we can all share. We need to support such initiatives by private members of the public, find the funds necessary, commission and pay moderate young Muslims to produce and distribute via all the media at our disposal a 21st-century, pluralist, inclusive, and progressive reading of Islam, as well as a confident, liberal, pluralistic idea of the kind of society we want to share. The potential audience is huge, and our fight for the market needs to be as entrepreneurial as that of the radicals and extremists. We need to counter them on every front: we need to place our moderate reading of Islam in the bookshops, we should be selling our Islamic DVDs online and claiming our social media space via YouTube, Twitter, Facebook, Instagram, Reddit, and Pinterest.

It is crucial too that we do not surrender the Internet. If you see a bigot on Twitter, it is no longer enough to chuckle at yourself and think, *What a moron!* Your private chuckle amounts to public acquiescence. As we have learned from Edmund Burke and others, all that is necessary for evil to triumph is that good men do nothing. For all Muslims, our responses matter, whether it is that of Abdullah-X or the many Muslims who took to social media after the Charlie Hebdo attack last year in Paris with a placard saying *"Je suis Charlie."* We all, whether we are Muslim or not, must not allow bigotry, intolerance, and violence to go unchallenged: we must not allow those who would sow fear and division to do so unimpeded, wherever this may happen, whether online or in real life.

The Internet is also a space where we can rebut the narrative that Muslims are under attack from the imperialism of the United States, Israel, and the West. We need to remind the Muslim community of the positive foreign policy achievements since the early 1990s: the liberation of Kuwait and the genuine attempts to alleviate the suffering of Muslims in Bosnia, Kosovo, and Afghanistan;[37] the efforts, which cost so many lives, to bring democracy to Iraq after the fall of Saddam

---

37 Ramakrishna, "Delegitimizing Global Jihadi Ideology in Southeast Asia." (p. 362)

Hussein's dictatorship; and the continuing attempts to find a solution to the seemingly intractable problem of Palestine. Okay, some of these attempts have ended in ignoble failure, but it cannot be denied that Western countries have made costly sacrifices in many well-meaning, if sometimes ill-fated, attempts to help the Muslim world. And Western governments do engage in charitable and humanitarian interests, Western civil society, charities, and NGOs, actual ordinary citizens of the West have been and continue to be an unambiguous force for good around the world and in the Islamic world.

To counter the "West against the Muslim world" narrative that feeds into global jihadi propaganda we must highlight such efforts as the donations given and the work done by Western aid agencies in response to natural disasters. The 2004 Boxing Day tsunami provides a good example; many countries with coastlines along the Indian Ocean were affected by this catastrophe, including Indonesia, a country with a huge Muslim population. We need to remind Muslims wherever and whenever we can that the response from the West was not disinterested because it happened to a country that followed the Islamic tradition; it was overwhelmingly a kind and generous response to suffering with a total of $14 billion in aid pledged and donated, with over half of governmental donations coming from Western countries in the European Union, and the United States, Australia, Germany, and Japan.[38] Whenever Muslim countries have suffered from natural disasters, famines, or other such human tragedies, Western governments and nongovernmental organizations have been there to help. And their help was no less enthusiastic, and no less effective, for it being directed towards the Muslim world.

In the end the kind of societies we live in comes down to whether we are happy to share our societies with each other or whether we are not. These recommendations are directed at those political leaders, religious leaders, cultural leaders, and ordinary folk going about their daily lives who want to live in a society where everyone has equal

---

38   M Flint and H Goyder, "Funding the tsunami response," (London: Tsunami Evaluation Coalition, 2006).

rights and equal duties of care for each other's rights, and where everyone is safe and lives in peace. Those infected by this radical virus do not share that vision of a shared society. Nor do some of those who claim to be "on our side." But when you fight fire with fire, everything gets burned. And the only society where no compromise needs to be made is a society where only one person is left. For as long as we shall live in shared societies, we will have to contend with diversity of opinions, beliefs, desires, and needs. The essence of social living is compromise. Let that social compromise be that we shall leave in peace with one another. Let the only thing we are intolerant about be *intolerance itself*!

EPILOGUE

slamic jihadism, underpinned by Salafist dogma, is one of the major threats to the modern world. Its adherents are prepared to slaughter innocents both in the Muslim world and in the West in pursuit of their dream of a pure Islamic state that will be purged of all the compromises and flaws accrued since the fall of the Rashidun caliphate. Most religious and secular movements tend to spawn a fringe that argues that the only solution to problems is a return to an earlier form of purity, or that the only reason an ideological solution has not worked is that it was applied with insufficient rigor. Islam is not unusual in this, but at the moment it has the problem that zealots are able to threaten both their coreligionists and any whom they believe threaten their goals. Let us be clear about this framing: Salafism (and its Wahhabist parent) is not a religious interpretation of the complex material in the Qur'an and the *hadiths*. It is a totalitarian ideology.

Equally, while Islamic terrorism is a contemporary problem, it is not that new. Not only do most broad belief systems spawn fundamentalist fringes but terrorism as a political tactic is probably as old as civilization.[1] The logic of opposing a powerful regime with violence

---

1   Mark Irving Lichbach, *The Rebel's Dilemna* (Michigan: University of Michagan Press, 1998).

is not new, nor are the tactics: when a regime is militarily powerful and the opposition is weak, the opposition can use a set of tactics to inspire or scare the wider population, attack, and kill those who collaborate. This asymmetric conflict can also include civil unrest or support from a friendly external power, but the goal is usually clear—to force the opponent to do something they would not otherwise agree to.[2] In this abstract sense it matters not one bit if we agree or disagree with the goals, as the range of options available to oppose a powerful state remains much the same.

Thus if we are to deal with such a revolt, we need to take into account two key issues. One is that it is not that our current problem is not without historic parallels in terms of violent domestic dissent. Yet on the other hand, while the current jihadist movement does share factors in common with other revolts, it will also have its own internal logic and stated goals. An early strand of commentary about AQ, especially post 9/11, was to identify it with the mostly left-wing and nationalist terrorism that had been a problem in Europe from the 1960s through the 1990s. Malise Ruthven, in *A Fury for God*,[3] makes this a core thesis. In my opinion, the book benefits from not presenting AQ as something new, but it still misses just exactly what was different about this new form of terrorist movement compared to movements in the past.

Studies of those earlier terrorist movements are discussed in detail earlier, where I argued that members of such groups tend to emphasize maintenance of in-group links over any real progress towards their goals. In other words, once they are assimilated into the ideology and accept violence, group stability and loyalty become of utmost importance. This gives such groups a degree of coherence and longevity. The Red Brigades were active as a terrorist group from 1974 to 1984[4] and

---

2   Tilly, *The Politics of Collective Violence.*

3   Ruthven, *A Fury for God: The Islamist Attack on America.*

4   Other dates can be chosen, but by 1984 they were no longer an organized threat to the Italian state, and before 1974 they were one of a cluster of radical groups on the Italian left that used violence during demonstrations etc. but were not, as such, engaged in terrorism.

the IRA in Northern Ireland from 1969 to 1992.[5] In both cases, they were opposed by a well-organized state that retained the loyalty of the vast majority of their populations. So such groups can survive in a hostile environment. How they ended is equally informative. The Red Brigades collapsed in part after internal disputes.[6] They were so full of informers that in-group loyalty fell apart. By the early 1990s, the IRA too was undermined from within—again, in-group loyalty was lost, and eventually its leadership accepted that there was no practical route to achieve their goal of a united Ireland through violence.

Some of this applies to groups such as AQ and ISIS, their local franchises, and those who are inspired by their propaganda. One strand to understanding their appeal is to understand why individuals enter such groups and then choose to remain.[7] If their tactics draw much on the (unacknowledged) approach of their predecessors, then so should our response—seeking to undermine that group loyalty. A major part of any sensible response should use earlier responses: treat them as a criminal justice problem, break down interorganizational trust, provide safe exit routes for those who wish to leave.

However, we need to be equally clear what is *different* about the current threat of jihadist violence. First it stems from an ideology that willfully misrepresents Islamic history and traditions in order to create a set of simple dogmas. This ideology is entwined with the oil-rich state of Saudi Arabia and exported by that regime in the seemingly benign form of mosques, madrassas, and imams who only espouse Wahabbi Salafist ideology. It is attracting a growing number of Muslims in part as it appears to offer such a simple and clear explanation for all that is wrong in the modern world. Fundamentally if we are to deal with violent jihadism, we need to clearly challenge this ideology.

---

5   Again, the dates are indicative—the IRA existed pre-1968 in a dormant form, and some of its original members carried out acts of terrorism after 1992.

6   The murder of the Italian prime minister Aldo Moro in 1978 proved to be too much for many militants in the organization, and the resulting factional splits left the remnant much more vulnerable to state infiltration.

7   Searle, "To defeat terrorists we have to get inside their minds".

And such a response needs care. Most who subscribe to the ideology are peaceful, using it as a means to frame their own lives. We may not like this, but in a democratic society tolerance of dissent is very important. But we can challenge it. And we should. That too is part of living in a pluralistic democratic society. This challenge has to be at the level of improving real knowledge of Islam and its early history, as well as helping the Saudis stop exporting Salafism (which in turn becomes a major threat to them in the hands of AQ and ISIS). So to break the hold of Salafism, we need to challenge it as an idea.

This cannot be done using the mind-set and slogans of Breitbart and the European and North American far right. They actually mirror the Salafist fallacy—that any deviation is a fundamental threat and that there was some golden age to which we can return—and the two reinforce each other. We need to challenge Salafism in its own right and on its own terms. It is my hope that this book is a step in that process.

REFERENCES

Aaronovitch, D. "What is IS ?" BBC, 2015 [Online]. http://www.bbc.co.uk/
  programmes/b06sdlmb. [Accessed 16 December 2015]

Abadie, A. "Poverty, Political Freedom, And The Roots Of Terrorism." *American
  Economic Review* 95, no. 4 (2005): 50-56.

Abrahms, M. "What Terrorists Really Want: Terrorist Motives and
  Counterterrorism Strategy." *International Security* 32, no. 4 (2008): 78-105.

Aburish, S. K. *The Rise, Corruption and Coming Fall of the House of Saud.* 2nd ed.
  London: Bloomsbury, 2005.

Ackerman, S., Stephen, C., and MacAskill, E. "US launches airstrikes against Isis
  in Libya " The Guardian, 2016 [Online]. https://www.theguardian.com/
  world/2016/aug/01/us-airstrikes-against-isis-libya-pentagon. [Accessed 23
  October 2016]

Acosta, B. T. "The Suicide Bomber as Sunni-Shi'i Hybrid." Middle East Forum,
  2010 [Online]. http://www.meforum.org/2743/suicide-bomber-sunni-shii-
  hybrid#.Vw_5u8joaiI.twitter. [Accessed 2 July 2016]

Ahmed, S. *What Is Islam? The Importance of Being Islamic.* New York: Princeton
  University Press, 2016.

Ahrens, D. A. *Christianity's Contribution to Just War Tradition.* Carlisle: Strategic
  Studies Institute, Army War College, 1999.

Al-Arian, A. "Why Western attempts to moderate Islam are dangerous." AlJazeera,
  2016 [Online]. http://www.aljazeera.com/indepth/features/2016/01/western-
  attempts-moderate-islam-dangerous-160118081456021.html. [Accessed 2
  July 2016]

Al-Fakhri, M., Cropf, R., Kelly, P., and Higgs, G. "E-Government in Saudi Arabia: Between Promise and Reality." *International Journal of Electronic Government Research* 4, no. 2 (2008): 59-85.

Alfred, C. "A Shocking Number Of Kids Are Fighting And Dying For ISIS." Huffington Post, 2016 [Online]. http://www.huffingtonpost.com/entry/isis-child-soldiers_us_56c779b9e4b0ec6725e28d90. [Accessed 27 January 2017]

Ali, L. "Why is ISIL able to find recruits in the West?" The National, 2016 [Online]. http://www.thenational.ae/opinion/comment/why-is-isil-able-to-find-recruits-in-the-west. [Accessed 2 July 2016]

Alibašić, A. "Globalisation and its impact on Bosnian Muslims practices." Paper presented at Democracy and Global Islam, UC Berkeley, 2005.

Aljebrin, M. A. "Labor Demand and Economic Growth in Saudi Arabia." *American Journal of Business and Management* 1, no. 4 (2012): 271-77.

Allen, C. *God's Terrorists: The Wahhabi Cult and the Hidden Roots of Modern Jihad.* Philadephia, PA: Da Capo Press, 2007.

Alsheha, B. "The e-government program of Saudi Arabia: Advantages and challenges." 8. Riyadh: King Fahd University of Petroleum and minerals, 2007.

Amman Message. "The Three Points of the Amman Message." 107. Amman, 2004.

Amnesty International. "Absolute Impunity: Militia Rule in Iraq." 28. London: Amnesty International, 2014.

———. "Saudi Arabia 2015/2016." London: Amnesty International, 2016.

Armstrong, K. "Wahhabism to ISIS: how Saudi Arabia exported the main source of global terrorism." New Statesman, 2014 [Online]. http://www.newstatesman.com/world-affairs/2014/11/wahhabism-isis-how-saudi-arabia-exported-main-source-global-terrorism. [Accessed 1 May 2015]

ARTIS. "General Information." 2016 [Online]. http://artisresearch.com/general-information/. [Accessed 1 May 2016]

———. "Theoretical Frames on Pathways to Violent Radicalization." 117. Arlington: Office of Naval Research, 2009.

Associated Press. "Saudi Arabia: beheadings reach highest level in two decades." The Guardian, 2016 [Online]. http://www.theguardian.com/world/2016/jan/02/saudi-arabia-beheadings-reach-highest-level-in-two-decades. [Accessed 10 January 2016]

Bahrawi, N. " Is Bosnian Islam going the way of Malaysia?" The Guardian, 2010 [Online]. https://www.theguardian.com/commentisfree/belief/2010/oct/05/bosnian-islam-malaysia. [Accessed 7 January 2017]

BBC. "US judge clears Saudi Arabia in 9/11 lawsuit." BBC, 2015 [Online]. http://www.bbc.co.uk/news/world-us-canada-34405451. [Accessed 11 January 2016]

BBC News. "Analysis: Palestinian suicide attacks." BBC, 2007 [Online]. http://news.bbc.co.uk/1/hi/world/middle_east/3256858.stm. [Accessed 25 January 2017]

————. "Bin Laden tape: Text." BBC, 2003 [Online]. http://news.bbc.co.uk/1/hi/world/middle_east/2751019.stm. [Accessed 23 January 2017]

Beaumont, P. "Abu Bakr al-Baghdadi: The Isis chief with the ambition to overtake al-Qaida." The Guardian, 2014 [Online]. http://www.theguardian.com/world/2014/jun/12/baghdadi-abu-bakr-iraq-isis-mosul-jihad. [Accessed 1 June 2016]

Beling, W. *King Faisal and the Modernisation of Saudi Arabia*. London: Croon Helm, 1979.

bin Abdul-Wahhab, M. *Explanation of "The Four Rules Regarding Shirk"*. New York: Al-Ibaanah Book Publishing, 2003. http://tawheednyc.com/aqeedah/tawheed/Shirk.pdf.

————. *Three Fundamentals of Islam*. New York: Al-Ibaanah Book Publishing, 2014. https://abdurrahmanorg.files.wordpress.com/2014/08/the-three-fundamental-principles-shaykh-bin-abdul-wahab-al-ibaanah-com.pdf.

Boteach, S. "Godlessness has doomed Britain." Jerusalem Post, 2011 [Online]. http://www.jpost.com/Opinion/Columnists/Godlessness-has-doomed-Britain. [Accessed 7 February 2017]

Bowen, W. H. *The History of Saudi Arabia*. Westport, CT: Greenwood Press, 2008.

Brehony, N. *Yemen Divided: The Story of a Failed State in South Arabia*. New York: IB Taurus, 2011.

Brogan, H. *The Pelican History of the United States of America*. London: Pelican, 1985.

Brown, R. *Social Psychology*. 2nd ed. New York: Free Press, 1986.

Bunzel, C. "The Islamic State of Disobedience: al-Baghdadi Triumphant." Jihadica, 2013 [Online]. http://www.jihadica.com/the-islamic-state-of-disobedience-al-baghdadis-defiance/. [Accessed 26 January 2017]

Butt, Y. "How Saudi Wahhabism Is the Fountainhead of Islamist Terrorism." Huffington Post, 2015 [Online]. http://www.huffingtonpost.com/dr-yousaf-butt-/saudi-wahhabism-islam-terrorism_b_6501916.html. [Accessed 30 June 2016]

Byman, D. L., and Williams, J. R. "ISIS vs. Al-Qaeda: Jihadism's global civil war." Brookings Institute, 2015 [Online]. https://www.brookings.edu/articles/isis-vs-al-qaeda-jihadisms-global-civil-war/. [Accessed 20 January 2017]

Cameron, D. "Muslim Brotherhood review: statement by the Prime Minister." UK Government, Cabinet Office, 2015 [Online]. https://www.gov.uk/government/speeches/muslim-brotherhood-review-statement-by-the-prime-minister. [Accessed 27 June 2016]

Chrisafis, A. "'Nothing's changed': 10 years after French riots, banlieues remain in crisis " The Guardian, 2015 [Online]. https://www.theguardian.com/world/2015/oct/22/nothings-changed-10-years-after-french-riots-banlieues-remain-in-crisis. [Accessed 1 July 2016]

Clapper, L. "The Saudi Connection in the Belgium Attacks." Geopolitical Monitor, 2016 [Online]. https://www.geopoliticalmonitor.com/the-saudi-connection-in-the-belgium-attacks/. [Accessed 26 June 2016]

REFERENCES

Cohan, A. *Theories of Revolution: An Introduction*. Exeter: Thomas Nelson, 1975.

Cohn, N. *The Pursuit of the Millenium*. 3rd ed. London: Paladin, 1970.

Coles, I., and Parker, N. "How Saddam's men help Islamic State rule." Reuters, 2015 [Online]. http://www.reuters.com/investigates/special-report/mideast-crisis-iraq-islamicstate/. [Accessed 21 January 2017]

Commins, D. *The Wahhabi Mission and Saudi Arabia*. New York: IB Taurus, 2009.

CounterJihad. "Special Ops Command to Pentagon: Stop Ignoring Jihad." CounterJihad, 2016 [Online]. https://counterjihadreport.com/tag/salafism/. [Accessed 18 December 2016]

Crawford, M. *Ibn 'Abd al-Wahhab*. London: Oneworld Publications, 2014.

Crenshaw, M. "The Causes of Terrorism." *Comparative Politics* 13, no. 4 (1981): 379-99.

Crossette, B. "Iraq Sanctions Kill Children, U.N. Reports." New York Times, 1995 [Online]. http://www.nytimes.com/1995/12/01/world/iraq-sanctions-kill-children-un-reports.html. [Accessed 23 January 2017]

Cummins, W. "Muslims are a threat to our way of life." The Telegraph, 2004 [Online]. http://www.telegraph.co.uk/comment/personal-view/3608849/Muslims-are-a-threat-to-our-way-of-life.html. [Accessed 18 December 2016]

DeAngelis, T. "Understanding terrorism." *American Psychological Association* 40, no. 10 (2009): 60-62.

Dell. "Youth Learning." 2016 [Online]. http://www.dell.com/learn/us/en/uscorp1/power-possible-learning. [Accessed 30 June 2016]

della Porta, D. "Left-Wing Terrorism in Italy." In *Terrorism in Context*, edited by Martha Crenshaw. 106-60. University Park, PA: Penn State Press, 2010.

Devji, F. *Landscapes of the Jihad: Militancy, Morality, Modernity*. 2nd ed. London: Hurst, 2017.

Dickens, A. G. *The Age of Humanism and Reformation: Europe in the Fourteenth, Fifteenth and Sixteenth Centuries*. London: Prentice Hall, 1977.

Donnelly, J. *Universal Human Rights in Theory and Practice*. 2nd ed. New York: Cornell University, 2003.

Duyvesteyn, I., and Peeters, B. "Fickle Foreign Fighters? A Cross-Case Analysis of Seven Muslim Foreign Fighter Mobilisations (1980-2015)." 37. The Hague: International Centre for Counter-Terrorism, 2015.

Dzidic, D. "Bosnia's Wartime Legacy Fuels Radical Islam." Balkan Transitional Justice, 2015 [Online]. http://www.balkaninsight.com/en/article/bosnia-s-wartime-legacy-fuels-radical-islam. [Accessed 8 January 2017]

Eager, P. W. *From Freedom Fighters to Terrorists: Women and Political Violence*. New York: Routledge, 2008.

El-Gomati, M. "How to tackle the EDL." The Guardian, 2013 [Online]. http://www.theguardian.com/commentisfree/2013/may/31/edl-english-defence-league-york-mosque. [Accessed 12 January 2016]

Ettinger, E. *Rosa Luxemburg: A Life*. Guernsey: Guernsey Press, 1995.

EU. "Syria crisis." 3. Brussels: European Union, 2016.

European Commission. "Joint Report from the Commission and the U.S. Treasury Department regarding the value of TFTP Provided Data pursuant to Article 6 (6) of the Agreement between theEuropean Union and the United States of America on the processing and transfer of Financial Messaging Data from the European Union to the United States for the purposes of the Terrorist Finance Tracking Program." Brussels: European Commission, 2013.

European Union. "The European Union Counter-Terrorism Strategy." Brussels: Council of the European Union, 2005.

Evening Standard. "We do use books that call Jews 'apes' admits head of Islamic School." The Evening Standard, 2007 [Online]. http://www.standard.co.uk/news/we-do-use-books-that-call-jews-apes-admits-head-of-islamic-school-7189965.html. [Accessed 1 December 2016]

Farrell, J. "Abdullah-X Cartoon Aims To Deter Jihadists." Sky News, 2014 [Online]. http://news.sky.com/story/1300364/abdullah-x-cartoon-aims-to-deter-jihadists. [Accessed 11 January 2016]

Fattah, H. A Brief History of Iraq. New York: Checkmark Books, 2009.

Fearon, J. D., and Laitin, D. D. "Violence and the Social Construction of Ethnic Identity." International Organization 54, no. 4 (2000): 845-77.

Ferracuti, F., and Bruno, F. "Psychiatric aspects of terrorism in Italy." In The mad, the bad and the different: Essays in honor of Simon Dinitz, edited by I. L. Barak-Glantz and C. R. Huff. Lexington, MA: Lexington Books, 1981.

Fisher, M. "How Saudi Arabia captured Washington." vox.com, 2016 [Online]. http://www.vox.com/2016/3/21/11275354/saudi-arabia-gulf-washington. [Accessed 2 July 2016]

Fisk, R. Pity the Nation: Lebanon at War. 3rd ed. Oxford: Oxford University Press, 2001.

Flint, M., and Goyder, H. "Funding the tsunami response." London: Tsunami Evaluation Coalition, 2006.

Flynn, P. "The Saudi Arabian Labor Force: A Comprehensive Statistical Portrait." The Middle East Journal 65, no. 4 (2011): 575-86.

Foran, J. "A Theory of Third World Social Revolutions: Iran, Nicaragua, and El Salvador Compared." Critical Sociology 19, no. 2 July 1, 1992 (1992): 3-27.

Friedman, T. L. "No Way, No How, Not Here." New York Times, 2009 [Online]. http://www.nytimes.com/2009/02/18/opinion/18friedman.html. [Accessed 22 March 2017]

Fukuyama, F. The End of History and the Last Man. New York: Free Press, 1992.

Future Learn. "What would you like to learn." 2016 [Online]. http://www.futurelearn.com. [Accessed 30 June 2016]

Gall, C. "How Kosovo was Turned into Fertile Ground for ISIS." New York Times, 2016 [Online]. http://www.nytimes.com/2016/05/22/world/europe/how-the-saudis-turned-kosovo-into-fertile-ground-for-isis.html. [Accessed 5 January 2017]

Gartenstein-Ross, D. "How Many Fighters Does the Islamic State Really Have?" War on the Rocks, 2015 [Online]. http://warontherocks.com/2015/02/how-many-fighters-does-the-islamic-state-really-have/. [Accessed 1 May 2016]

George, M. "Iran's Revolutionary Guards commander says its troops in Syria." Reuters, 2012 [Online]. http://www.reuters.com/article/us-iran-syria-presence-idUSBRE88F04C20120916?feedType=RSS&feedName=Iran&virtualBrandChannel=10209&utm_source=dlvr.it&utm_medium=twitter&dlvrit=59365. [Accessed 30 August 2016]

Ginsborg, P. A History of Contemporary Italy: 1943-1980. London: Penguin, 1990.

——. Italy and Its Discontents: 1980-2001. London: Penguin, 2001.

Glenny, M. The Fall of Yugoslavia. London: Penguin, 1996.

——. McMafia: Crime Without Frontiers. London: Bodley Head, 2008.

Goldstein, R. J. Political Repression in 19th Century Europe. London: Routledge, 1983.

Gove, M. Celsius 7/7. London: Weidenfeld and Nicolson, 2006.

Gramsci, A. Selections from Prison Notebooks. Translated by Geoffrey Nowell Smith and Quintin Hoare. Southampton: Lawrence Wishart, 1971.

Gurr, T. R. Why Men Rebel. Princeton, NJ: Princeton University Press, 1970.

Hasan, M. "Suicide attacks are un-Islamic." In New Statesman, 2009.

Hegghammer, T. "Should I Stay or Should I Go? Explaining Variation in Western Jihadists' Choice between Domestic and Foreign Fighting." American Political Science Review 107, no. 1 (2013): 1-15.

Hennessy, P. The Secret State: Whitehall and the Cold War. London: Penguin, 2002.

Hobsbawm, E. "Dr Marx and the Victorian Critics." In How to Change the World: Tales of Marx and Marxism, edited by Eric Hobsbawm. 199-210. London: Little Brown, 2011.

Holt, R. "Only 6pc of Imams are Native English Speakers." The Telegraph, 2007 [Online]. http://www.telegraph.co.uk/news/main.jhtml?xml=/news/2007/07/06/nislam106.xml. [Accessed 28 January 2016]

Honore, T. "The Right to Rebel." Oxford Journal of Legal Studies 8, no. 1 (1988): 34-54.

Hopwood, D. Syria 1945–1986. London: Routledge, 2013.

Horgan, J. "From Profiles to Pathways and Roots to Routes: Perspectives from Psychology on Radicalization into Terrorism." The Annals of the American Academy of Political and Social Science 618, no. 1 (2008): 80-94.

Hosking, G. A History of the Soviet Union. 2nd ed. London: Fontana, 1990.

Hubbard, B., and Sheikh, M. E. "WikiLeaks Shows a Saudi Obsession With Iran." New York Times, 2015 [Online]. http://mobile.nytimes.com/2015/07/17/world/middleeast/wikileaks-saudi-arabia-iran.html?referrer=&_r=1. [Accessed 10 February 2016]

Human Rights Watch. "Iraq: Women Suffer Under ISIS." Human Rights Watch, 2016 [Online]. https://www.hrw.org/news/2016/04/05/iraq-women-suffer-under-isis. [Accessed 10 June 2016]

REFERENCES

Ibrahim, A. "The Resurgence of Al-Qaeda in Syria and Iraq." 80. Washington: SSI, 2014.

Ingersoll, G. "REPORT: Saudi Arabia Sent 1,200 Death Row Inmates to Fight in Syria." Business Insider, 2013 [Online]. http://www.businessinsider.com/saudi-arabia-sent-inmates-against-assad-2013-1?IR=T#ixzz35jkuX7QX. [Accessed 27 January 2017]

Jankowski, J. P. *Nasser's Egypt, Arab Nationalism and the United Arab Republic.* Boulder, Co: Lynne Rienner, 2001.

Jehl, D. "C.I.A. Says Berg's Killer Was Very Probably Zarqawi." *The New York Times*, 2004 [Online]. http://www.nytimes.com/2004/05/14/world/struggle-for-iraq-beheader-cia-says-berg-s-killer-was-very-probably-zarqawi.html. [Accessed 24 November 2014]

Jones, A. "Genocide and Mass Killing." In *Security Studies: An Introduction*, edited by Paul D Williams. 190-99. London: Routledge, 2008.

Jreisat, J. E. "Administrative Reform and the Arab World: Economic Growth." *Review of Policy Research* 16, no. 2 (1999): 19-40.

Kabbani, S. H. "Jihad, Terrorism and Suicide Bombing: The Classical Islamic Perspective." The Islamic Supreme Council of America, 2017 [Online]. http://www.islamicsupremecouncil.org/understanding-islam/legal-rulings/21-jihad-classical-islamic-perspective.html?start=15. [Accessed 31 March 2017]

Kamali, M. H. *Principles of Islamic Jurisprudence.* London: Islamic Texts Society, 2005.

Kemp, J. "Saudi Arabia's dwindling oil revenues and the challenge of reform." Reuters, 2016 [Online]. http://www.reuters.com/article/saudi-oil-kemp-idUSL8N1553PO. [Accessed 14 June 2016]

Khan Academy. "You can learn anything." 2016 [Online]. https://www.khanacademy.org. [Accessed 30 June 2016]

Kirdar, M. "Al-Qaeda in Iraq." 15. Washington: Center for Strategic and International Studies, 2011.

Kristof, N. "The Terrorists the Saudis Cultivate in Peaceful Countries." *The New York Times*, 2016 [Online]. http://mobile.nytimes.com/2016/07/03/opinion/sunday/the-terrorists-the-saudis-cultivate-in-peaceful-countries.html?_r=1&referer=http://m.facebook.com/. [Accessed 3 July 2016]

Krueger, A. B. "The National Origins of Foreign Fighters in Iraq." 18: NBER, 2006.

Lebovich, A. "How 'religious' are ISIS fighters? The relationship between religious literacy and religious motivation." Brookings Institute, 2016 [Online]. http://www.brookings.edu/research/papers/2016/04/how-religious-are-isis-fighters-lebovich. [Accessed 1 July 2016]

Lewis, P. "Kosovo PM is head of human organ and arms ring, Council of Europe reports " The Guardian, 2010 [Online]. https://www.theguardian.com/world/2010/dec/14/kosovo-prime-minister-llike-mafia-boss. [Accessed 8 January 2017]

REFERENCES

Lia, B. "The al-Qaida Strategist Abu Mus'ab al-Suri: A Profile." 5. London: OMS, 2006.

Library of Congress. "Al-Qaeda in Libya: A Profile." 54. Washington: Federal Research Division, 2012.

Lichbach, M. I. *The Rebel's Dilemna*. Michigan: University of Michagan Press, 1998.

Lund, A. "Divided, they may fall." Carnegie Middle East Center, 2016 [Online]. http://carnegie-mec.org/diwan/66413. [Accessed 25 January 2017]

———. "Syria's Salafi Insurgents: The Rise of the Syrian Islamic Front." 51. Stockholm: Swedish Institute of International Affairs, 2013.

Maalouf, A. *The Crusades Through Arab Eyes*. London: Al Saqi, 1983.

Mason, R. "Nigel Farage: British Muslim 'fifth column' fuels fear of immigration." The Guardian, 2015 [Online]. http://www.theguardian.com/politics/2015/mar/12/nigel-farage-british-muslim-fifth-column-fuels-immigration-fear-ukip. [Accessed 1 June 2015]

McCants, W. "How Zawahiri Lost Al-Qaeda." Washington: Brookings Foreign Affairs, 2013.

McCants, W., ed. *Militant Ideology Atlas*. West Point: Combating Terrorism Center, 2006.

McElroy, D. "Ireland 'leads the world in Islamic values as Muslim states lag'." The Daily Telegraph, 2014 [Online]. http://www.telegraph.co.uk/news/worldnews/europe/ireland/10888707/Ireland-leads-the-world-in-Islamic-values-as-Muslim-states-lag.html. [Accessed 10 January 2016]

Meijer, R., ed. *Global Salafism: Islam's New Religious Movement*. Oxford: Oxford University Press, 2009.

Memri. "Saudi Government Paper: 'Billions Spent by Saudi Royal Family to Spread Islam to Every Corner of the Earth'." The Middle East Media Research Institute, 2002 [Online]. http://www.memri.org/report/en/0/0/0/0/0/0/638.htm. [Accessed 26 June 2016]

Meserole, C. "The French Connection." Religion.org, 2016 [Online]. https://religional.org/2016/04/05/the-french-connection-part-i-backstory/. [Accessed 30 June 2016]

Mohammed, R. *Caliphate Reloaded: Past, present and future Muslim discourse on Power*. 2016.

Murray, D. "'Religion of peace' is not a harmless platitude." The Spectator, 2015 [Online]. http://www.spectator.co.uk/2015/01/religion-of-peace-is-not-a-harmless-platitude/. [Accessed 2 July 2016]

Naji, A. B. *The Management of Savagery: The Most Critical Stage Through Which the Umma Will Pass*. Translated by William McCants. John M. Olin Institute for Strategic Studies, Harvard University, 2006.

Nel, P., and Righarts, M. "Natural Disasters and the Risk of Violent Civil Conflict.". *International Studies Quarterly* 52, no. 1 (2008): 159-85.

REFERENCES

Office for Standards in Education. "Ebrahim Academy." London: The Office for Standards in Education, Children's Services and Skills, 2015.
———. "Marahirul Uloom School." London: The Office for Standards in Education, Children's Services and Skills, 2014.

Offord, D. *The Russian Revolutionary Movement in the 1880s.* Cambridge: Cambridge University Press, 1986.

One laptop. "One laptop per child." One laptop per child, 2016 [Online]. http://one.laptop.org/. [Accessed 30 June 2016]

OSCE. "Preventing Terrorism and Countering Violent Extremism and Radicalization that Lead to Terrorism." Vienna: Organization for Security and Co-operation in Europe, 2014.

Palestinian Central Bureau of Statistics. "Estimated Population in the Palestinian Territory." Palestinian Central Bureau of Statistics, 2016 [Online]. http://www.pcbs.gov.ps/Portals/_Rainbow/Documents/gover_e.htm. [Accessed 1 May 2016]

Pantucci, R. *"We Love Death As You Love Life": Britain's Suburban Terrorists.* London: C.Hurst & Co, 2015.

Parekh, B. "Is Islam a Threat to Europe's Multicultural Democracies?". *Religion in the New Europe* (2006): 111-21.

Partos, G. "Bosnia's Islamic heritage." BBC, 2003 [Online]. http://news.bbc.co.uk/1/hi/talking_point/3104130.stm. [Accessed 7 January 2017]

Paterson, T. G., Kisatsky, D., Maddock, S. J., Clifford, J. G., Hagan, K. J., Brigham, R., and Donoghue, M. *American Foreign Relations: Since 1895.* Vol. 2, Belmont CA: Wadsworth, 2009.

Paton, G. "Universities 'to reform Islamic teaching'." *The Telegraph*, 5 June 2007.

Peace, T. "Who becomes a terrorist, and why?" *The Washington Post*, 2016 [Online]. https://www.washingtonpost.com/news/monkey-cage/wp/2016/05/10/who-becomes-a-terrorist-and-why/. [Accessed 1 July 2016]

Peek, A. L. "The Roots of Lone Wolf Terrorism: Why the West's Homegrown Jihadists Are All Sunni." Foreign Affairs, 2016 [Online]. https://www.foreignaffairs.com/articles/middle-east/2016-01-12/roots-lone-wolf-terrorism?cid=soc-tw-rdr. [Accessed 2 July 2016]

Perliger, A. *Challengers from the Sidelines: Understanding America's Violent Far-Right.* West Point: Comating Terrorism Center, 2012.

Phillips, M. *Londonistan: How Britain is Creating a Terror State Within.* London: Encounter Books, 2006.

Podesta, J., and Ogden, P. "The Security Implications of Climate Change." *The Washington Quarterly* 31, no. 1 (2007): 115-38.

Pons, A. "E-Government for Arab countries." *Journal of Global Information Technology Management* 7, no. 1 (2004): 30-46.

Ramadan, T. *The Messenger.* Oxford: Oxford University Press, 2007.

Ramady, M. *The Saudi Arabian Economy: Policies, Achievements and Challenges.* 2nd ed. London: Springer, 2010.

Ramakrishna, K. "Delegitimizing Global Jihadi Ideology in Southeast Asia." *Contemporary Southeast Asia* 27, no. 3 (2005): 343-69.

Ramet, S. P. "Bosnia-Herzegovina since Dayton." In *Bosnia-Herzegovina since Dayton: Civic and uncivic values*, edited by Ola Listhaug and Sabrina P. Ramet. 9-48. Ravenna: Angelo Longo Editore, 2013.

Razmetaeva, Y. "The Right to Resist and the Right of Rebellion." *Oxford Journal of Legal Studies* 21, no. 3 (2014): 758-84.

Reinmann, J. "Saudi Arabia vs. Iran: Predominance in the Middle East." Washington: Foreign Policy Journal, 2016.

Richardson, H. "'Radicalisation risk' at six Muslim private schools, says Ofsted." BBC, 2014 [Online]. http://www.bbc.co.uk/news/education-30129645. [Accessed 12 December 2015]

Robertson, N., Cruickshank, P., and Lister, T. "Documents give new details on al Qaeda's London bombings." CNN, 2014 [Online]. http://edition.cnn.com/2012/04/30/world/al-qaeda-documents-london-bombings/?c=&page=0. [Accessed 2 February 2017]

Rockmore, T. *Marx after Marxism: The Philosophy of Karl Marx.* Oxford: Blackwell, 2002.

Roex, I. "Should we be Scared of all Salafists in Europe? A Dutch Case Study." *Perspectives on Terrorism* 8, no. 3 (2014).

Ross, W. "Geert Wilders: The 'Prophet who hates Muhammad'." Newsweek, 2015 [Online]. http://europe.newsweek.com/geert-wilders-prophet-who-hates-muhammad-300266?rm=eu. [Accessed 30 June 2016]

Rubin, A. "Legal borrowing and its impact on Ottoman legal culture in the late nineteenth century." *Continuity and Change* 22, no. 2 (2007): 279-303.

Russell, A. "Unforgiven, unforgotten, unresolved: Bosnia 20 years on." Financial Times, 2012 [Online]. https://www.ft.com/content/8a698dbe-73af-11e1-aab3-00144feab49a. [Accessed 5 January 2017]

Ruthven, M. *A Fury for God: The Islamist Attack on America.* London: Granta, 2002.

Sadi, M. A. "The Implementation Process of Nationalization of Workforce in Saudi Arabian Private Sector: A Review of "Nitaqat Scheme"." *American Journal of Business and Management* 2, no. 1 (2013): 37-45.

Sambidge, A. "Saudi king approves $312m payout to poor." ArabianBusiness.com, 2010 [Online]. http://www.arabianbusiness.com/567647-saudi-king-approves-312m-payout-to-poor. [Accessed 4 August 2010]

Samuel, H. "Le Pen found guilty of Holocaust denial." The Telegraph, 2008 [Online]. http://www.telegraph.co.uk/news/worldnews/1578053/Le-Pen-found-guilty-of-Holocaust-denial.html. [Accessed 11 January 2016]

Sassoon, D. *One Hundred Years of Socialism: The West European Left in the Twentieth Century.* London: Fontana, 1997.

Saul, H. "Life as a woman under Isis: Document reveals for the first time what group really expects from female recruits living in Syria and Iraq." The

Independent, 2015 [Online]. http://www.independent.co.uk/news/world/ middle-east/life-as-a-woman-under-isis-document-reveals-for-the-first- time-what-group-really-expects-from-female-10025143.html. [Accessed 27 January 2017]

Schmid, A. "Foreign (terrorist) fighter estimates: conceptual and data issues." The Hague: International Center for Counter-Terrorism Policy, 2015.

Sciascia, L. *The Moro Affair.* Translated by Sacha Rabinovitch. 2nd ed. London: Granta, 1987.

Scubert, A., and Davey-Attlee, F. "Abdullah X:' Former extremist's cartoon aims to stop young Muslims joining ISIS." CNN, 2014 [Online]. http://edition.cnn. com/2014/10/07/world/abdullah-x-cartoon/. [Accessed 18 December 2015]

Searle, N. "To defeat terrorists we have to get inside their minds." The Guardian, 2017 [Online]. https://www.theguardian.com/commentisfree/2017/mar/17/ defeat-terrorists-terrorism. [Accessed 17 March 2017]

Shane, S. "Saudis and Extremism: 'Both the Arsonists and the Firefighters'." New York Times, 2016 [Online]. http://www.nytimes.com/2016/08/26/world/ middleeast/saudi-arabia-islam.html?_r=0. [Accessed 5 January 2017]

Shubert, A. "The women of ISIS: Who are they?" CNN, 2015 [Online]. http:// edition.cnn.com/2015/05/29/middleeast/who-are-the-women-of-isis/. [Accessed 27 January 2017]

Shultz, R. H. "Global Insurgency Strategy and the Salafi Jihad Movement." INSS Occasional Paper 66, 2008.

Simms, B. *Unfinest Hour: Britain and the Destruction of Bosnia.* London: Penguin, 2001.

Skells, M. "Wahhabist Ideology: What it is and why it's a problem." Huffington Post, 2016 [Online]. http://www.huffingtonpost.com/entry/585991fce4b014e 7c72ed86e?timestamp=1482266088767. [Accessed 21 December 2016]

Smucker, P. "Iraq builds 'Mother of all Battles' mosque in praise of Saddam." The Telegraph, 2001 [Online]. http://www.telegraph.co.uk/news/worldnews/ middleeast/iraq/1335735/Iraq-builds-Mother-of-all-Battles-mosque-in- praise-of-Saddam.html. [Accessed 23 January 2017]

Stewart, K. "How Christian fundamentalists plan to teach genocide to schoolchildren " The Guardian, 2012 [Online]. https://www.theguardian. com/commentisfree/2012/may/30/christian-fundamentalists-plan-teach- genocide. [Accessed 7 February 2017]

Sudetic, C. "The bullies who run Kosovo." Politico, 2015 [Online]. http://www. politico.eu/article/kosovo-hashim-thaci-un-special-court-tribunal-organ- trafficking-kla-serbia-milosevic-serbia-ramush/. [Accessed 8 January 2017]

Tahir-ul-Qadri, M. "Fatwa on Terrorism and Suicide Bombings." 512. London: Minhaj-ul-Quran, 2010.

Tarantelli, C. B. "The Italian Red Brigades and the structure and dynamics of terrorist groups." *The International Journal of Psychoanalysis* 91, no. 3 (2010): 541-60.

Taylor, A. "20 Years Since The Bosnian War." The Atlantic, 2012 [Online]. http://www.theatlantic.com/photo/2012/04/20-years-since-the-bosnian-war/100278/. [Accessed 5 January 2017]

Taylor, J. "Sheikh issues fatwa against all terrorists." The Independent, 2010 [Online]. http://www.independent.co.uk/news/uk/home-news/sheikh-issues-fatwa-against-all-terrorists-1915000.html. [Accessed 22 March 2017]

Tétreault, M. A. "Globalisation and Islamic Radicalism in the Arab Gulf Region." In *The Transformation of Politicised Religion: From Zealots Into Leaders,* edited by Hartmut Elsenhans, Rachid Ouaissa, Sebastian Schwecke and Mary Ann Tétreault. 57-74. London: Routledge, 2015.

The London Declaration. "The London Declaration." 2011 [Online]. http://www.londondeclaration.com/. [Accessed 24 March 2017]

Tilly, C. *The Politics of Collective Violence.* Cambridge: Cambridge University Press, 2003.

Toaldo, M. "Europe's options on Libya: no easy way out." Aspenia, 2015 [Online]. https://www.aspeninstitute.it/aspenia-online/article/europe%E2%80%99s-options-libya-no-easy-way-out. [Accessed 29 October 2016]

Tomlinson, C. "Islamic Scholar: Europe may be heading toward Civil War." Breitbart, 2016 [Online]. http://www.breitbart.com/london/2016/09/11/islam-scholar-europe-may-heading-toward-civil-war/. [Accessed 18 December 2016]

Travis, A. "MI5 report challenges view on terrorism in Britain." The Guardian, 2008 [Online]. http://www.guardian.co.uk/uk/2008/aug/20/uksecurity.terrorism1. [Accessed 29 June 2016]

United Nations. "The human rights situation in Iraq in the light of abuses committed by the so-called Islamic State in Iraq and the Levant and associated groups." 51. Geneva: UNHCR, 2015.

———. "Rome Statute of the International Criminal Court." UN, 2002 [Online]. http://legal.un.org/icc/statute/romefra.htm. [Accessed 23 February 2014]

———. "Universal Declaration of Human Rights,." 8. New York: UN General Assembly, 1948.

Urban, J. B. *Moscow and the Italian Communist Party: From Togliatti to Berlinguer.* Ithaca: Cornell University Press, 1986.

Urban, M. "Bosnia: The cradle of modern jihadism?" BBC, 2015 [Online]. http://www.bbc.co.uk/news/world-europe-33345618. [Accessed 8 January 2017]

Victoroff, J. "The Mind of the Terrorist." *Journal of Conflict Resolution* 49, no. 1 2005/02/01 (2005): 3-42.

Warf, B., and Vincent, P. "Multiple geographies of the Arab Internet." *Area* 39, no. 1 (2007): 83-96.

Watson, D. " The Terrorist Threat Confronting the United States." FBI, 2002 [Online]. https://archives.fbi.gov/archives/news/testimony/the-terrorist-threat-confronting-the-united-states. [Accessed 7 February 2017]

REFERENCES

Wight, C. "Theorising Terrorism: The State, Structure and History." *International Relations* 23, no. 1 March 1, 2009 (2009): 99-106.

Wiktorowicz, Q. *Radical Islam rising: Muslim extremism in the West*. London: Rowman & Littlefield Publishers, 2005.

Willan, P. *Puppet Masters: The Political Use of Terrorism in Italy*. 2nd ed. New York: Authors Choice Press, 2002.

Winter, C. "Libya: The Strategic Gateway for the Islamic State." 15. London: Quilliam Foundation, 2015.

Wynabrandt, J. *A Brief History of Saudi Arabia*. 2nd ed. New York: Infobase Publishing, 2010.

Zelin, A. Y. "Abu Bakr al-Baghdadi: Islamic State's driving force." BBC, 2014 [Online]. http://www.bbc.co.uk/news/world-middle-east-28560449. [Accessed 10 March 2015]

INDEX

A

Abbasid Caliphate, 26–32
Abbasid dynasty, ix, 25, 29–32
Abbasid Empire, 29–32, 90
Abduh, Muhammad, 8
Abdullah-X, 266–267
"Abode of peace," ix, 79–80, 86–87,
   125. *See also Dar al-Islam*
"Abode of war," ix, 79–80, 83–84, 86,
   152. *See also Dar al-harb*
Abu Bakr, 19–21, 104, 134, 237–239
Abu Ghraib, 249, 258
Afghanistan, 201, 207, 210, 218–220,
   227, 259
Al-Awda, Salman, 65
Al-Baghdadi, Abu Bakr, 19–21, 104,
   134, 237–239
Al-Battani, 28
Al-Din Ahmad, Taqi, 79
Al-Faisal, Abdullah, 148–151
Al-Ghazali, 29–30
Al-Hawali, Safar, 55, 65
Al-Haytan, 28
Al-Kashi, 28
Al-Khwarizmi, 28
Al-Latif, Shaikh 'Abd, 46
Al-Maliki, Nouri, 89, 209
Al-Masri, Abu Hamza, 149, 151
Al-Muhajiroun, 152–153
Al-Nusra, 141, 203, 213–221, 225, 228

Al-Qaeda (AQ)
   acceptance of, 225
   characteristics of, 216–218, 224–
      225, 228–229
   creation of, 139, 207
   defeat of, 78, 88, 201–202, 216
   global offensive of, xi–xii
   goals of, 218–219
   ISIS and, 93, 121, 216–220, 223–
      231, 258, 272–274
   modern jihadism and, 113
   offspring of, 216–220
   rejection of, 225
   rise of, 139, 242
   roots of, xi
   spread of, xi–xii
   threats from, xix–xx
   at war with, 235
Al-Qaeda Central (AQC), 217
Al-Qaeda in Iraq (AQI)
   characteristics of, 210, 217
   creation of, 207–208
   ISIS and, 217–220
   leadership of, 202–203
   rebranding of, 219
   tactics of, 207–210
Al-Salam Faraj, Muhammad 'Abd, 80
Al-Saud family, 43, 45
Al-Saud, Muhammad bin Salman, 245
Al-Shaam, Ahrar, 211

Al-Shaikh, 'Abd Allah Al, 53
Al-Shaikh family, 43, 44
Al-Sharia, Ansar, 225
Al-Shishani, Abu Omar, 238
Al-Tusi, 28
Al-Wahhab, Muhammad ibn 'Abd, 36–46, 51–52, 71, 85
Al-wala' wa al-bara', 45, 86, 95–96
Al-Zarqawi, Abu Musab, 207–209, 218
Al-Zawahiri, Ayman, 82, 85–86, 104, 238
Al-Zayat, Montasser, 82
Albania, 183–184, 186–190, 193–196, 198
Alexander the Great, 21–23
Amal, 58, 208
Amman Message, 121–125
Antidote
    for conflicts, 235–269
    expectations of, 265–266
    recommendations for, 235–269
Antimodernism, 3–4
Apostates, x–xv, 37–38, 67, 86–88, 95, 106, 122–124
AQ. *See* Al-Qaeda
AQI. *See* Al-Qaeda in Iraq
Ash'arism, 123
Askari, Hossein, 8
Assad regime, 39, 203, 210–214, 217, 223
Atran, Scott, 157, 172–173, 176
Atta, Muhammad, 149
Azzam, Abdallah Yusuf, 81, 151, 238

B
Ba'ath regime, 57, 88, 202–206, 209–210, 230
Bakri, Omar, 148–149, 152–153, 266
Balkans, 183–198, 220, 239
"Band of brothers," 171–174, 178
Beck, Glenn, 236
Bigotry
    ending, 265–269
    hate preaching and, 140, 145–147, 155

    ideology of, 94, 111, 118, 252
    as infectious disease, 236
    inoculation against, 236–237, 255–256
    spread of, 230, 236
    war against, 235–236
Bin 'Abd al-'Aziz, Faisal, 55
Bin 'Abd al-'Aziz, Sa'ud, 55
Bin 'Abdul 'Aziz, Nayef, 55
Bin Baz, Shaykh 'Abd al-'Aziz, 64–67, 84, 96, 135
Bin Laden, Osama, 45, 53–55, 63–66, 82–86, 96, 103–104, 148–149, 206–207, 238
Bin Salman al-Saud, Muhammad, 245
Blair, Tony, 152, 250
Boko Haram, 35, 155, 160, 229
Bosnia, xvii, 183–198, 201, 229
Brotherhood, idea of, 162, 171–174, 178. *See also* Muslim Brotherhood
Brzezinski, Zbigniew, 81
Bunzel, Cole, 217
Burke, Edmund, 267
Bush, George, xi, 97
Byzantines, 7, 18–21, 25, 90

C
Caliphates, x, xii, xv, 3–6, 18–32
Catholicism, xvi–xvii, xx, 91, 189
Celsius 7/7, 165
Charlie Hebdo attack, 267
Christianity, xv, xx, 6–7, 18, 22–25, 36, 90–99, 103, 188, 252–254
Cicero, 129
Clinton, Bill, 193
Cold War, 57–59, 169
Communism, 58–59, 81, 156, 170–171, 183, 259
Communist Party, 94, 114, 116, 151, 159, 205, 223, 263, 264
Constitution of Medina, 12–18, 23–24, 246
Counter-Terrorism and Security Act, 250
Criminal gangs, 175, 186, 196

D

Daesh. See Islamic State in Iraq and Syria

Dar al-harb, 79–80, 83–84, 86, 106

Dar al-Islam, 46, 63, 79–80, 83, 86–87, 106

Davis, Richard, 157, 172–173

Dayton Accords, 185–186, 192, 195

"Dead men walking," 109

Death, love of, 108–110

Declaration of Human Rights, 129. *See also* Human rights

Declaration of Jihad on the Jews and Crusaders, 85

Declaration of War against the Americans Occupying the Land of the Two Holy Places, 85

Discrimination, xv, 5, 18, 109, 153, 222

Doctrines, 44–45, 50, 86–87

Drug trade, 196, 207

E

Education
coeducation, 194–195
control of, 222–223
importance of, 55, 251–252, 261–262
Islamic education, 40, 104
low education, 74–75
religious education, 68, 103, 145, 178, 207, 250–252
standards in, 251
for women, 61–63, 194–195

English Defense League, 247–248

EU-US Terrorist Finance Tracking Programme, 250

European Union (EU), 183–187, 197–198, 226, 229, 250, 259, 266–268

F

Face veils, 162, 166, 195

Fahd, King, 63–64, 84

Fascism, 110, 114, 156, 223, 259

Fatwa
of Bin Baz, 65

Mardin Fatwa, ix, 79–84, 123, 125, 127, 129
of Tahir-ul-Qadri, 121–122, 125–126

Final Solution, xvii

Free Syrian Army (FSA), 203, 211–212, 217

Fury for God, A, 272

G

Gadhafi, 225

Gangs, 175, 186, 196

Gazi al-Haj, Al-Amir, 215

Gender segregation, 62, 195

Ghannoushi, Rachid, 261

Ghazali, 29–30

Ginges, Jeremy, 157

Global jihadism, xii–xx, 148, 227–229, 237–241, 259–261, 265. *See also* Jihadism

Global repercussions, 223–226

Gove, Michael, 165

Graham, Bob, 140, 240

Greek Empire, 31

Grievance politics, 106–110, 115, 169

Grievance theology, 148, 245, 249

Group identity, 77, 162–164, 173–175

Guantanamo Bay, 249, 258

Gulf Wars, 152, 205, 230, 273–274

H

Hadiths, 27, 37, 40, 87, 130, 134, 246, 271

Hajj, 17–18

Hamas, 74, 93, 208

Hamza, Abu, 148, 149, 151, 266

Hanif, Asif Muhammad, 153

Hate
belief systems and, 143
ideology of, 137–140, 149–151, 153–154
implications of, 153–156
message of, 149–151, 153–154
preachers of, 105, 140, 144–151, 155–158, 178
spread of, 137–180

Hawkins, Harold, 157
Headscarf, 162, 190
Hijra, 13–14, 19
Hindu Tamil Tigers, xiii, 93
Hitler, Adolf, 239
Hizb ut-Tahrir (HT), 148, 152
Hizbollah, 58, 74, 208, 211, 214, 216
Holbrooke, Richard, 195
Holocaust, 239, 260
House of Saud, xix, 39, 42–53, 64–71,
    85, 94, 100, 139–141, 240, 242
House of Wisdom, 27, 29
Human rights
    abuses of, 196
    declaration of, 129
    democracy and, 8
    protection of, 126, 129, 133, 150
    respect for, 112, 125–126
Hungarian Empire, 183
Hussein, Saddam, xi, 45, 58, 64, 84,
    88, 152, 202, 205–206, 235, 268

I
Ibn 'Abd al-Wahhab, Muhammad,
    36–46, 51–52, 71, 85
Ibn 'Abd Allah ibn Muhammad,
    Sulayman, 45, 50, 63
Ibn Abi Sufyan, Muawiya, 23–25
Ibn Abi Talib, Ali, 20–21, 23
Ibn Ali, Hasan, 23, 26
Ibn Hayyan, Jabir, 28
Ibn Saud, Abd al-'Aziz, 47–51, 67–68
Ibn Saud, Khalid, 45–46
Ibn Saud, Muhammad, 42–43
Ibn Sina, 28
Ibn Taymiyya, 79, 80–82
Iconoclasm, 37, 43
Idolatry, 37, 46
Ignorance, 18, 30, 40, 257–258
Ikhwan, 49–53
Imperialism, 223, 267
Infidels, 45–48, 67–68, 143, 214, 239
Intolerance
    ending, 235–237, 255–256, 265–269
    hate preaching and, 140, 145–147,
        155

ideology of, xv–xvi, 35, 39, 87,
    94–98, 111, 118, 252
spread of, 230, 236
Iran, 32, 36, 49, 58–61, 202–207, 211–
    213, 230, 244
Iraq, 32, 201–210, 214–226, 229–230,
    235–241, 259
ISIS/ISIL. *See* Islamic State in Iraq and
    Syria
Islam
    belief systems, xvi–xvii, 31–32,
        85–97, 103–118
    birth of, 9–10
    branches of, 20–21
    description of, 7–8
    history of, 4–7
    ideology of, 4–7, 35–36, 87–100,
        103–107
    mainstream Islam, xv, xx, 5, 31, 43,
        52, 102, 106, 121, 148, 158
    reactionary Islam, 3–7, 30, 35–38,
        92–98, 102, 113
    revolutionary Islam, 38–41
    rise of, 4–5
    theology and, 103–107
    understanding of, 4–5, 35–36
    violent Islam, 4–7, 53–57, 121–123,
        126–130, 153–161, 164–179
Islamic age, beginning of, 13–14
Islamic Alliance, 211
Islamic challenge
    Amman Message and, 121–125
    condemning terrorism, 121–136
    laws of war and, 125, 129–134
    London Declaration and, 121–125
    rejection of Salafism, 125–133
    right to rebel and, 125–129, 133
Islamic dynasty, ix, x
Islamic extremism. *See also* Jihadism;
    Radicalism
    approach to, xii–xiv, xviii, 263–
        266
    belief systems, 31–32, 85–97, 194–
        195, 210–212, 264, 271–272
    ideology of, xii, 5
    interpretation of, 127

root of, 32
violence and, 175–178, 250–251
Islamic Front, 211–214, 217, 221, 228
Islamic Golden Age, xv, 1–30, 37, 41, 168, 255
Islamic radicalism, xi–xx. *See also* Radicalism
Islamic state, establishment of, xii, 12–18
Islamic State in Iraq and Syria (ISIS)
   AQ and, 93, 121, 216–220, 223–231, 258, 272–274
   AQI and, 217–220
   Assad regime and, 217
   characteristics of, 216–218, 224–225, 228–229
   establishment of, xii, 7, 12–18
   goals of, 87–89, 224–226
   ideology of, 87–89, 224
   joining, 142–145
   members of, 160
   modern jihadism and, 113
   rise of, 139–145, 242
   self-identification with, 157–158
   threats from, xix–xx
   at war with, 235
   women and, 221–223
Islamophobia, 257–258

J

Jahiliya, 18, 23, 30, 40, 100, 102
Jaish al-Islam, 212
Jewish community, xv, xvii, 6–7, 15–16, 22–25, 85, 90–99, 150, 238, 251–254
Jihad definition, ix. *See also* Jihadism
Jihadi-Salafism, 64–67, 71, 241–243. *See also* Salafism
Jihadism. *See also* Islamic extremism; Radicalism
   activism and, 106, 158, 168, 172–174
   basis for terrorism, 63–67, 78–79, 107, 115–116
   current threats of, 273–274
   defensive jihad, 67
   definition of, ix
   doctrines of, 87
   global jihadism, xii–xx, 148, 227–229, 237–241, 259–261, 265
   goals of, 87
   ideology of, 87, 238, 265–266, 271–274
   jihadi Salafism, 64–67, 71, 113, 241–243
   modern jihadism, 63–65, 69–118, 176
   offensive jihad, 67
   rhetoric and, 153–154, 158, 168–169, 174–175, 265
   violent jihad, xiii–xx, 3, 66, 88–95, 112–116, 130, 145–153, 161–167, 174–177, 201–209, 240, 258, 273–274
Journalists, role of, 256–258
Jurisprudence, schools of, 122, 127, 129, 133–134
Just War, 86–89, 128–129. *See also* War

K

Ka'aba, 12, 17–18, 42
Karadzic, Radovan, 184
Khadija, 10–11
Khan, Genghis, 79
Khan, Mohammad Sidique, 108, 150
Kharijites, 43, 99, 127–134
Khayyam, Omar, 28
Khimar, 162
Khomeini, 58
Kosovo, xx, 184–190, 192–198, 201, 229
Kosovo Liberation Army (KLA), 186, 195–197
Kuffar, 106, 118, 152

L

Law, rule of, 126, 150–151
Laws of war, 125, 129–134
Legal schools, 122–124, 127–129, 133–134
Leninism, 111, 114, 223–224, 231
Liberalism, 98, 111, 129, 252
Libyan Islamic Fighting Groups (LIFG), 225
Lindsay, Germaine, 150

Liwa al-Islam, 212
Liwa' al-Tawhid, 212
London Declaration, 121–125
Londonistan: How Britain is Creating a Terror State Within, 165
"Lone wolf" attacks, 35, 179, 224, 227–228, 236

M
Mahdi, 237
Major, John, 152
Maliki, Nouri, 89, 209
Management of Savagery, The, 239
Mardin Fatwa, ix, 79–84, 123, 125, 127, 129
Martyrdom operations, 67, 95, 152, 174, 216
Marx, Karl, 111, 146
Marxism, 76–77, 111–116, 169, 223–224, 230–231
Mathahib, 123
McCants, William, 217
Mecca, 13, 17–18, 39–43, 48–49, 51
Medina, 18, 39–43, 48–49, 51
Mein Kampf, 239
"Messengers of death," 49–50
Milošević, Slobodan, 185
Modern jihadism, 63–65, 69–118, 176. *See also* Jihadism
Mongols, 26, 29, 32, 43, 79–81
"Moral purity," xviii, 5, 23
Moussaoui, Zacharias, 150, 151
Mubarak, Hosni, 81
Muhammad, Omar Bakri, 148–149, 152–153, 266
Muhammad, Prophet
  birth of, 9
  birthplace of, 51
  death of, 18–19
  family of, 9–10
  marriage of, 10–11
  Mecca migration and, 13
  Mecca return of, 17–18
  message of, 11–14, 18, 23–24, 29–30
  mission of, 11–12

reputation of, 10–11
  tomb of, 42–43
Mujahedeen, 66, 82–86, 110, 149–151, 173–174, 192, 237, 243
Muslim Brotherhood, ix, 35, 54–55, 78, 81, 146, 212
"Muslim cause," 17, 158, 167, 173
Muslim countries, 8, 139–141, 159, 183–192, 268
Muslim populations, 24–25, 139–141, 147, 159, 183–184, 188–192, 198, 268
Muslims, "true," xv–xvi, 45–53, 79–80, 87, 96–97, 106, 152
Mussolini, Benito, 73
Mysticism, 123

N
Naji, Abu Bakr, 239
Napoleon, Louis, 146
Narodniks, 3, 113
Nasser, Gamal, 54–55, 57, 80, 123
NATO, 183, 185–187, 197–198
Nazism, xvii, 99–100, 144, 165, 260
Neglected Duty, The, 80
Neo-Nazis, 260
Niqab, 162
Nonbelievers, 106, 118, 152, 158, 163

O
Oil production, 48, 56–60, 68, 242–246, 273
Oppression, 5, 55, 80, 126, 143, 155–170
Organ trafficking, 196
Organization for Security and Co-operation in Europe (OSCE), 250
Orthodox Marxism, 111, 114–116, 223, 230–231
Orthodoxy, 25, 47–49, 103, 188–190, 252
Ottoman Empire, 41, 47, 50, 84, 102, 187–188
Ottomans, 30, 39–50, 63, 79, 84–85, 107, 183

P

Paganism, 7, 13–14, 17–19, 23, 27, 128–129

Palestinian terrorists, 74, 93, 113–114, 208

Pasha, Muhammad Ali, 43

Peace/Islam, "abode of," ix, 79–80, 86–87, 125

Phillips, Melanie, 165

Pinochet, Augusto, 146

Policy makers
challenge for, 92, 161, 166, 240
recommendations for, 107, 253
role of, 166, 253, 258–265

Political repression, 113–115, 141, 248–249. *See also* Repression

Polytheism, 37, 40–44, 52, 79, 96

Poverty, 57, 74, 115, 170, 263

Prejudice, 29, 98, 209, 236, 247–249, 255. *See also* Bigotry

Preventing Terrorism and Countering Violent Extremism and Radicalization that Lead to Terrorism, 250

Propaganda
celebration of, 113
invention of, 93
losing war against, 142–143
spread of, 3, 93, 98, 142–145, 153, 157–160, 217, 235–236, 245
videos of, 142–144, 266–268

Psychopaths, 75–76, 112, 116, 142, 175

Pull factors, xiv, 76

Push factors, xiv, 76

Putin, Vladimir, 259

Q

Qatada, Abu, 148–150

Quietists, 163, 193–194, 228

Qur'an, 5, 8, 12, 20, 37, 40, 87, 91–93, 101–104, 143, 246–247, 271

Qur'anic law, 22, 101–104

Qutb, Sayyid, 55, 82, 237–238

R

Racial equality, 22, 24, 27, 101

Racism, 29, 151, 247–249. *See also* Prejudice

Radicalism. *See also* Islamic extremism; Jihadism
activism and, 106, 158, 168, 172–174
alienation and, 3, 26, 108, 145, 168–172, 175, 206–209, 222, 228, 247, 252
description of, xi–xx
origins of, 35
rhetoric and, 153–154, 158, 168–169, 174–175, 265
understanding, xi–xx, 3–4

Radicalization
research on, 117–118, 156–178
self-radicalization, xviii, 146, 157–159, 179, 224
stages of, 156–178

Rashidun Caliphate, x, 19–23, 31, 40, 248, 271

Reactionary fundamentalism, 94–98

Realistic fundamentalism, 261

Reid, Richard, 149, 150, 151

Religious leaders, role of, 246–252

Reporters, role of, 256–258

Repression, 13, 24–26, 50, 113–115, 141, 248–249

Revolutionary Islam, 38–41. *See also* Islam

Rhetoric, 153–154, 158, 168–169, 174–175, 265

Rijpkema, Rogier, 157

Rituals, 65, 108, 162, 237

Roex, Ineke, 162, 163

Roman Empire, 19, 22, 31, 90

Rule of law, 126, 150–151

Ruthven, Malise, 272

S

Sadat, Anwar, 57, 80

Safavid Empire, 58

Sageman, Marc, 157, 174, 176

Salafism. *See also* Wahhabism
in Balkans, 183–198
belief systems, 85–97, 194–195, 210–212, 271–272

challenging, 110–113, 179, 183, 273–274
definition of, x, xiv–xvi
description of, xviii, xx, 52–53
development of, 63–65
doctrines of, 87
embracing, 103, 117, 145, 161–164, 204
enemies of, 83–86
global repercussions on, 223–226
goals of, 87, 101–103
hate preaching and, 105, 140, 144–151, 155–158, 178
ideology of, x, xiv–xvi, xviii, xx, 3–4, 87–100, 110, 156, 223–225, 265–266, 271–274
in Iraq, 205–210
jihadi Salafism, 64–67, 71, 113, 241–243
laws of war and, 125, 129–134
logic of, 78
mainstream Salafism, 53, 64–67, 71, 84, 87, 94–99, 116, 129, 140, 148, 213, 230
Muslim Brotherhood and, 63–65
origins of, 32, 39, 52–54
propaganda and, 142–145, 153, 157–160
"quietest Salafism," xix, 94, 135, 166, 178, 240
rejection of, 125–133
response to, xx
right to rebel and, 125–129, 133
in Syria, 210–211
teachers of, 145
understanding of, 3–4
Sassanid Empire, 19, 21, 90
Saudi Arabia
challenges of, 60–63
financial reserves of, 60–61
ideological war in, 100–101
Jihadi-Salafism in, 66–67, 241
labor force in, 61–63
modernization program in, 61–63, 68

oil production and, 48, 56–60, 68, 242–246, 273
role of, 240–246
Wahhabism and, 33–68
Secularism, xvi–xvii, 25, 55, 88, 110, 113, 205, 213, 242
Self-identification, xvi, 58, 157–158
Self-radicalization, xviii, 146, 157–159, 179, 224
Serbia, 183–188, 190–193, 196–198
Sharia law, xvii, 87, 101–103, 163, 213, 216, 228
Sharif, Omar Khan, 153
Shi'a Muslims, xiii–xiv, 20–21, 31, 40–42, 48–49, 58–60
Shirk, 37, 40, 52, 65
Social media, xx, 61, 142–143, 179, 222, 267
Socialism, 55–59, 81, 111, 123, 129, 205–206, 242
Sociopathy, 75, 99
Soviet Empire, 83
Stalin, Joseph, 143
Stalinism, 99, 110
Sufism, 123
Suicide bombings. *See also* Terrorist attacks
beginnings of, 93
catalysts for, xiii–xiv
children and, 223
reliance on, 117
support of, 161
tactics of, 121–122, 131–132, 153, 207–208, 214, 221–223
women and, 221–223
Sunni Muslims, xii–xiv, 20–21, 31, 36
Suqur al-Shaam, 211–212
Syria, 202–230, 235–241, 244, 249, 259–260

T
Tahir-ul-Qadri, Muhammad, 121, 122, 125–126, 128
Takfir, x, 37–38, 41, 67, 122–124, 149, 163–164

INDEX

Takfirism, x, 82, 86–88, 106–110, 176, 179
Taliban, xi, 85, 103, 153, 218–219, 235
Tamil Tigers, xiii, 93
Teachers, role of, 253–256, 261
Terror, war on, xi–xii, 97–101, 152
Terrorism
　basis for, 63–67, 78–79, 107, 115–116
　catalysts for, xiii–xiv, xix, 72–74
　condemning, 53, 121–136
　dynamics of, 177–179, 263–265
　fighting, 97
　funding, 139–145, 250
　logic of, 71–78
　pull factors of, xiv, 76
　push factors of, xiv, 76
　rejection of, 124–129
　rise of, 139–145
　"terrorist types," 74–76, 115–116
　understanding of, 263–265
Terrorist attacks. *See also* Suicide bombings
　7/7 London bombings, 103, 108, 150, 165
　9/11 terrorist attacks, xi, 67, 86, 104, 140, 149, 152, 159, 192, 201, 218, 237, 240–241, 246
　Charlie Hebdo attack, 267
　Hebron terrorist attack, 157
　Hofstad terrorist attack, 157
　"lone wolf" attacks, 35, 179, 224, 227–228, 236
　Madrid terrorist attack, 157
Terrorist Finance Tracking Programme, 250
Terrorists
　background of, xix, 74–76, 170, 207–209, 224
　study of, 74–76
　types of, 74–76, 115–116
Theology, role of, 103–107
Theoretical Frames on Pathways to Violent Radicalization, 156–157
Tito, Josip, 183, 188

Totalitarian ideology, 87, 98, 113, 143, 156, 165, 271
"True believers," xii, xiv–xv, 86–89, 95
"True faith," 31–32, 45–46, 89–97
"True Muslims," xv–xvi, 45–53, 79–80, 87, 96–97, 106, 152
Trump, Donald, 166, 236, 259–260
TV pundits, role of, 256–258
"Two Mosques," 39–43, 48–49

U
Umar, 21
Umayyad Caliphate, 23–26
Umayyad dynasty, x, 6, 23–26, 31–32
Umayyad Empire, x, 28–29, 212
Ummah, 7, 14, 18–19, 22, 37–38, 238
UN charter, 125–126, 133
United Nations (UN), 85, 129, 191–192, 197–198
"Us" vs. "Them," 94, 117, 140, 143, 155–157, 169, 256–257
Uthman, 21

V
Vigilantism, 121–122
Violence. *See also* Suicide bombings; Terrorist attacks
　catalysts for, xiii–xiv, xix, 72–74
　current threats of, 273–274
　glorifying, 108
　ideology and, 3, 95, 156, 273–274
　of Islam, 4–7, 53–57, 121–123, 126–130, 153–161, 164–179
　justification for, xiv, xvii, 75–82, 108, 112, 115, 121–132, 159–160, 227, 241
　pull factors of, xiv, 76
　push factors of, xiv, 76
　rejection of, xvii, 166, 209, 227–228
　violent jihad, xiii–xx, 3, 66, 88–95, 112–116, 130, 145–153, 161–167, 174–177, 201–209, 240, 258, 273–274

W
Wahhabi emirates, 42–49

Wahhabism. *See also* Salafism
    definition of, x, xiv–xv
    description of, 7
    first wave of, xviii–xix
    ideology of, 36, 52, 235, 256,
       271–274
    Ikhwan revolt and, 49–53
    mainstream Wahhabism, 50–53,
       67–68
    movement of, 38–41
    origins of, 36–37
    phases of, 38–40
    revolutionary Islam and, 38–41
    Saudi Arabia and, 33–68
    Wahhabi emirates, 42–49
War
    against bigotry, 235–236
    against ideology, 97–101, 235–236,
       259
    Just War, 86–89, 128–129
    laws of, 125, 129–134
    on terror, xi–xii, 97–101, 152

War/heresy, "abode of," ix, 79–80,
    83–84, 86, 152
"War on Terror," xi–xii, 97–101, 152
Warden, Francis, 42
Wiktorowicz, Quintan, 248–249
World order, 86, 168
World War I, 47, 49
World War II, xvii, 130, 239, 259
Wright, Dominick, 157

X
Xenophobia, 45–46, 51, 111, 144,
    257–258, 260

Y
Yugoslavia, 183–185, 187–189, 193–195
Yusuf 'Azzam, 'Abdallah, 81, 151, 238

Z
Zarqawi, Abu Musab, 207–209, 218
Zawahiri, Ayman, 82, 85–86, 104, 238
Zoroastrians, 6–7, 18, 22–25, 90